JOURNAL FOR THE STUDY OF THE OLD TESTAMENT SUPPLEMENT SERIES
288

Sheffield Academic Press

Revisions of the Night

Politics and Promises in
the Patriarchal Dreams of Genesis

Diana Lipton

Journal for the Study of the Old Testament
Supplement Series 288

For Peter
דּוֹדִי לִי וַאֲנִי לוֹ

Jacob and Jonah
יְשִׂמְךָ אֱלֹהִים כְּאֶפְרַיִם וְכִמְנַשֶּׁה

Copyright © 1999 Sheffield Academic Press

Published by Sheffield Academic Press Ltd
Mansion House
19 Kingfield Road
Sheffield S11 9AS
England

Printed on acid-free paper in Great Britain
by Bookcraft Ltd
Midsomer Norton, Bath

British Library Cataloguing in Publication Data

A catalogue record for this book is available
from the British Library

ISBN 1-85075-958-8

CONTENTS

PREFACE

This study first saw light of day as a PhD thesis submitted to the Divinity School, Cambridge University, and I am deeply indebted to my supervisor, Professor Robert Gordon, who retained his excellent humour while reining me in. I am also grateful to my examiners, Dr Graham Davies and Professor John Rogerson, who gave me helpful suggestions for future revisions (and approved my PhD).

I owe a great deal to friends too numerous to mention, but I must mention Dr Meira Polliack, supporter and chavrutah; she inspired me with her wonderfully sensitive approach to Hebrew texts, and taught me how to read the rabbinic commentaries that so greatly enriched my own reading of the Bible.

I thank the Principal and Fellows of Newnham College, Cambridge for welcoming me into their community. Although I would have finished this manuscript much more quickly without my duties as Admissions Tutor, I would have been much less happy without an intellectual home. I also thank the members of Beth Shalom Reform Synagogue, Cambridge for providing a warm spiritual home. I am extremely grateful to my superb proof-reader, Ruth Phillips; any errors that remain were introduced by me after the manuscript left her capable hands. Thanks are also due to Sheffield Academic Press for publishing this monograph.

Above all, I acknowledge the great contribution of my peerless sons, Jacob and Jonah, who never get exasperated, and my incomparable husband, Peter Lipton, without whose unlimited supply of enthusiasm, stability, love and absolute confidence, this project would have been a qualified pleasure.

ABBREVIATIONS

AOAT	Alter Orient und Alte Testament
BDB	Frances Brown, S.R. Driver and Charles A. Briggs, *A Hebrew and English Lexicon of the Old Testament* (Oxford: Clarendon Press, 1907)
BibInt	*Biblical Interpretation*
BZ	*Biblische Zeitschrift*
BZAW	Beihefte zur *ZAW*
CBQ	*Catholic Biblical Quarterly*
ExpTim	*Expository Times*
GR	*Genesis Rabbah* (C. Albeck [ed.], Jerusalem: Wahrmann Books, 1965 [1929])
HSM	Harvard Semitic Monographs
HUCA	*Hebrew Union College Annual*
IBS	*Irish Biblical Studies*
JANESCU	*Journal of the Ancient Near Eastern Society of Columbia University*
JAOS	*Journal of the American Oriental Society*
JBL	*Journal of Biblical Literature*
JJS	*Journal of Jewish Studies*
JQR	*Jewish Quarterly Review*
JSOT	*Journal for the Study of the Old Testament*
JSOTSup	*Journal for the Study of the Old Testament*, Supplement Series
JSS	*Journal of Semitic Studies*
MG	*Mikraot Gedolot* (New York: Pardes Publishing House, 1951)
NJPS	New Jewish Publication Society
NRSV	New Revised Standard Version
Or	*Orientalia*
OL	*Orientalische Literaturzeitung*
OTP	James Charlesworth (ed.), *Old Testament Pseudepigrapha*
SBLMS	SBL Monograph Series
SJOT	*Scandinavian Journal of the Old Testament*
TynBul	*Tyndale Bulletin*
VT	*Vetus Testamentum*
VTSup	*Vetus Testamentum*, Supplements
ZAW	*Zeitschrift für die alttestamentliche Wissenschaft*

INTRODUCTION

The book of Genesis contains ten clear-cut cases of dreaming: Abimelech (20.1-18); Jacob at Bethel (28.10-22); Jacob and the speckled
flock (31.10-13); Laban (31.24); Joseph (37.5-8 and 37.9-11); Pharaoh's butler (40.5-15); Pharaoh's baker (40.16-22); and Pharaoh (41.1-
4 and 41.5-8). With the exception of Jacob's dream at Bethel, which is
announced by the verbal form 'and he dreamed' (ויחלם), all these texts
include at least one occurrence of the noun 'dream' (חלום). There are,
in addition, two episodes that have dream-like characteristics but are, in
fact, called visions: Abraham's 'vision' (מחזה) in 15.1-21, and Jacob's
'visions of the night' (מראת הלילה) in 46.2. Scholars have speculated
that the revelations received by Hagar (21.17-19) and Isaac (26.23-24)
were based on dream reports, but evidence for this view seems to me
too weak to justify a consideration of these episodes in a discourse on
dreams.

This monograph will focus on the four patriarchal texts that include
an explicit reference to dreaming, together with the report of the vision
in ch. 15. Although the dreams of the Joseph narrative will be mentioned in connection with other dream reports, stylistic and theological
differences suggest that they do not belong with the dreams of the
patriarchal narratives; they seem to reflect an Israelite view of how
dreams were perceived in Egypt, rather than a distinctively Israelite
conception of dreaming. Furthermore, perhaps because of their crucial
role in the Hebrew Bible's[1] closest approximation to a novella, the
Joseph dreams have often been the subject of close readings of the type
offered here.

A Survey of Recent Literature

Aside from some recent psychoanalytically-inspired considerations,[2]
irrelevant to this study, there is a surprising dearth of material on the

1.   The terms 'biblical' and 'Bible' will always refer here to the Hebrew Bible.
2.   See, for instance, A. Resch, *Der Traum im Heilsplan Gottes: Deutung und
Bedeutung des Traums im Alten Testament* (Freiburg: Herder, 1964).

dreams of Genesis. What work has been undertaken in the past 40 years has been based on the larger unit of biblical dreams, with the result that a close reading of the dreams in Genesis, or even an acknowledgment that this group deserves separate consideration, is almost entirely lacking in existing studies. There are, of course, numerous commentaries on Genesis, but, while these provide detailed exegesis of at least some of the dream texts, they often say little about the special nature of dream revelations. Indeed, many proceed with scant regard for the fact that the text in question is a dream report. The following chronological survey of the recent literature will be confined to works that treat Genesis dream texts with dreams as their starting point.

E.L. Ehrlich

E.L. Ehrlich's *Der Traum im Alten Testament*[3] attempts a comprehensive survey of biblical dreams, presenting six thematic chapters which deal respectively with incubation, symbolic dreams, divine orders and instructions transmitted through dreams, dreams as vehicles of divine revelation, dreams in comparison, and the rejection of dreams as vehicles of revelation. Each chapter provides introductory remarks on the topic in question, and proceeds to analyse a number of relevant dream texts. The fact that no dream text is considered in detail in more than one chapter highlights a flaw in Ehrlich's approach to the subject. Moreover, some of his divisions seem artificial. This is particularly evident in his decision to include a discussion of Gen. 28.10-22 in the chapter on incubation primarily because *other* scholars have treated it as an incubation text. That having been said, however, most of Ehrlich's categorizations are logical, and his adherence to the perspective of his chosen theme makes for straightforward reading. Under the heading of incubation, he discusses Genesis 15; 28.10-22 and 46.1-5. Genesis 37.5-8, 9-10; 40, and 41 are discussed as symbolic dream reports, while Genesis 20; 31.10-13 and 31.24 are considered as message dreams.

   Ehrlich's research is conducted within the parameters of conventional source criticism, and he attributes most dream texts to the Elohist, in whose work God's speech is directed from a distance (p. 135). The source-critical approach has, in particular, influenced his analysis of chs. 15 and 28. In ch. 15 he envisages two distinct revelations, the first being the vision (v. 1) in which Abraham is asked to go outside and

---

3.   Berlin: Alfred Töpelmann, 1953.

count the stars, and the second being a divine revelation (v. 7) which, for the sake of a smooth transition from one narrative to the next, is not specifically announced by the redactor. Verses 13-16 are seen as a later addition which interrupts the progress of the action. Ehrlich condemns Wellhausen's view that these verses describe a form of incubation, but claims that this reading has some merit if not restricted to vv. 13-16. This more comprehensive claim requires him to see Abraham's division of the pieces (v. 10) as a type of sacrifice, without which the text could not properly be said to represent an incubation ritual.[4]

Ehrlich sees ch. 28 as the culmination of a series of stories surrounding the holy site of Bethel. He includes this narrative in his chapter on incubation only because it has traditionally been seen as an incubation text, and not because he regards it as such. On his reading, incubation cannot have been intended here since Jacob only *discovers* the holy place, coming across it quite by chance. He does concede, however, that incubation may have been present in an earlier Canaanite level of the narrative, whose existence he surmises. An energetic defence of the traditional source-critical reading of 28.10-22 is provided, and Ehrlich is especially hostile towards the more holistic reading of Volz which, he claims, fails to distinguish between an account that was originally a Canaanite legend about the discovery of a holy place, and a real dream experience.

Ehrlich's own reading follows the conventional division of the Bethel narrative into 'J' and 'E' strands, with J's contribution being an angel apparition (not necessarily a dream revelation) with a speech, and E's being a silent angel apparition whose meaning Jacob must comprehend. The ladder is described as an image from the mythological topography of Bethel, originally unconnected with Jacob's experience there. He sees a clear relationship between the dream vision and Jacob's vow, which he characterizes as three requests (protection, food and clothes [counting as one], and safe return to his father's house), followed by three promises (the acceptance of God, the erection of a house of God, and the tithing of goods received from God). Given God's specific assurance in relation to the three requests in v. 15

---

4. In order to fulfil Ehrlich's conditions for incubation the text must report preparatory steps taken prior to sleeping in a holy place with the intention of inducing a dream.

Ehrlich finds a link between vv. 13-15 and vv. 20-22 untenable. Jacob's vow, in his view, makes sense only as a response to the silent vision of the ladder, and not to the promises of vv. 13-15.

While he finds no evidence of incubation in ch. 28, Ehrlich does regard 46.1-4 as an incubation report, arguing that the sacrifices are intended to persuade God to send an oracle or revelation to Jacob at a time of uncertainty. In contrast to ch. 28, Jacob knows that he is in a holy place, and thus two of Ehrlich's conditions for incubation (awareness of the holy nature of the place and sacrifice) have been met. The absence of an explicit reference to dreaming in this text presents no cause for concern, and he notes that the Bible scarcely distinguishes phenomenologically between words for dream and vision. The discussion of 46.1-4 concludes with a summary of its retelling by Josephus, apparently to emphasize how the latter successfully blurred the incubation issue by inserting an account of Jacob's thoughts after making the sacrifices and before falling asleep.

Genesis 20, 31.10-13 and 31.24 are classified as direct-message dreams. Ehrlich sees ch. 20 as the work of the Elohist and, as elsewhere, notes the occurrence of the הנה (behold) typical of dream reports. Much of his discussion of this text is devoted to an elaboration of the differences between this and the other two wife-sister texts (chs. 12 and 26). Laban's dream in 31.24 is identified as a warning dream, and is ascribed to the Elohist. Jacob's dream (31.10-13), he claims, is to be regarded as a later addition which may have originated with either the Elohist or the Yahwist.

The frequency with which Ehrlich's work is cited by other scholars testifies to its influence in the field. In particular, his definition of incubation and its application to biblical dreams have been widely accepted, and his views seem not to have been superseded significantly in the past 40 years. Given the extent to which his analyses would have benefited from Oppenheim's study (see below), had it been available to him, this is somewhat surprising. His emphasis on source criticism means that much of his discussion is of limited use to scholars not working from this vantage point, and his decision to treat all the biblical dream texts precludes a close textual analysis of any one. With a few notable exceptions (such as Abimelech's dream, which is discussed in relation to the other wife-sister texts), little attention is paid to the wider context in which each dream report appears.

A.L. Oppenheim

For scholars interested in comparing biblical dreams with their ancient Near Eastern counterparts, A.L. Oppenheim's work is indispensable.[5] It should be noted at the outset, though, that the Bible is not the focus of his interests: it was the author's original intention to produce a scholarly edition of an Assyrian dream book, and this evolved into a wide-ranging analysis of dreams in the ancient Near East. Since Oppenheim devotes comparatively little space to biblical dreams, and since his discussion of other ancient Near Eastern dreams is long and complex, this survey will focus primarily on aspects with obvious relevance to the dreams of Genesis.

Oppenheim claims that dream experiences were reported on three distinct planes: the dream as divine revelation, the dream reflecting its dreamer's spiritual and bodily health and the mantic dream that prognosticates events. He suggests that only the dreams in which a divine message is revealed to a king or priest can be studied properly, since no other type of dream report is adequately attested, but he is adamant, against Dodds and Gadd, that these dreams cannot be taken as 'initiation' dreams because they do not establish the cultic or social standing of the dreamer. He makes the obvious point that the message dreams recorded in royal inscriptions are not suitable material for a psychoanalytic approach, both on account of the linguistic difficulties they present, and because they have been shaped according to rigid restrictions of form, content and mood. Even if they were based on individual experience, little trace of it remains, and literary considerations have submerged the personality of the dreamer. In a similar vein, he points out that the modern psychoanalyst can glean little from dream symbols whose significance is no longer accessible to us. Although Oppenheim's research focuses mainly on dreams from Mesopotamian (Syrian and Akkadian) sources, he includes pertinent Egyptian, Hittite and biblical texts, as well as Greek literature, for the purposes of elucidation.

In his analysis of message dreams, Oppenheim envisages the division of dream reports into two distinct sections: the dream's setting, who dreamt it, when, where and under what circumstances; and the actual content of the dream. Since no dream report contains all the characteristic features, each text must be studied in detail in order to separate its

5. 'The Interpretation of Dreams in the Ancient Near East: With a Translation of an Assyrian Dream Book', *Transactions of the American Philosophical Society* NS 46 (1956), pp. 179-373.

formulaic from its individual traits. He notes that we must take account of authorial preference when studying the distribution of dream reports in the ancient Near East. This, he suggests, explains the fact that the so-called autobiography of the Hittite king Hattusilis and the inscriptions of the Assyrian king Assurbanipal offer most or all of the dream reports of their respective types. Similarly, he attributes the majority of biblical dreams to the Elohist.

Oppenheim claims that few actual incubation incidents are recorded in works originating in the ancient Near East, although Solomon's dream at Gibeon (1 Kgs 3.5 and 2 Chron. 1.5), and the dream of Daniel in the Legend of Aqht are classified as 'provoked incubation dreams experienced by kings'. He suggests that the dreams of Thutmose IV in the shadow of the great sphinx, and Jacob's dream at Bethel may be described as unintentional incubation dreams.[6] A distinction is made between incubation dreams and the unprovoked dreams received by priests sleeping in a sanctuary, such as the dream of Samuel. Despite the sparsity of uncontested instances of incubation in ancient Near East literature, Oppenheim sees the incubation dream as the prototype for many dream reports that do not feature incubation. Thus, he claims that the characteristic incubation setting has been incorporated into non-incubated dream reports in the commonplace descriptions of apparitions of towering size:

> The sleeper in the cella, lying at the feet of an image, conditioned by appropriate ritual which nourish his apprehensions and by reports which channel his imagination, distorts this image in his dream into towering size and hears his name called in the stillness of the night.[7]

An important feature of many dream reports is the precise account of the dreamer's awakening. Oppenheim provides an interesting discussion of the shock element in ancient Near Eastern dreams, focusing particularly on the characteristic image of the deity entering the dreamer's room. He takes the biblical phrase 'God came to NN in a dream by night' (Gen. 20.3, 31.24; 1 Kgs 3.5, 9.2) as a replacement for the expression 'to see (a dream)', and suggests that this may account for the dreamer's surprise upon awakening. Several theories are offered to

---

6.   'In both cases, the devotee chances upon the numinous place where the god who has his abode in this very locality appears to him in a dream' ('The Interpretation of Dreams', p. 187).

7.   Oppenheim, 'The Interpretation of Dreams', p. 190.

explain the emphasis on a surprised awakening which concludes many ancient Near Eastern dream reports, such as the second dream of Gudea: 'He woke up with a start, it was (but) a dream!' The sudden awakening may mark the distinction between one dream and any other which might follow it, while the dreamer's surprise testifies to the dream's vividness and thus—Oppenheim posits—its validity. He points out that many Sumerian, Akkadian, Hebrew and Greek dreams include a phrase indicating that the deity stands at the head of the dreamer and awakens him. This is linked to the calling of the dreamer's name (cf. 1 Sam. 3 and Gen. 31.11), which may be seen as preparing the dreamer to receive the dream revelation. Indeed, it is noted that the Egyptian word for dream (*rswt*), written with the symbol of an open eye, is etymologically connected with a root meaning 'to be awake'.

With rare exceptions, the central figures of ancient Near Eastern dream reports are divine, and Oppenheim sees theophany as the proto-type of the message dream. The notion of dream-demons or messengers belongs to the classical world, and dream visions of the dead, or indeed of the living, are very rare.[8] Likewise, conversations between dreamer and deity, and gestures and actions by either, are seldom reported. This accords with the essentially passive nature of the dreamer. It is noted, however, that dreams are often used to provide the dreamer with inspiration, or even detailed information, regarding the design of an artifact or building. Gudea's dream[9] may be the best example of this, but 1 Chron. 28.11-19, where David gives Solomon the pattern of the temple, is also cited. (See also Exod. 25.9 and Num. 8.4.) Jacob's dream in Gen. 31.10 is, perhaps, an inspirational dream regarding shep-herd-lore. In a similar category are inspirational message dreams about the birth of a royal heir or important hero, and dreams containing medi-cal advice, particularly regarding infertility. These issues are occasion-ally fused, as in the case of the Egyptian Setme Khamuas, whose dream about the naming of a child is preceded by his wife's dream regarding a cure for infertility.

8.　This observation may highlight an important difference between the Joseph dreams and other ancient Near Eastern dream reports. God's intervention is more subtle. Furthermore, the characters are not passive, reflecting the fact that God acts through them, not simply on their behalf.

9.　Oppenheim's discussion of Gudea's dreams will be presented in detail in the light of possible parallels with Gen. 28.

The 'autobiography' of the Hittite king Hattusilis contains more dream-stories than any other ancient Near Eastern document. Many of the dreams reported here are attributed to the king's wife and his uncle, showing the importance attached to the dreams of people surrounding a significant figure, as well as by him.[10] While dreams are seldom attributed to women in the ancient world, the Hattusilis document refers both to the dreams of the king's wife, and to the fact that he married her following advice given in a dream.[11]

In his discussion of symbolic dreams Oppenheim makes the odd claim, repeated by others after him, that symbolic dreams in the Bible are reserved for Gentiles. He must have meant symbolic dreams in need of interpretation, since there is otherwise no explanation for Joseph's own dreams. Various methods of demonstrating the validity of symbolic dreams are discussed, such as the sending of a separate sign, but he notes the use of repetition, in the Bible and elsewhere, to show that a dream is 'true' and should be heeded. Some texts indicate that the intelligence of the dreamer may be a factor in determining who should receive symbolic dreams. Thus, in the Gilgamesh epic, Ea defends himself against accusations of betrayal by pointing out that he did not reveal the secret plan of the gods, but only sent a dream to Uta-naphistim, who was able to interpret it.

Many interesting observations are made about interpretation, and about the difficulty of identifying the precise meaning of this concept in the ancient world. Evidence suggests that the process of interpretation involved the removal of a dream's evil consequences (or at least the removal of its dreamer's sense of foreboding), as well as the explanation of the dream's literal meaning. This fits well with the emphasis on Pharaoh's anxiety prior to Joseph's interpretation of his dreams, although fear may follow a dream even when its meaning is clear (cf. Jacob in 28.17). Oppenheim links the Hebrew root פתר with the Semitic *psr*, whose range of meanings, he claims, are best suggested by the English 'to solve' and its derivatives 'to dissolve' and 'to absolve'. He sees three basic methods of dream interpretation in the ancient Near East, the first being closest to modern psychoanalytic methods, and

10. The dreams of Abimelech (Gen. 20) and Laban (Gen. 31) will be discussed in this light.

11. It is notable that this use of dreams does not feature in Genesis, although other types of divine intervention occur with regard to the choice of a wife (cf. 24.12-14).

based on an intuitive understanding of the dreamer and his situation; the second involving the use of dream omina, and requiring a scholarly outlook on the part of the interpreter; and the third involving divine assistance, either from the deity who sent the dream, or from an agent of the deity, as in Gudea's dream. His etiology of the meaning of dream in the ancient world suggests that words for dreams are often derived from words meaning sleep, as in the Akkadian *suttu* (dream), from *sittu* (sleep), or from words meaning to see, as in the Arabic *ru'a* from *ra'a*.

M. Lichtenstein
M. Lichtenstein's article, 'Dream Theophany and the "E" Document',[12] opens with an analysis of the problems arising from the popular identification of dream revelations with the Elohist. He notes that traditional source-critical divisions of Genesis 15 and 28 suggest that revelation during sleep is a feature of both the E and the J contributions to these texts, from which it follows that dreams cannot be the sole province of the Elohist.

The primary motivation for this article is encapsulated in the following question:

> Is there a genuine qualitative and chronological distinction in the Pentateuch between dream-theophany and corporeal theophany (or manifestation)?[13]

Lichtenstein claims that the most natural distinction regarding dream revelations in the ancient Near East is to be made between symbolic and direct-message dreams. He suggests that disparaging references to dreams in the Bible may be directed at the former in contrast to the latter, and not to dreams in general as opposed to some form of corporeal theophany. He makes the excellent point that the hierarchy of revelation implied in Num. 12.4-9 suggests that the Pentateuch allows for the coexistence of various types of revelation, and this surely presents a problem for those scholars who assume the existence of an evolution of revelation. Similarly, while, at first glance, evidence from the Gilgamesh epic suggests that dreams are valued less than direct revelation, there are no cases of direct-message dream theophany in the entire epic, and the contrast here is based on the lower esteem accorded to symbolic or ambiguous dreams as opposed to direct-message dreams.

---

12. *JANESCU* 1–2 (1969), pp. 45-54.
13. Lichtenstein, 'Dream Theophany', p. 48.

This distinction is also implied in the dreams of Gudea, who first receives a symbolic dream from Ningirsu, and must then earn a direct-message dream by building a chariot for the god. It is somewhat surprising when, after emphasizing the distinction between symbolic and direct-message dreams, Lichtenstein concludes that the choice of symbolic dream, direct-message dream or corporeal revelation is primarily a matter of literary preference in the ancient Near East. He is surely correct, however, in asserting that the existence in some ancient Near Eastern documents (such as the Mari 'prophetic' documents and the annals of Assurbanipal) of a variety of theophanies and revelations, should make scholars sceptical both about attributing dream-revelations to a single Israelite school of thought, and about envisaging an evolutionary approach towards modes of revelation in the Pentateuch.

R.K. Gnuse

R.K. Gnuse approaches the dreams of the Bible with a specific focal point—the dream of Samuel.[14] He does not allow this to influence unduly his analysis of other biblical dreams, and each is presented in its own right, with no attempt to interpret it according to 1 Samuel 3. Samuel's experience is understood not as a prophetic call, but as a dream report in the ancient Near Eastern tradition. This view was previously expounded in an article,[15] and what the book adds is primarily an expansion of his reading of 1 Samuel 3 and a more detailed independent discussion of other biblical dreams. Heavy use is made of Oppenheim's work, but since the latter refers only occasionally and briefly to biblical dreams, there is no substantial overlap. Gnuse, like Ehrlich, is committed to source criticism, and includes several discussions of the Elohist. He is, however, adamant that evidence for the existence of the Elohist source should not be based upon its apparent preference for dreams as vehicles of revelation alone, but also on use of images, expressions, proper names and theological concepts. He outlines a presumed similarity between the Elohist's treatment of dreams

---

14. *The Dream Theophany of Samuel: Its Structure in Relation to Ancient Near Eastern Dreams and its Theological Significance* (Lanham: University Press of America, 1984).

15. 'A Reconsideration of the Form-critical Structure in 1 Samuel 3: An ANE Dream Theophany', *ZAW* 94 (1982), pp. 379-89.

and the components of ancient Near Eastern dreams as described by Oppenheim.[16]

The book opens with an introductory account of the types of dream reports which existed in the ancient Near East (auditory message, symbolic message, mantic and psychological status dreams), and proceeds with a brief discussion of dreams in various cultures (Babylonia, Hittite, Egypt, Ugarit, Assyria and Chaldean Babylon). Chapter 2 provides a brief account of all recognized dream reports in the Bible. Gnuse makes a concerted attempt to incorporate the ancient Near Eastern elements presented in chapter 1, but, as in Ehrlich's work, the dreams are not considered in their broader context, nor are they related to one another.

With the exception of the Joseph dreams, all the dreams of Genesis are discussed under the heading 'Structure of the Dream Report'. Each consideration begins with a reference to the sources, with most being attributed to the Elohist or to a conflation of Elohistic and Yahwistic sources. He notes von Rad's view that it may be inappropriate to identify ch. 15 with either source on account of the cultic language, the

---

16. 'Oppenheim's outline of the ancient Near Eastern message dream contained the following components:

   I. Setting
      A. Who
      B. When
      C. Where
      D. Conditions under which the dream came
  II. Dream Content
 III. End of the dream and reaction
 IV. Fulfilment

This author has observed and formulated a similar pattern in the Elohist, which can be outlined as follows:

    I. Theophany
   II. Recipient
  III. Dream reference
  IV. Time
   V. Auditory address formula
  VI. Message
      A. Introductory formula, or particle <u>hinneh</u>
      B. Divine self-identification
      C. Assurance and promise/warnings/commands
      D. Dialogue
 VII. Formal termination' (Gnuse, *Dream Theophany of Samuel*, p. 75).

oracle of salvation, declaration of righteousness, and the metaphor of
God as a shield. Gnuse allows that incubation may be possible in this
case, but only if the cutting of the animals constitutes a sacrifice, and
the location is regarded as a sacred shrine. The repetition in ch. 20 of
the Yahwist accounts in chs. 12 and 26 is taken as further confirmation
of the existence of the Elohistic source, and this highlights a general
problem with Gnuse's approach. Once he has explained away any textual difficulties or inconsistencies by reference to the sources, he looks
no further.

The discussion of ch. 28 is similar to Ehrlich's, focusing on source
criticism, and possible Canaanite influences. An attempt is made to
interpret the ladder in the light of ancient Near Eastern concepts, such
as the ladder upon which deceased pharaohs ascended, and the Sumerian stairway that linked the underworld and the gate of Anu, Enlil and
Ea. While Gnuse is not alone in considering Gen. 46.1-7 as a dream
report, his decision to include Gen. 21.16-19, 22.1-2 and 26.24 is
slightly more unusual. In each case, however, he makes it clear that
there is scant justification for regarding these texts as dream reports.
With the exception of Gen. 22.1-2, which he compares with Samuel's
dream, he sees possible evidence of incubation in these texts. 31.10-17
is interpreted as the Elohist's sanctioning of Jacob's trickery by giving
it divine origin in a dream, and Gnuse shares Ehrlich's view that 31.24
constitutes both a warning and a command. The bulk of the brief discussion of this dream is devoted to the question of whether Laban worshipped the LORD.

M.G. Robinson

M.G. Robinson's 'Dreams in the Old Testament'[17] is a comprehensive
study, providing an extensive consideration of biblical dreams in relation to their ancient Near Eastern counterparts. Although she emphasizes the literary nature of ancient dream reports, her outlook is more
anthropological and sociological than textual. She is interested in what
role dreams may, in actuality, have played in Israelite society, claiming
that it may have been much greater than the Bible suggests. She also
discusses the changing attitude towards dreams and their significance as
reflected in the Bible.

17. Unpublished PhD thesis; Faculty of Theology, University of Manchester,
1987.

Robinson begins with the problem of how to identify a biblical dream. This is partly a matter of terminology; the Bible presents no clear view of the distinction between a vision and a dream, sometimes suggesting that they are parallel terms (Num. 12.6; Job 7.14), and sometimes implying that they reflect different psychological experiences. The matter is complicated further by the characteristics of the experiences described. Ezekiel's visions in chs. 1 and 37 have all the features normally associated with dreams, while Abimelech's dream in Gen. 20.6-7 does not.

Robinson presents a detailed treatment of biblical dreams from a psychological point of view. Much of this is necessarily speculative, but her conclusion that dreams were seen as the product of divine intervention and not as a creation of the dreamer's soul seems plausible. Dream interpreters are also considered from a vantage point which is both psychological and sociological, and she claims that dream interpretations were sought out in the ancient world with much more urgency than they are today. This may be misleading. While there is reason to believe that kings and military figures were anxious to have their dreams interpreted, it would be wrong to assume that the common man sought dream interpretations with equal enthusiasm. Indeed, the sense of urgency may be the product of a literary convention. Robinson proceeds with a discussion of the people and institutions associated with dream interpretation in surrounding cultures, with a view to building up a possible picture of the situation in Israel. While respecting her scepticism about the 'argument from silence', it must be acknowledged that the image of a class of professional dream interpreters ignored by the Bible is highly speculative.

Robinson's anthropological and social interests are particularly evident in the chapter on incubation, which does not confine itself to ancient Near Eastern texts, but draws upon evidence from other cultures in an effort to build a picture of the actual practice of incubation rituals in Israel (as opposed to the impression conveyed by the Bible). In her opinion, claims that incubation is incompatible with Israelite theology[18] are not supported by the text, and she concludes with a

---

18. Robinson cites L. Köhler (*Old Testament Theology* [trans. A.S. Todd; London: Lutterworth Press, 1957], p. 103): '...there is no human process, no prayer, sacrifice or technique of any kind, whereby man could induce a divine apparition. Man is always the recipient only, never the author of the revelation' ('Dreams in the Old Testament', p. 99).

discussion of biblical narratives which may reflect incubation practices. It is noted that typical features of incubation rituals can be found in Gen. 46.1-4:

> the visit to the sanctuary, the offering of sacrifices, the night visions ... and the promises made by the deity.[19]

Robinson concurs with Ehrlich that the sacrifices and visions are explicitly connected, and that weeping may be seen as a purification ritual in preparation for incubation. Similarities between this text and the dream of Keret in the Ugaritic epic poem suggest possible Canaanite influences. She tentatively suggests that Gen. 28.10-22 may incorporate an incubation experience, and that the verses which contradict this reading (such as vv. 11 and 16) may represent a deliberate attempt to cloud the issue. Although sceptical about Jaros's claim that the biblical story is essentially a Canaanite legend recast for the purpose, she does not dismiss Nyberg's theory, based partly on a reading of Hos. 12.4, that the Ephraimites sought oracles from a stone at Bethel (p. 132). Robinson's consideration of Genesis 15 opens with an outline of Lohfink's reading of an incubated dream in v. 13, the result of a sacrifice in a holy place. She associates the terebinth of Moreh with 'an indwelling spirit or numen', seeing this as further evidence for the possibility that incubatory practices may have continued at local shrines even after the removal of their original deities. Obermann's view that this (and other 'pre-natal' texts) may contain faint echoes of incubation episodes such as those described in the Ugaritic episodes of Aqht and Keret is ultimately rejected. In the two distinct narratives which, in Robinson's view, comprise ch. 15, childlessness occurs only in the first and possible incubation only in the second.

In her chapter on royal dreams, Robinson emphasizes the literary nature of the dream reports, and doubts that they have much relation to actual experience. She does, however, note the value of the texts as a source of information about the perceived role of kings in the ancient world. In particular, the dream reports confirm the view of a king as an intermediary between people and the gods, simultaneously representing the former in heaven and the latter on earth. The ensuing survey of royal dream reports emphasizes, in particular, the function of the dream as a legitimizing device. Robinson attributes the widespread use of

---

19. Robinson, 'Dreams in the Old Testament', p. 122.

dreams, as opposed to other methods of divination, for this purpose to the fact that many types of divination were difficult to falsify and, unlike dreams, would have required accomplices.

As well as legitimizing claims to the throne, dreams also played an important role in temple building. Robinson claims that:

> dream reports relating to temple building probably form the largest single category of dreams recorded in Ancient Near Eastern literature and are to be found in virtually every region of the area over a wide timespan.[20]

Indeed, she sees temple building partly as another legitimizing device, intended to forge the relationship between god and king, and takes 1 Chron. 22.10 as biblical evidence for this.

In her chapter on the literary form of biblical dreams, Robinson considers Oppenheim's view that the formulaic presentation of biblical dream reports may owe something to real dreams resulting from incubation rituals. She shares Richter's opinion that the complex pattern discernible in the symbolic dreams of the Bible may suggest the existence of an institution of professional dream interpreters, and finds further evidence for this in the occurrence of specific formulaic phrases in biblical dream reports. Given that most of the relatively small number of symbolic dreams in the Bible occur within two narratives, one of which may be influenced by the other, one should, perhaps, be wary of inferring too much from a certain amount of structural conformity here. Moreover, some of Robinson's examples of texts which support her theory (Gen. 41.16, for instance) are not entirely convincing.

The final chapter deals with the attitude towards dreams in the Bible. Robinson notes the obvious ambivalence, but rightly emphasizes that it was shared by many cultures. While it is possible that this ambivalence results from an increasingly sophisticated theological outlook on the part of the biblical narrators, it may also stem from the difficulty of assessing the value of dreams. Robinson's citation from Aristotle makes the point well: 'As for prophecy which takes place in sleep and which is said to proceed from dreams, it is not an easy matter either to despise it or to believe in it'.[21]

20. 'Dreams in the Old Testament', p. 169.
21. 'Dreams in the Old Testament', p. 215.

J.M. Husser

J.M. Husser's *Le songe et la parole: Etude sur le rêve et sa fonction dans l'ancien Israël*[22] is not intended to be a comprehensive work, but rather combines a consideration of selected dream texts with a discussion of the attitude towards dreams which prevailed during different periods of Israelite history. Recognizing the value of treating Israelite dreams in their ancient Near Eastern context, Husser commences with an analysis of royal dreams and incubation in Ugaritic texts, against which background he discusses Solomon's dream at Gibeon (1 Kgs 3) and Jacob's dream at Bethel (Gen. 28.10-22). He emphasizes the role of these two dreams as legitimizing devices of the kind reported in connection with royal figures throughout the ancient Near East, and sees the latter as part of 'un chemin initiatique'[23] which begins at Bethel and ends at Penuel. Although Husser is concerned primarily with the transformation that Jacob undergoes as a result of his experience at Bethel, he envisages several different layers of redaction, each with its own distinct interests. Thus a putative deuteronomistic redactor alludes to the Jerusalem Temple with a repetition of the word 'place',[24] and a postexilic editor inserts the reference to angels of God. Husser claims that ultimately the text's various interests in the sanctuary of Bethel and the person of Jacob combine with others arising from Gen. 32.23-33 to form the basis of the patriarch's role as Israel's eponymous ancestor.

Somewhat surprisingly, Husser does not consider the dream of the flocks (31.10-13) alongside his analysis of the dream at Bethel, but treats it separately as an example of a part exilic, part postexilic insertion of prophetic material into the patriarchal narrative. He compares certain linguistic and structural elements of the dream with the visions of Zechariah, but also identifies it with a tradition of prophetic call narratives which he illustrates by reference to Exodus 3.[25] It is Husser's opinion that the similarity between these two texts forges a link between Jacob and Moses, thus contributing to a more general attempt to recast Jacob's tenure with Laban in Paddan Aram as a forerunner of the Exodus.

In view of its introduction of the term 'prophet' (נביא), one might have expected Husser to consider Abimelech's dream in Genesis 20 in

---

22. Berlin: W. de Gruyter, 1994.
23. *Le songe et le parole*, pp. 116.
24. *Le songe et le parole*, pp. 110-11.
25. *Le songe et le parole*, pp. 134.

relation to prophecy. In fact, however, he discusses possible links with the wisdom tradition, influenced in part by perceived parallels between the question of Abimelech's guilt, or lack of it, and issues of apparent divine injustice which arise in Job. Once again, Husser's reading entails a postexilic date for the Genesis material, and the relative lateness of his attributions may make it difficult for some scholars to accept other aspects of his interpretations of the Genesis dreams.[26]

As this survey suggests, it is not among the aims of any of these studies to provide detailed considerations of the dream texts of Genesis. Despite the obvious imbalance in the number of dreams reported, and the significance attached to them, between Genesis and the rest of the Bible, they are not singled out for special treatment, and little attention is paid to their distinctive literary characteristics. Certainly, the charts and graphs that punctuate Gnuse's text are helpful in enabling us to recognize the particular language of dream reports, but they fall short of enhancing our understanding of its meaning. Indeed, none of these works emphasizes the unity of the dream reports, either as individual literary creations, or in terms of their role in the book in which they appear. (This may be accounted for partly by the adherence to traditional source criticism, at least by Ehrlich and Gnuse.) This study will attempt to provide a detailed textual analysis of the dreams of Genesis, incorporating an assessment of their role in the context in which they appear and their relationship to each other, which could not be achieved in works of greater scope.

A Survey of the Dreams in the Patriarchal Narratives

Before proceeding to the detailed analysis, I will set the stage with a brief overview of each of the five 'dream' texts, highlighting some of the themes and questions I will examine and address.

Abimelech's Dream (20.1-18)

Genesis 20 opens with a brief description of Abraham's journey to Gerar. During his sojourn there, Abraham announces that Sarah his wife is, in fact, his sister, upon which Abimelech, king of Gerar, has her

---

26. Husser mentions Gen. 31.24 only in passing, and includes no reference at all to Gen. 15, which he does not identify with the patriarchal dreams.

brought to him. The force of the Hebrew וַיִּקַּח אֶת שָׂרָה[27] (and he took Sarah) indicates that the king took Sarah for a wife, although the narrator's claim in v. 4 that Abimelech had not approached her (וַאֲבִימֶלֶךְ לֹא קָרַב אֵלֶיהָ) suggests that the union, or intended union, was not consummated. God comes to Abimelech in a dream of the night and the chapter proceeds with an account of a conversation in which the latter protests his innocence and the former threatens death. Ultimately, God concedes that, provided Abimelech returns Sarah to her husband, Abraham will intercede for him. The next morning Abimelech demands an explanation of Abraham, who cites his fear about what might have happened to him in Gerar on Sarah's account, and claims that, in any case, Sarah is his father's daughter, though not his mother's. Abimelech plies Abraham with animals, servants and a thousand pieces of silver, and the 'prophet' prays to God with the result that the king and his household are healed of the sterility with which, we now learn, God had afflicted them. Von Rad and others see at the heart of this narrative the issue of Abimelech's innocence and Abraham's guilt. The present study will argue against this interpretation, following Sternberg's reading to show how a recognition of the temporal disorder at work in this text can alter our perceptions of the apparently virtuous king.

The announcement of the dream in v. 3 is interesting for several reasons, not least for its use of 'and God came' (וַיָּבֹא אֱלֹהִים). Given the obvious distinction between dreams containing symbolic or visual images and those which report speech, one might have expected a formulaic introduction suggestive of a purely verbal exchange, as in 46.2. It is noteworthy that, while 'and God came' is among the least cerebral of the formulaic dream announcements, it occurs in Genesis only here and in the equally non-visual dream of Laban the Aramean in 31.24. The description of the deity entering the dreamer's room is a common feature of ancient Near Eastern dream reports, and it is possible that the non-Israelite status of these two dreamers discouraged the narrators from attempting to disguise the pagan formula.

C. Westermann has suggested that the content of Abimelech's dream is singularly inappropriate for its framework.[28] It is possible that the

---

27. All Hebrew Bible quotations are taken from *Biblia Hebraica Stuttgartensia* (Stuttgart: Deutsche Bibelgesellschaft, 1967/1990).

28. *Genesis 12–36: A Commentary* (trans. J.J. Scullion; London: SPCK, 1985): 'The dialog is introduced as a dream, or more accurately set within the framework

narrator prepared for this sort of criticism by providing, after the initial exchange between God and Abimelech, a rare reminder that God's subsequent words are still part of the dream (v. 6). With 31.10-13, this is one of the two occasions in Genesis when the activity of dreaming is mentioned both at the beginning of a dream and in the middle.[29] This may represent an attempt to compensate for an unconvincing narrative, but it may equally well confirm the narrator's commitment to the dream as a vehicle of revelation. At any rate, while it is true that Abimelech's is the only certain case of a dream in Genesis involving a dialogue between God and the dreamer,[30] it seems unreasonable to question the appropriateness of the vehicle on this account, particularly given the extent to which the dream report follows the conventions of royal dreaming in the ancient Near East.

Yet it is clear that God's message to Abimelech could have been conveyed by means other than a dream; a timely plague (12.17) or glance from a window (26.8) would have sufficed to alert Abimelech to the true situation. It is thus appropriate to ask why the narrator persisted with a dream narrative here. (Indeed, the existence of versions of the story with no reference to the dream motif makes it difficult to claim, as some exegetes have done of Jacob's dream at Bethel, that it was simply a traditional element of the story that was maintained even after it was no longer appropriate.) This question has no simple answer, but it does encourage a search for an aspect of God's message that could not have been conveyed naturalistically, and which is, indeed, particularly suited to its dream format. The answer may be found partly in v. 7, particularly given the obvious links between chs. 20 and 18, where Abraham also fulfils an intercessory role.

Jacob's Dream at Bethel (28.10-22)
28.10-22 describes Jacob's momentous experience upon leaving his father's house. Arriving at a place, as yet unnamed, he takes a stone for a pillow and lays down to sleep. He dreams of a ladder or stairway extending from earth to heaven upon which angels are moving up and

---

of a dream (vv. 3a, 6a, 8). No exegete has seen that what is within the framework does not suit the frame' (p. 321).

29. In the Joseph stories we are dealing with pairs of dreams, so this point does not apply there.

30. Gen. 15 also contains a dialogue between God and the 'dreamer', but Abraham's experience there is described as a vision not a dream.

down. God is standing next to him,[31] promising land and offspring who
will spread out in every direction over the earth; he further claims that
all the families of the earth will bless themselves through Jacob and his
descendants. Jacob awakes, shaken by the experience, and sets up the
stone pillow as a pillar which he anoints. He renames the place, previously called Luz, Bethel. Jacob then vows that, provided God protects
and cares for him, and returns him safe to his father's house, the stone
will become a house of God, and that he will offer a tenth of all God
gives him. This dream, although it contains the striking visual image of
the ladder, is not 'symbolic' in the style of the Joseph dreams.

Much of the extensive scholarship on Gen. 28.10-22 has focused on
whether or not it features incubation. Although the context is propitious, in that the narrative immediately preceding it suggests that Jacob
may have been uncertain on account of his duplicitously won blessing,
and the instruction to find a wife,[32] scholarly opinion seems to weigh in
against incubation. It is a generally acknowledged prerequisite of dream
incubation that the dreamer should be aware of the holiness of the place
before falling asleep,[33] and thus, according to Ehrlich,[34] Jacob's failure
to recognize the holiness of Bethel until God revealed himself there
rules out dream incubation in this text. The notion of an 'unintentional'
incubation,[35] which did not depend on the dreamer's knowing that the
place was holy, fails to convince.

Exegetes applying source-critical techniques to this text might posit
substantially different attitudes towards incubation in the two narrative
sources usually presumed here. Such scholars generally view vv. 16 and

31. The Hebrew והנה יהוה נצב עליו may be translated as meaning that the LORD
was standing next to him or above him, referring to Jacob, or that the LORD was
standing next to it or above it, referring to the ladder. In view of similarities to other
ancient Near Eastern dream reports, one of the two former readings seems preferable.

32. A. Jeffers, 'Divination by Dreams in Ugaritic Literature and in the Old Testament', *IBS* 12 (1990), pp.167-83, suggests that dreams are sought by means of
incubation in cases of extreme necessity, particularly regarding the lack of an heir.

33. T.H. McAlpine, *Sleep, Divine and Human, in the Old Testament* (JSOTSup,
38; Sheffield: JSOT Press, 1987): 'Based on Deubner's definition, Ehrlich takes at
least the following to be necessary conditions for incubation: (1) intention to elicit a
divine revelation (2) to be received in sleep (3) in a holy place (4) after specific preparatory steps' (p. 158).

34. *Der Traum im Alten Testament*, p. 32.

35. Gnuse, *The Dream Theophany of Samuel*, p. 67.

17 as the work of the so-called Yahwist and Elohist respectively, partly because the former uses יהוה (usually rendered in English 'LORD' or 'YHWH') and the latter אלהים (usually rendered 'God'), and partly because the two verses overlap in function, both expressing what appears to be Jacob's immediate response to his dream. If Jacob denies his prior awareness of the holiness of the place only in 'J' (v. 16), it would be misleading to claim, on that basis, that 'E' precludes incubation.[36] The analysis offered here will, however, consider the text in its final form, proposing that the Bethel narrative is based on the model of those ancient Near Eastern dream reports, exemplified by the dream of Gudea of Lagash, which provide the dreamer with the plan, or at least the authorization and inspiration, for a temple. The סלם (described variously as a ladder stemming from the mythological topography of Bethel,[37] a ramp or stairlike pavement,[38] or some sort of ziggurat, akin to the Tower of Babel)[39] is the biblical equivalent of the monstrous figure that provides Gudea with his architectural blueprint.

36. A.W. Jenks, *The Elohist and North Israelite Traditions* (SBLMS, 22; Montana: Scholars Press, 1977).

37. Ehrlich, *Der Traum im Alten Testament*: 'Diese Leiter stammt aus der mythologischen Topographie von Bethel. "Für das volkstümliche Denken ist die Himmelsleiter eine Realität und hat ursprünglich mit der Stiftungssage des Heiligtums durch Jakob nichts zu tun" (Westphal, Jahwes Wohnstätten, 1908, S. 233)' (p. 30).

38. Von Rad, *Genesis* (trans. J.H. Marks; London: SCM Press, 1961–1987): 'When we think of the "ladder to heaven", however, we should not think of an actual ladder, for such a simultaneous mounting and descending of wingless divine messengers on it would not be easily conceivable' (p. 284).

39. N. Sarna, *Understanding Genesis: The Heritage of Biblical Israel* (New York: Schocken Books, 1966–1972): 'The dream imagery reflects a decidedly Mesopotamian background already familiar to us from the "Tower of Babel" episode. The stairway that Jacob saw connecting heaven and earth recalls at once the picture of the ziqqurat (sic) with its external ramp connecting each stage of the tower to the other. The note that "its top reached the sky" (28.12) and the identification of the sight of the dream as "the gateway to heaven" (28.17), is reminiscent of the stereotyped phraseology used in connection with the Babylonian temple-towers. But it differs from pagan mythology in that the stairway of Jacob's dream is not a channel of communication between man and God. The deity does not descend by it to the human realm and man does not ascend to the divine sphere. The chasm between the two is unbridgeable by physical means. Indeed, the background presence of the angels serves to highlight this fact, for the stairway is obviously for them alone. They are merely ornamental, playing no role in the theophany' (p. 193).

Finally, and briefly, on Jacob's experience at Bethel, it should be noted that the dream contains God's promise that all the families of the earth will be blessed through Jacob and his offspring (28.14). This may connect with Abraham's intercessory powers in chs. 15 and 20; with Joseph's role as the interpreter of Pharaoh's dreams; and, of course, with Jacob's own interactions with Laban. This study will consider the possible significance of the fact that most of the Genesis dream texts deal, in one sense or another, with the relationship between Israelites and non-Israelites.

Jacob and the Speckled Flock (31.10-13)
Chapter 30 contains the strange and confusing account of Jacob's use of elaborate selective breeding techniques at the expense of his father-in-law, Laban. The references to shoots of poplar, almond and plane make it seem likely that pagan customs played as large a part as rational observation in this account. In ch. 31 Jacob relates a dream in which an angel of God has confirmed God's role in the business of the speckled flock, and the dream may thus have been intended to sanitize the pagan elements introduced in the previous chapter. In addition, it enabled Jacob to blame God for any false-dealings with Laban, and provided him with a justification for removing his wives from their father's house.

The dream is interesting on several counts. First, it is the only Genesis dream that is not announced by the narrator. While it may simply be the case that God's instructions in v. 3 and the dream reported in v. 10 were regarded as one and the same event, thus diminishing the need for a specific dream announcement, this omission may have greater narrative significance. Although it is not the only dream in which angels appear, it is the only one in which an angel of God speaks to the dreamer instead of (or possibly as well as) God himself. The use of the idiom concerning raised eyes is also unusual: although this image is commonplace, particularly when preceding a narrative turning point or introducing an event or object of particular importance, it does not usually feature in dream announcements. Furthermore, no mention is made of the dreamer's falling asleep or awakening, the time of day, nor the fear or awe with which the dream, or its subsequent narration, was received.

The Dream of Laban the Aramean (31.24)

Shortly after Jacob's dream of the speckled flock, God comes to Laban in a dream. Laban is by now a familiar figure, which makes the formal appellation, 'Laban the Aramean', a little surprising, and it is possible that the narrator wished to emphasize Laban's non-Israelite status. As with Abimelech's dream (20.3), the revelation is called a dream of the night. The dream's message is as mysterious as it is brief:

הִשָּׁמֶר לְךָ פֶּן תְּדַבֵּר צִם יַעֲקֹב מִטּוֹב עַד רַע:
Beware of attempting anything with Jacob, good or bad.

Various attempts have been made to translate this verse, but none is entirely satisfactory. It seems unlikely that God is simply advising Laban against speaking to Jacob,[40] or against having any dealings whatsoever with him (NJPS), particularly since Laban proceeds immediately to do both. More plausibly, טוב (good) and רע (evil) may carry the weight of blessing and curse;[41] God is warning Laban that the shoe is on the other foot. Indeed, it may be more of a reminder than a warning; Laban has previously made a strikingly similar point to Abraham's servant (24.50).

The Covenant of the Pieces (15.1-21)

In Genesis 15, which includes the events usually known as the Covenant of the Pieces, God comes to Abraham[42] in a vision, promising protection and reward. Abraham, on account of his childlessness, is sceptical about the nature of the reward, and God responds by taking him outside to count the stars, assuring him that his descendants will be as numerous. God further promises that Abraham will possess the land already assigned to him (12.7), and again Abraham expresses doubt. This time God instructs him to bring three animals and two birds, and Abraham cuts the animals, but not the birds, in half and sets the pieces opposite each other. Birds of prey descend upon the carcasses and Abraham drives them away, at which point the sun sets and he falls into a deep sleep. God speaks again, warning of oppression for Abraham's

40. NRSV: 'Take care that you say not a word to Jacob, either good or bad'.

41. Cf. Balaam's words in Num. 24.5. מַה טֹּבוּ אֹהָלֶיךָ יַעֲקֹב (how good are your tents O Jacob) is clearly to be read as a blessing, in contradistinction to the curse which Balak has asked him to deliver.

42. For the sake of simplicity, the first patriarch will be referred to as 'Abraham' even where Genesis indicates 'Abram'.

offspring, but promising peaceful old age for the patriarch himself. A smoking oven and a flaming torch then pass between the divided carcasses, and God makes a covenant with Abraham in which he reconfirms his promise of the land.

Much of the scholarly exegesis of ch. 15 has centred on the breakdown of the text into Yahwistic and Elohistic components. The present analysis will deal with the text in its final redacted form, and it will be argued that many of the difficulties it poses (such as the confusion over the time of day at which the events occurred, and the omission of instructions to Abraham regarding what he should do with the animals) may be resolved by treating the entire episode as a dream report which begins with the announcement of the vision in v. 1. Further evidence for this view may be found both in the specific language of the account ('fear not', v. 1, and 'behold', v. 4 often appear in dream reports), and in its subject matter (dreams often concern the lack of an heir). The prophecy encapsulated in vv. 13-16 fits well in the context of a dream, the connection between dreaming and prophecy being well attested in the Bible and elsewhere.

Some Sign Posts

Although I have made extensive use of studies of ancient Near Eastern dream literature and rabbinic Bible interpretation, not to mention modern Bible scholarship, I have been particularly keen to provide a 'close reading' of the dream reports treated here. This close reading has highlighted six clear-cut themes which are, I believe, shared by all five texts. A brief summary of these themes at the outset may help the reader to trace their development through the ensuing analysis:

(1)   Each dream is received during a period of anxiety or danger (for the dreamer, for the person for whom the dream is actually intended, i.e., Abraham in 20.1-18 and Jacob in 31.24, or for both).

(2)   Each dream concerns the descendants (immediate or eventual) of the dreamer, of the person for whom the dream was intended, or both, and is received at a time when the continuation of a line seems to be in jeopardy.

(3)   Each dream signals a change in status for the dreamer or for the person for whom the dream is intended, or for both.

(4) Each dream recasts recent events to reveal divine involvement in what had previously appeared as an exclusively human affair.

(5) Each dream deals with at least one aspect of the relationship between non-Israelites and Israelites.

(6) Each dream is connected with absence from the land.

Naturally, I do not mean to suggest that these themes are the exclusive property of dream reports, but rather that dream reports contain these themes in a particularly vivid and concentrated form which merits the close scrutiny I have attempted to provide.

Chapter 1

ABIMELECH'S DREAM
(GENESIS 20.1-18)

The Wife-Sister Narratives: Treading the Textual Minefield

Much of the scholarly attention devoted to the so-called 'wife-sister' texts of Genesis (12.10-20; 20.1-18; 26.1-12) has sought to describe and account for the threefold repetition of a markedly similar story. Traditional source criticism has played a central role in the analysis of these texts, although scholars have differed significantly in their attributions. In his commentary on Genesis, G. von Rad regards 12.10-20, a particularly problematic narrative for him, as the work of the Yahwist, and 20.1-18 as an attempt by the more theologically sophisticated Elohist to iron out some of the difficulties of the earlier account. While noting evidence of redaction by a later hand, he ascribes most of 26.1-12 to the Yahwist. Following Wellhausen and Noth, he does not rule out the possibility that the account of Isaac and Rebekah in Gerar may be the oldest of the three wife-sister texts.[1]

In his more detailed discussion of these texts, J. Van Seters grapples with the problem of how both 12.10-20 and 26.1-12 can be seen as the work of the Yahwist, particularly in the face of the common assertion that doublets indicate separate sources. For reasons which need not be elaborated here, the resulting confusion persuades him that 20.1-18 cannot be ascribed to the Elohist, and he therefore designates both 12.10-20 and 20.1-18 as pre-Yahwistic, claiming that only 26.1-12 is the work of the Yahwist as traditionally defined. The relevant sections of chs. 20 and 26 are seen as literary, rather than oral, variants of 12.10-20.[2] For rather different reasons, C. Westermann is equally dismissive

1. *Genesis*, pp. 167-70, 225-39, 268-73.
2. *Abraham in History and Tradition* (New Haven: Yale University Press, 1975), pp. 167-91.

of the view that 26.1-12 may be the oldest of the three sources, arguing that its proponents have failed to come to terms with H. Gunkel's depiction of 12.10-20 as a classical example of an early folk narrative. He asserts that only this account can be ascribed to the Yahwist, and that the other two were incorporated into the Priestly and Yahwistic material at a later stage.[3]

In an article dealing with the literary composition of the wife-sister texts, T.D. Alexander is critical of all these theories and, given their extreme complexity, the uncertainty with which they are presented, and the extent to which they contradict one another, he has little difficulty in finding chinks, if not gaping holes, in their armour. With this in mind, perhaps, it is only in passing that he risks his own proposal, namely that the wife-sister texts may be the work of one author.[4]

The waters are muddied still further by the fact that, whereas Van Seters finds reason here to claim that ch. 20 cannot be ascribed to the Elohist, others, such as von Rad[5] and Gnuse,[6] have taken it as compelling evidence for the existence of this source. Quite apart from the objections raised by Van Seters specifically in regard to ch. 20, M. Lichtenstein has made a more general claim advocating a highly sceptical approach to the so-called Elohist's supposed preference for dream theophany.[7] When all this is taken into account, it is difficult to see how any advances in the debate over the attribution of these texts can be made within the scope of this monograph. Yet, given the impossibility of proceeding with an analysis of Abimelech's dream in ch. 20 without a hypothesis of some kind about the wider context in which it appears, a proposal is required.

At this point it is necessary to return to Gunkel's claim, clearly a continuing influence on Westermann and others, that 12.10-20 represents the earliest form of the 'folktale' upon which the other two were

3. *Genesis 12–36*, pp. 159-68, 316-29, 420-30.

4. 'Are the Wife/Sister Incidents of Genesis Literary Compositional Variants?', *VT* 42 (1992), pp. 145-53.

5. See *Genesis*, pp. 26-27, where the Elohist's interest in prophecy is mentioned alongside his preference for dream theophany, and p. 226, where von Rad claims that 20.1-18 is unanimously ascribed to the Elohist by scholars who recognise the existence of this source.

6. See *The Dream Theophany of Samuel*, pp. 64-65. The author claims here that, as a doublet of the Yahwist accounts in chs. 12 and 26, 20.1-18 provides evidence for the existence of the Elohist source.

7. Lichtenstein, 'Dream-Theophany and the "E Document"', pp. 45-54.

based.[8] The problem here is that one expects to find in a story of the sort outlined by Gunkel a narrative coherence which is patently lacking in ch. 12, and this suggests that, oldest or not, it cannot be relied upon to provide the essential characteristics of the account on which it was based. The story related in ch. 12 makes sense only when information gleaned from the narratively later accounts is read back into it, but although biblical scholars seem content with this form of reading-with-hindsight, it is unlikely to have satisfied those unversed in modern literary theory. Van Seters argues that the 'proleptic and resumptive style' of 20.2 'is not a feature of oral storytelling', and that the economy of detail here makes it unlikely that it is an independent account of the story told in ch. 12.[9] If one were to apply the same arguments to 12.10-20, it would be the case that, in its failure to explain how Pharaoh learned that Sarah was Abraham's wife and that God had sent plagues on her account, this text should also be seen as too economical to stand alone as a full account of an oral story or an independent literary version. This leaves us with the possibility that all three wife-sister texts are based on an earlier account of an event whose precise details we are unlikely ever to ascertain. The Genesis versions may then be regarded as reworkings of that account, which make use of only those elements considered relevant to the narrative context in which they appear. It seems probable that each version omitted features of the original account, and that each added details not present there. An attempt will now be made to reconstruct the basic elements of this earlier account, in the hope that this will reveal something of the significance of its biblical renditions.

This approach differs markedly from that adopted by most exegetes of these texts, who, if they refer at all to an earlier version of the story, make no attempt to distinguish its contents from either 12.10-20 or 26.1-12, depending on their theory of source attribution. Exceptional in this respect is K. Koch, who formulates various theories of literary development and arrives at the following conclusion:

> The original version will thus have run: Because of famine Isaac travelled from the desert in southern Palestine to the nearby Canaanite city of Gerar to live there as a 'sojourner', i.e. to keep within the pasturage rights on the ground belonging to the city. He told everyone that his wife was his sister so that his life would not be endangered by those who

8. H. Gunkel, *Legends of Genesis* (New York: Schocken Books, 1964), p. 100.
9. *Abraham in History and Tradition*, p. 171.

desired her. However, Rebekah's beauty could not pass unnoticed. The king of the city, Abimelech, took Rebekah into his harem, amply compensating Isaac. As a material sin was about to be committed, God struck the people of the palace with a mysterious illness. Through the medium of his gods, or a soothsayer, Abimelech recognised what had happened. Abimelech called Isaac to account: 'What is this you have done to me?' He then restored him his wife and sent him away, loaded with gifts.[10]

Koch bases his conclusion that the original version concerned Isaac and Abimelech on the general assumption that in the transmission of a saga the least known figure is the original. Yet, aside from the troubling translation of a rule of thumb into an absolute here, his theory takes no account of other plausible explanations for the duplication of one story with two different heroes, such as the identification of father and son, or the desire to emphasize the extent to which both were the victims of circumstance. The presumed involvement of gods or a soothsayer is also worrying, and the reference to the sleeping children and settled cattle who may have formed the backdrop to the telling of this tale raises concerns about the role played by imagination in the construction of this theory.

Yet a form-critical analysis of the three narratives is a reasonable starting-point, and a similar, though abbreviated, analysis will follow:

1	2	3
Famine		Famine
Visit to king	Visit to king	Visit to king
Wife/sister	Wife/sister	Wife/sister
Wife's beauty		Wife's beauty
King plagued	King plagued	
Discovery (?)	Discovery (dream)	Discovery (window)
King's rebuke	King's rebuke	King's rebuke
Wealth (from king)	Wealth (from king)	Wealth (from God)
	Fear of God	Fear of God
	Dispute over well	Dispute over well
	Covenant with king	Covenant with king

For the purposes of this discussion, it will be assumed that the original story included only those elements which occur in all three versions

10. 'The Ancestress of Israel in Danger', in *idem, The Growth of the Biblical Tradition: The Form-Critical Method* (trans. S.M. Cupitt; London: A. & C. Black, 1969), pp. 111-28 (126).

available to us.[11] While this process of selection may be, in some respects, as random as that chosen by Koch, it lacks the imaginative element which is troubling there, and does not involve unprovable assumptions regarding external data and the identity of the original protagonists. The result is a coherent narrative whose plot may be summarized as follows: (1) the patriarch visits a foreign king and, (2) prior to arrival, tells his wife to pretend that she is his sister. (3) The king discovers that she is, in fact, his wife, and (4) rebukes the patriarch. (5) The patriarch is wealthier after the event than he was before. In essence, then, this is the story of the patriarch's entry into a difficult, and potentially dangerous situation, which he is able to turn to his own advantage. The famine, the wife's beauty and the reference to the absence of fear of God may be taken as dispensable justifications, and no guesses need be made about whether Abraham or Isaac was the story's original hero.

It may be helpful at this stage to ask whether this narrative sequence is more likely to have been derived from a story about one of the patriarchs or from the knowledge of an actual practice. N. Sarna refers to other ancient stories in which a wife is taken on account of her great beauty and must be restored to her rightful husband.[12] Yet although one of them tells of a man's appropriation of his brother's wife, suggesting, perhaps, a confusion between wife and sister,[13] none of the stories available to us justifies the biblical emphasis on the wife-sister motif. If, on the other hand, the narratives were based on a practice, what kind of practice might it have been? E.A. Speiser attempted to explain the wife-sister motif with reference to a supposed Hurrian custom in which a man adopted his wife as a sister, thereby raising her status.[14] Yet

11. Van Seters, *Abraham in History and Tradition*, pp. 183-91, includes the descriptions of the disputes over the wells and subsequent covenants in 21.22-33 and 26.12-31 in his discussion of the wife-sister texts, and the same principle has been followed here.

12. *The Jewish Publication Society Torah Commentary, Genesis* (Philadelphia: Jewish Publication Society, 1989), pp. 94-95, 410. Sarna draws parallels with the Ugaritic legend of King Keret, who lost the beautiful wife through whom he was destined to continue his line, and with the Greek story of Helen of Troy.

13. Sarna, *JPS Torah Commentary*, p. 410, describes the Egyptian tale of the brothers Anubis and Bata. It should be noted, however, that, although Sarna mentions this tale in connection with 12.10-20 (p. 95), the extended reference here is given in the more appropriate context of 39.7-20.

14. 'The Wife-Sister Motif in the Patriarchal Narratives', in A. Altmann (ed.),

although, as Sarna also suggests,[15] this may have special application to
20.12, it does not fit well with the general context of the Genesis stories. At any rate, Van Seters has argued convincingly that the Nuzi
texts should not be taken as the basis for patriarchal custom here,[16] and
many objections have been raised against Speiser's reading of them.[17]
Even the possibility that the custom of giving one's wife to a foreign
king to secure his favour was widespread at the time fails to explain the
biblical wife-sister deception. Had Abraham wanted to give his wife to
curry favour, he could have done so without claiming that she was his
sister, and, furthermore, Isaac tells the same lie while showing no inclination to give Rebekah to Abimelech. More plausible than any of these
theories, perhaps, is the notion that the story was rooted in the idea of
the patriarchs' need for self-protection among alien peoples. We cannot
know whether or not the use of this particular device was widespread,
but the facts that identical deceptions are practised by both Abraham
and Isaac, and that Abraham may have used it throughout his travels,[18]
suggests a certain breadth of application. Even if, however, these stories were based on a general need rather than a specific occurrence in
patriarchal history, the imaginative appeal of this plot should not be
underestimated. It exploits the thrilling narrative touchstones of unusual
beauty, disguise, sex, wealth and narrowly averted danger, and we cannot exclude the possibility that, at one level, its repetition owes much to
this fortuitous combination of themes.

The Central Themes of the Wife-Sister Texts

The task of analysing the issues raised and addressed by the repetition
of the wife-sister motif has, of course, been undertaken by many exegetes. R. Polzin writes of two sets of 'transformations', the first of

Biblical and Other Studies (Cambridge, MA: Harvard University Press, 1963),
pp. 15-28.

    15. *Understanding Genesis*, pp. 102-103.

    16. *Abraham in History and Tradition*, pp. 71-76 (see p. 76 for this precise
point).

    17. See, for instance, M. Selman, 'The Social Environment of the Patriarchs',
TynBul 27 (1976), pp. 114-36, especially pp. 119-21.

    18. This is Nachmanides's reading of 20.13, *MG, ad loc*. He suggests that,
although this was Abraham's procedure wherever he went, it is only mentioned
when something significant happens on account of it.

which concerns the relationship of promised wealth and progeny to adultery, and the means by which the monarch discovers Sarah's true identity. The second set answers questions about the nature of blessing and curse.[19] In a psychoanalytic reading of the wife-sister texts, J.C. Exum emphasizes the playing out of a voyeuristic male fantasy confirming his wife's desirability. She too envisages a transformation, beginning with Abraham's act of making Sarah available to Pharaoh, and ending with Abimelech's observation of a sexual encounter between Isaac and Rebekah.[20] D.J.A. Clines's interest in transformation extends to the entire Genesis narrative and beyond.[21] He shows how the identity of the endangered party changes with each text, beginning with Abraham in ch. 12, moving to a crucially pregnant Sarah in ch. 20,[22] and ending with Isaac in ch. 26. Clines sees Lot and Ishmael as potential threats, removed as the narrative progresses, to the transmission of the blessing to Abraham's own descendants, and concludes with the unexplored suggestion that relations between Isaac and the Philistines may have implications for narratively later biblical encounters, such as those described in Judges 13–17, and throughout 2 Samuel. The present analysis will elaborate upon Polzin's account of the theme of blessing and curse in these texts, suggesting that they deal with the specific question of how the patriarchs can avert curse and bring blessings upon non-Israelites, and will explore the additional questions of how the patriarchs will be able to live peaceably with the existing inhabitants of the land, and how God will operate in this context.

The exegetical device of the 'leading word' (*Leitwort*), first outlined by M. Buber[23] and used extensively, albeit loosely, by modern literary

19. ' "The Ancestress of Israel in Danger" in Danger', *Semeia* 3-4 (1975), pp. 81-97.

20. 'Who's Afraid of the Endangered Ancestress?', in J.C. Exum and D.J.A. Clines (eds), *The New Literary Criticism and The Hebrew Bible* (JSOTSup, 143; Sheffield: Sheffield Academic Press, 1993), pp. 91-124.

21. *What Does Eve do to Help? And Other Readerly Questions to the Old Testament* (JSOTSup, 94; Sheffield: 1990), pp. 67-84.

22. Not all scholars would share Clines's confidence in the 'arithmetic of the narrative': 'For if there were twelve months to run from 17.21 to the birth of Isaac, and nine months from 18.10 to the birth of Isaac, and Isaac is to be born immediately the wife-sister narrative concludes—which is to say: promptly and explicitly "at the season of which YHWH had spoken" (21.2)—Sarah has to be pregnant during the dangerous incident of ch. 20' (pp. 75-76).

23. 'Leitwort Style in Pentateuch Narrative', in M. Buber and F. Rosenzweig,

critics of the Bible,[24] provides a useful starting point for a discussion of the coexistence of the patriarchs and the land's permanent residents. In an interesting discussion of this concept, Y. Amit[25] draws a careful distinction between the 'leading word' and the 'key word', and enumerates the difficulties inherent in the use of this tool of biblical exegesis. She emphasizes, in particular, the necessity of demonstrating that a presumed 'leading word' is used in the 'highly significant' manner prescribed by Buber, and that its significance can be established by alternative methods of analysis.

Sarna describes גור (sojourn), which occurs in various forms 15 times in Genesis, as a 'key word',[26] and although he may not be using this term in the strict sense outlined by Amit, it is interesting to note that the word occurs in all three of the wife-sister texts.[27] In 12.10 Abraham goes to Egypt 'to sojourn there' (לגור שם); in 20.1 he 'sojourns in Gerar' (ויגר בגרר); and in 26.3 God instructs Isaac to sojourn 'in this land' (גור בארץ הזאת).[28] The notion that the verb has special significance here is reinforced by what appears to be a particular emphasis on its usage in chs. 20 and 26. Genesis 20.1 reads as follows:

ויסע משם אברהם ארצה הנגב וישב בין קדש ובין שור ויגר בגרר:
Abraham journeyed from there to the region of the Negeb; he settled between Kadesh and Shur and sojourned in Gerar.[29]

Scripture and Translation (trans. L. Rosenwald; Bloomington: Indiana University Press, 1994), pp. 114-28.

24. See, for instance, J.P. Fokkelman, *Narrative Art in Genesis: Specimens of Stylistic and Structural Analysis* (Biblical Seminar, 12; Sheffield: JSOT Press, 1991 [1975]).

25. 'The Multi-Purpose "Leading Word" and the Problems of its Usage', *Prooftexts* 9 (1989), pp. 99-114.

26. See *JPS Torah Commentary*. It should be noted here that it is not clear from Sarna's discussion whether he is using this term in the technical sense outlined by Amit, or merely as an exegetical expression.

27. Cf. other occurrences of 'sojourn' in 17.8, 21.23, 21.34, 35.27, 47.4, 49.9.

28. Presumably for stylistic reasons, *JPS* does not invariably translate גור as 'sojourn'. 26.3 reads 'reside in this land' but, to avoid confusion in this discussion, I will use 'sojourn'.

29. I depart slightly here from *JPS*, which does not follow the Masoretic Hebrew punctuation in this verse.

Abraham '*settled*' (וישב) between Kadesh and Shur, but he '*sojourned*' (ויגר) in Gerar,[30] and one might note here the extent to which the verb is emphasized by its use in conjunction with a place name derived from the same root. Chapter 26.1-12 contains three different verbs meaning 'dwell'. In v. 2 God tells Isaac to 'stay in the land which I point out to you' (שכן בארץ אשר אמר אליך). Clearly this statement needs clarification, and some is duly given in v. 3: 'Sojourn in *this* land and I will be with you' (גור בארץ הזאת ואהיה עמך). God's temporary unwillingness to name the precise location (cf. 22.2) has heightened suspense, and we are somewhat surprised when Isaac is told merely to stay where he is, 'in this land'. What, then, has been achieved by God's stalling tactic? The only significant change is in the precise definition of the terms of Isaac's residence in Gerar; he will reside there as an outsider. Neither is the plausibility of this reading compromised by the third use of a verb meaning 'dwell' in v. 6: 'So Isaac stayed in Gerar' (בגרר וישב יצחק). 'Sojourn' (גור) is simply a quasi-technical term defining conditions of residence, which is perfectly compatible with other similar words. Thus, whereas 'stayed' (ישב), for instance, is neutral, denoting a stay of no particular duration or quality, 'sojourn' (גור) applies to what is often described as a 'resident alien'; a guest rather than a citizen.[31]

The significance of 'sojourn' (גור) in the context of the wife-sister texts is further revealed by the circumstances in which Abraham and Isaac are required to dwell in Egypt and Gerar. An obvious *Leitmotif* of two of these narratives is the announcement of famine.[32] Famine, or at

---

30. For an outline of scholarly approaches to the geographical difficulties raised by this verse, see Westermann, *Genesis 12–36*, p. 320.

31. See Gen. 23.4 and Lev. 25.47 for uses of גר that support this reading.

32. Famine is, of course, unmentioned in ch. 20, but 26.1 implies that there may have been, at one stage, a tradition of famine in Gerar as well as in Egypt:

ויהי רעב בארץ מלבד הרעב הראשון אשר היה בימי אברהם וילך יצחק אל
אבימלך מלך פלשתים גררה:

There was famine in the land—aside from the previous famine that had occurred in the days of Abraham—and Isaac went to Abimelech, king of the Philistines, in Gerar.

The announcement of famine in ch. 12 drives Abraham down to Egypt but, even before God tells Isaac not to go to Egypt (26.2), the patriarch has made the decision to go to Gerar. In view of the identification of father with son in this episode, one

least the lack of food or water, in the Bible often coincides with a more
direct manifestation of God's intervention in the human sphere, as the
lack of natural sustenance increases human dependence upon divine
good-will.[33] In the wife-sister narratives, however, the extent of the
patriarchs' dependence on God is not immediately obvious, and it
seems possible that the generosity of a foreign ruler will be the source
of their material salvation. Yet we need not wait long for the first indication that reliance upon foreign kings has little to recommend it.

From the outset, then, the wife-sister texts are dealing with conditions of residency, and in this context it is no accident that the narratively earlier version takes place in Egypt as opposed to Canaan. As
noted by von Rad,[34] 12.10-20 presents the story in its bleakest and most
disturbing form. Abraham's deception almost certainly results in actual
adultery between Sarah and Pharaoh, Pharaoh and his house are plagued
and the great wealth with which Abraham returns to Lot, besides being
a source of friction between them, is tainted by its dubious origin. Yet
aside from the wealth, which Abraham is allowed to keep, we can
hardly fail to note how little the ensuing narrative is affected by the
patriarch's sojourn in Egypt.[35] The one subsequent reference to this episode in Abraham's life occurs in 26.1-2, and here primarily so that
Isaac will not repeat his father's history. One might argue that the striking absence of repercussions from this potentially damaging, if not
disastrous, error of judgment on Abraham's part is partly attributable to
its occurrence in Egypt, which is primarily a point of exodus in Israelite
history, rather than the location of long-term integration.

As noted above, Van Seters sees the dispute over the wells and subsequent covenant as an integral part of the wife-sister texts in chs. 21
and 26. At first glance, it appears that this element of the story is

might make 26.1 the basis for a theory that, at least in Isaac's mind, Gerar was
associated with refuge from famine.

33. See Gen. 41 (especially v. 25), where the famine is the backdrop against
which Joseph, with God's help, rises to power and saves his brothers from starvation in Canaan. See also Exod. 16 and 17, where the Israelite dependence upon
God is emphasized by the lack of natural sustenance.

34. *Genesis*, pp. 167-70.

35. *MG, ad loc.*, suggests that the patriarch's sojourn in Egypt is intended to
mirror the later experience of the Israelites there: everything that happened to them
had already happened to Abraham. While acknowledging the subjectivity of this
view, one should note the extent to which it accommodates the repetition of the
theme of plagues in connection with Pharaoh.

missing from ch. 12, but, in fact, precisely the same concerns are raised in ch. 13 in connection with Lot. All three narratives address the question of how the land will support the patriarch alongside other inhabitants whose wealth and blessing do not come directly from God. Yet, whereas in chs. 21 and 26 the dispute over the wells involves the protagonists of the wife-sister text which precedes it, in chs. 12 and 13 the role which should belong to the foreign king is assumed by Lot. A clue to the significance of this may be found in O. Sforno's commentary on 13.7.[36] Having noted the extreme difficulty, for lack of pasture, of coexistence in the land, Sforno directs his comment to the impression conveyed by the dispute between Abraham and Lot to the Canaanites and the Perizzites, who were already dwelling there. If these two kinsmen cannot coexist peacefully together in the land, the Canaanites and Perizzites observe, according to Sforno, how much harder will it be for them to coexist with the other people who are already living there! Taken together, 12.10-20 and 13.1-12 are directly related to what is emerging as a central theme of the wife-sister texts; the relationship between two peoples dwelling together in one land. Yet the ideal of peaceful coexistence is by no means the only issue at stake here. Immediately before Abraham leaves for Egypt God tells him:

ואברכה מברכיך ומקללך אאר ונברכו בך כל משפחת האדמה:

I will bless those who bless you and curse him that curses you; and all
the families of the earth shall bless themselves through you (12.3).

This verse contains the three elements—divine blessing, divine curse, and the self-blessing of non-Israelites through the patriarch—which constitute the complex relationship envisaged between the Israelite and non-Israelite inhabitants of the land.

The ensuing narrative contains a graphic demonstration of what will befall those who curse Abraham: for the crime of taking Abraham's wife, the LORD 'afflicted [struck] Pharaoh and his house with mighty plagues' (נגע נגעים). The verb 'afflict/strike/touch' (נגע) is relatively unusual in the Pentateuch, and a brief examination of its occurrences in chs. 20 and 26 will help to reveal its significance. In 12.17 the LORD *strikes* (וינגע) Pharaoh and his house with great plagues; in 20.6 God tells Abimelech, 'I did not let you *touch* (לנגע) her'; and in 26.11 Abimelech warns that whoever *touches* (הנגע) Isaac or his wife will die.

36. *MG, ad loc.*

These represent three of the eight occurrences of this verb in Genesis (3.3; 26.29; 28.12; 32.26; and 32.33).

It is immediately clear that the verb is used quite differently in each of the three texts. In 12.17 it refers to plagues, in 20.6 it describes a sexual approach, and should probably be seen as a pair with v. 4, 'Now Abimelech had not approached her' (ואבימלך לא קרב אליה),[37] and in 26.11, where it applies both to Isaac and to Rebekah, it means neither 'plagues' nor 'molests', but something closer to 'lays a hand on'. Yet although the three occurrences of the verb carry three distinct meanings, they are almost certainly used interactively. It should be noted here that, elsewhere in Genesis, it is rarely used in a neutral sense, usually appearing in a context where a touch inflicts harm or, at the least, has harmful repercussions. In 3.3 it may reflect Eve's subconscious acknowledgment of what could happen to her if she touches the tree; in 32.26, 33 it is the strike which lames Jacob; and in 26.29 Abimelech is almost certainly harking back to his own words in 26.11.[38] The exception is 28.12 (מגיע), where it probably means no more than 'touched' or 'reached'.

What, then, is the precise nature of the interplay between the various occurrences of the verb 'strike/touch' in the wife-sister texts? One might begin to answer this question by asking another: how did Pharaoh determine the causal relationship between the plagues and Sarah? Van Seters[39] suggests that the narrator saw Abimelech's dream as a solution to this problem but, in the context of ch. 12 itself, this is not entirely helpful. The same may be said of the soothsayers or heathen gods envisaged by Koch in ch. 12.[40] The rabbinic commentators offer a

37. The pairing of these two phrases may explain the unusual use in v. 6 of the preposition 'unto' (אל)—'I did not allow you to touch [unto] her'—as opposed to the more common 'against' (ב). 'It is possible that 'unto' (אל) may indicate the sexual nature of Abimelech's intended 'touch' here.

38. See also Ps. 105.15, where the parallelism indicates that 'touch' is equivalent to 'harm'.

39. *Abraham in History and Tradition*: 'The first set of questions raised by 12.17 (story A) is why God should have punished Pharaoh, who did not know that Sarah was Abraham's wife, and how it was that the king knew that Sarah was the cause of divine displeasure. Ch. 20.3-7 answers these questions by suggesting that God appeared to the king in a dream and accused him of his fault, and when the king protested his innocence God provided a way by which the consequences of his action could be averted' (p. 173).

40. *The Growth of the Biblical Tradition*: 'How can a Pharaoh determine the

rather different solution: Pharaoh's plagues were of a sexual nature, and this led the monarch to infer that a woman was the source of his affliction.[41] Yet even here questions remain unanswered. How did Pharaoh know that Sarah was Abraham's wife, and how does this reading account for the fact that his house was also affected? The former cannot be answered without assuming that the plagues were accompanied by some form of explicit announcement by God, or that the text omits an interrogation of Abraham by Pharaoh in which the truth is revealed. The latter question, on the other hand, may have seemed redundant in the context of the ancient Near East, where it was taken for granted that a plague upon the king would affect his people. The notion that the plagues of 12.17 were sexual works well, however, with the unmentioned fact that Pharaoh had enjoyed sexual relations with Sarah.[42] Pharaoh can infer that he was plagued because he touched Sarah.

In ch. 20 we find the opposite situation. The verb 'strike/touch' is used to describe Abimelech's (thwarted) sexual intentions towards Sarah, but it is unmentioned in the context of the sexual affliction (sterility and barrenness) suffered by Abimelech and his house. It is for Abimelech to infer the connection: in attempting to touch Sarah, he was plagued. In ch. 26, on the other hand, the sexual aspect has been removed altogether,[43] and Abimelech merely warns his people against touching (harming) Isaac or Rebekah. This reading is confirmed in 26.29 where Abimelech reminds Isaac that he has not been harmed, and requests similar treatment. The removal of the sexual threat is also

---

reason for his misfortune? Only through his gods, through the medium of a soothsayer; but that heathen gods could have told Pharaoh the truth was considered suspect by the writer and he has left it out. This has created a gap in the story' (p. 123).

41. See, for instance, Nachmanider *MG, ad loc.* The Sforno, *MG, ad loc.*, suggests that, in all of Pharaoh's house, only Sarah was immune to the plagues, and thus it was possible to infer that they had been brought on her account.

42. Commentators differ on this point, but one should note the distinction between Pharaoh's 'and I took her [Sarah] *for a wife*' (וָאֶקַּח אֹתָהּ לִי לְאִשָּׁה), and the less explicit report about Abimelech: 'and he took Sarah' (וַיִּקַּח אֶת שָׂרָה).

43. Van Seters, in *Abraham in History and Tradition*, sees word-play here based on the dual usage of 'strike/touch' (נגע): '...there is an interesting use of the verb *nga* since for a man it means "to inflict bodily injury", but for a woman it means "to approach sexually". In story B, 20.6, it has the latter meaning while in A, 12.17, it has to do with bodily harm in the sense of the divine plague. This rather ingenious double entendre provides the conclusion of the episode for this author' [i.e. of 26.11] (p. 181).

underlined by the reference to the long duration of Isaac's stay in the land before Abimelech's discovery that Rebekah is the patriarch's wife and not his sister. One might thus observe a development or a transformation in which extreme divine punishment and human sexual threats are gradually removed, so that, in ch. 26, the difficulties have become more hypothetical than actual. In ch. 12 God *strikes* a foreign king with plagues (וינגע יהוה את פרעה נגעים גדלים) as a punishment for sexual attentions towards Sarah. In ch. 20 he thwarts these by not letting the king *touch* her (לא נתתיך לנגע אליה). In ch. 26 it is the foreign king's threat of death to any one of his people who *touches* Isaac and Rebekah (הנגע באיש הזה ובאשתו מות יומת) which both protects the patriarch and paves the way for a shared blessing.

Interpreting Chapter 20

In the unfolding development of the role of blessing and curse in the three-way relationship between God, Israel and the non-Israelite inhabitants of the land, ch. 20 marks a crucial turning-point. Polzin makes the valid point that blessing, in the context of the wife-sister tales, is inextricably bound up with material wealth and the fulfilment of God's promise of offspring,[44] but his reason for making this connection arises from what he envisages as essentially moralistic concerns in the text. Abraham must have the right kind of wealth (i.e. not riches gained at the expense of his wife's honour), and the threat of adultery must be removed before God can bless him with offspring. Apart from the fact that the train of Polzin's argument seems to be derailed in ch. 26, where he fails to acknowledge that Isaac is blessed *before* he accumulates great wealth (see 26.12-14),[45] one must ask whether he is on the right

44. See ' "The Ancestress of Israel in Danger" in Danger', pp. 88-93: 'Two essential signs or actualizations of God's blessing appear to be the acquisition of great wealth and the obtaining of progeny. God's blessing is seen as a *process* and the process is essentially complete when wealth and progeny are obtained under certain conditions'.

45. ' "The Ancestress of Israel in Danger" in Danger': 'We are specifically told in Gen. 26.12-13: "The LORD blessed him, and the man became rich, and gained more and more until he became very wealthy." Already having progeny, and already having rectified the potentially adulterous situation of Gen. 26.1-12, Isaac now receives God's blessing in the form of great wealth' (p. 91). This 'blessing in the form of great wealth' is troubling given that Polzin assumes elsewhere that the blessing comes only *after* the wealth.

track at all with this emphasis on morality. While Abimelech's payment (20.14-16) appears to be motivated partly by a desire to protect Sarah's honour (although the Hebrew is too difficult to be certain), as far as Abraham is concerned, it is only tangentially connected with adultery and is, in fact, made primarily so that he will intercede in the matter of the king's impotence. It is only after these payments have been made that Abraham begins to pray (v. 17). Yet despite the possibility that the removal of the adulterous element in ch. 20 arises from the necessity of establishing that Abraham and not Abimelech is the father of Isaac (whose conception is announced in 21.1-2), Polzin is correct in equating fertility with blessing in this context. And if fertility is equated with blessing, then its opposite, impotence and barrenness, must be seen as a form of curse. Thus we return to the combined promise/threat of 12.3. Having taken the patriarch's wife, without whom, we may assume for the purposes of this text, Abraham is effectively impotent (cursed), Abimelech is cursed with impotence. Returning Sarah is not enough to guarantee a cure, and Abraham must intercede on his behalf. Abimelech is then cured (blessed) when the wombs in his household are opened, and Abraham and Sarah are also blessed with the opening of Sarah's womb. Because of certain peculiarities in the narration of ch. 20, the centrality of Abimelech's impotence (curse) is often overlooked. M. Sternberg, however, sees it clearly.[46]

Among the most striking features of ch. 20 is the narrative's unusual temporal order, or disorder. Statements that are, at first glance, confusing or positively misleading are clarified and elaborated as the story unfolds, and information that is revealed late in the narrative alters entirely our perspective on the earlier state of affairs. Sternberg argues that, for instance, the supposedly unwitting adulterer deserves less sympathy than appearances initially suggest. Verse 4 reports that Abimelech had not approached Sarah but, following Sternberg's analysis, this is explained not by the king's good behaviour, or even by his good fortune. It is because, as we learn in vv. 17 and 18, God had prevented Abimelech's approach by making him impotent:

ויתפלל אברהם אל האלהים וירפא אלהים את אבימלך ואת אשתו
ואמהתיו וילדו: כי עצר עצר יהוה בעד כל רחם לבית
אבימלך על דבר שרה אשת אברהם:

46. *The Poetics of Biblical Narrative: Ideological Literature and the Drama of Reading* (Bloomington: Indiana University Press, 1987), pp. 315-16.

> Abraham then prayed to God, and God healed Abimelech and his wife
> and his slave girls, so that they bore him children; for the LORD had
> closed fast every womb of the household of Abimelech because of
> Sarah, the wife of Abraham.

It is typical of the temporal disorder in this narrative that we learn of
Abimelech's affliction (reported, in the end, with all the casual finality
of one of Virginia Woolf's 'deaths in brackets')[47] only after our discovery that he has been healed. As vv. 17 and 18 confirm, Abraham
intercedes because God has cursed Abimelech and his entire household
with impotency and barrenness, and it is by means of this intercession
that God transforms the curse into a blessing.

Reading Chapter 20 in Context

Koch suggests that, like 12.10-20, ch. 20 may be taken out of context
and read in isolation.[48] He believes this partly because he sees ch. 20 as
an Elohistic narrative surrounded by the work of the Yahwist, and partly
because of technical difficulties such as that presented by the words
(v. 1) 'And Abraham journeyed *from there*' (ויסע משם אברהם). From
whence has Abraham departed, and what explains the geographical confusion about the precise location of Gerar? In fact, obvious linguistic
similarities between 20.1 and 12.9 suggest that, in some respects, the
two episodes were seen as interchangeable. Indeed, the opening verses
of ch. 26 are similarly obscure: where precisely is Isaac when famine
strikes, and why, if he is already in Gerar, does he need to go to Abimelech? Koch's more serious mistake, however, is to neglect the important connections between ch. 20 and the narratives that precede and
follow it. As well as providing a graphic illustration of God's promised
blessing and curse, it is clear that ch. 20 relates to the chapters surrounding it in other respects. Most obvious is the link, mentioned

47. See, for instance, *To the Lighthouse* (London: The Hogarth Press, 1977
[1927]): '(Mr. Ramsay stumbling along a passage stretched his arms out one dark
morning, but, Mrs. Ramsay having died rather suddenly the night before, he
stretched his arms out. They remained empty)' (pp. 199-200).
48. *The Growth of the Biblical Tradition:* 'A look at the overall context shows
that B can be taken out of its present position just as easily as A. Before it is the
story of Sodom and Gomorrah, which certainly has nothing to do with the ancestress of Israel. (Originally chapter 20 must in any case have had a different context,
for it appears to have been written by the Elohist. Chapter 19 is by the Jahwist—but
we will look into this later.)' (pp. 117-18).

above, between the denial that Abimelech had sexual relations with
Sarah (v. 4), the infertility that befalls him and his house on her account
(v. 18), and the announcement of her conception (21.1). There exists, in
addition, a rather more complex relationship between ch. 20 and the
events described in chs. 18 and 19, where the subject of curses averted
and blessings acquired through Abraham arises directly in connection
with the destruction of Sodom and Gomorrah. In 18.17 God asks himself whether he should conceal from Abraham his planned destruction
of Sodom and Gomorrah. Perhaps because he speaks of the usually
negative act of concealing rather than the positive act of revealing, the
substance of God's answer is predictable; he will not conceal his plans.
God's reasoning, by contrast, is less predictable. He will reveal his
intentions because (18.18) 'Abraham is to become a great and populous
nation and all the nations of the earth are to bless themselves by him'
(ואברהם היו יהיה לגוי גדול ועצום ונברכו בו כל גויי הארץ). It should be
noted that 'nations [peoples] of the earth' (גויי הארץ) has replaced the
term that occurred in God's similarly worded promise to Abraham in
12.3: 'all the *families of the earth* (משפחת האדמה) shall bless themselves by you'. Given Abimelech's reference in 20.4 to himself and
his nation as an 'innocent people' (גוי צדיק), we cannot exclude the
possibility that this signals an intentional parallel between Abraham's
intercession on behalf of the people of Sodom and his subsequent intercession for Abimelech.[49] Indeed, this reading becomes increasingly
plausible when one considers that the word 'innocent' (צדיק)[50], rare
enough in Genesis, occurs in one form or another seven times in ch. 18.
(Who can forget this when Abimelech asks if God will slay an innocent
people [הגוי גם צדיק]?) Moreover, the episode at Sodom illustrates a
clear modification, motivated by Abraham, in God's attitude towards
punishment by means of swift destruction, and this is hardly irrelevant

---

49. H. Gossai, *Power and Marginality in the Abraham Narrative* (Lanham:
University Press of America, 1995), pp. 111-39, sees another less positive parallel
between these texts: 'The narrative impels us to draw a parallel between the action
of Lot in giving his daughters to the men of Sodom (Genesis 19) and the sacrifice
of Sarah. Whether it is for the protection of the men in Genesis 19 or the protection
of Abraham in the land of Gerar, the woman's life is endangered. However, the
issue at stake is even greater than the unprincipled actions of Abraham and Lot.
Both Sarah and the daughters of Lot (19:31-38) are the ones who would be bearers
of future generations' (p. 117).

50. צדיק is much more often translated as 'righteous', but I will follow the *JPS*
use of 'innocent' here.

in view of his leniency towards Abimelech in contrast to Pharaoh. A glance at *Genesis Rabbah*'s commentary on ch. 20 shows that much of this was evident to the rabbis, who drew explicit parallels between Abimelech and the victims of the flood and the builders of Babel. Indeed, in the rabbinic account, the king himself draws God's attention to the similarities and their implications.[51] The reaction of Abimelech's servants when he tells them about the dream (20.8) may thus be more than a typical response to a king's uninterpreted dream (cf. Pharaoh's response to his own dream in 41.8). Even if the monarch is proved righteous, and is duly saved on that account, precedent does not bode well for them.

Royal Dreams in the Ancient Near East

Before proceeding with an examination of Abimelech's dream in ch. 20 and its role in the wife-sister texts, it may be helpful to provide a brief discussion of royal dreams in the ancient Near East. As M. Robinson has pointed out, the predominance of royal dream reports may be partly an accident of survival; the dreams of kings were more likely to be recorded and preserved than the dreams of peasants. In addition, since divinely sent dreams were seen as confirmation of a king's right to rule, or as a higher authorization for royal decisions regarding military endeavours or the location of a new temple, their widespread use is not surprising.[52] This suggests that many royal dream reports in the ancient Near East should be regarded as literary productions based on political need, rather than the result of actual dream experiences.[53] It should be noted, however, that while numerous royal dream reports have survived, we find relatively few examples of reports of other types of divination used by, or in connection with, kings.[54]

51. See *GR, ad loc.* In the rabbinic account Abimelech dares to question whether the generations of the flood and of the dispersion may also have been righteous.

52. 'Dreams in the Old Testament', pp. 155-56.

53. S. Zeitlin, 'Dreams and their Interpretation from the Biblical Period to the Tannaitic Time: An Historical Study, *JQR* 66 (1975–76), pp. 1-17, observes that, prior to the Tannaitic period, recorded dreams usually concerned leaders or royalty. Only the Tannaim, who 'did not regard dreams as acts of divination' and who 'had some understanding of the psychology of dreaming' began to show an interest in recording the dreams of ordinary people (p. 15).

54. See Oppenheim, 'The Interpretation of Dreams', pp. 179-373.

Broadly speaking, there are three distinct issues that arise in connection with the dreams of kings in the ancient Near East. The first concerns the king's right to rule. Succession was rarely straightforward in the ancient world, and it is hardly surprising that a tradition should have developed in which dreams were used to lend divine authority to a monarch's claim to the throne. The second concerns fertility. That fertility is a common theme of ancient dream reports is well attested, and this was of particular importance when a throne was at stake. Predictably, evidence of incubation rituals is often found in dream reports pertaining to fertility.[55] The third issue concerns building. Sometimes the building in question is a city or palace for the king, but more frequently it is a temple built as a dwelling for a particular god. Clearly, the building of a significant edifice was seen as validation of the king's claim to the throne, and proof that he was favoured by the gods.[56] Partly because evidence of divine intervention was desirable in matters of statecraft, the king's role as a mediator for divine communication was of paramount importance in the ancient Near East. More importantly, however, kings were regarded as spokesmen for their people, and it was assumed that divinely bestowed favour would be channelled through the monarch. One need hardly say that this element, too, is abundantly present in ch. 20. Upon hearing Abimelech's report of his dream (v. 8), the king's servants exhibit entirely justifiable fear; his fate is, in their view, inseparable from their own. Abimelech shares this view: he reprimands Abraham for having brought great sin upon himself and his kingdom (v. 9) and, indeed, his entire house is cursed when he takes Sarah.

In this light, it is clear that the prevalence of royal dreams in the ancient Near East may have significant implications for the study of biblical dreams. Three of the eleven dreams in Genesis are dreamt by kings, while a king, Pharaoh, is the subject of two additional dreams. Westermann and others have questioned the suitability of the dream of Abimelech on the basis that its content does not fit its form,[57] but, given

55. See Jeffers, 'Divination by Dreams', pp. 167-83.

56. For a detailed discussion of divine participation in building projects see V.A. Hurowitz, *I Have Built You an Exalted House: Temple Building in the Light of Mesopotamian and Northwest Semitic Writings* (JSOTSup, 115; Sheffield: JSOT Press, 1992), pp. 135-63.

57. See *Genesis 12–36*: 'The dialog is introduced as a dream, or more accurately set in the framework of a dream (vv. 3a, 6a, 8). No exegete has seen that

the predominance of royal dreams, it is hardly surprising that the biblical narrators thought in terms of a dream when divine intervention was required to limit the potential damage. Robinson's observation that dreams received by kings were particularly likely to be lucid and non-symbolic may also be relevant here.[58] If royal dreams were used for the quasi-political purposes suggested above, the premium on direct speech as opposed to ambiguous symbolism is hardly surprising. Dreams which allowed too much room for interpretation would have had limited value as indications of divine support for kingly actions. Thus, the straightforward dialogue between God and Abimelech may reflect a tradition of royal dreams in the ancient world. Sceptics will object that this is patently not the case with the dreams of Pharaoh, but it is clear both that a tradition of symbolic royal dreams clearly existed alongside the tradition of direct-message dreams received by kings in the ancient Near East, and that the impenetrability of Pharaoh's dream symbolism is crucial to the plot of the Joseph narrative. Furthermore, the fact that Pharaoh ruled in Egypt, where dream interpretation and the study of dream symbols had been elevated to scientific proportions, may account for the symbolic nature of his dream.

Finally, while Abimelech's dream (together with Laban's) stands apart from the other Genesis dream reports in that the dreamer is not its main beneficiary, one might argue that the king benefits more from his dream than appearances suggest. Since this is the dream of a non-Israelite king reported in an Israelite narrative, one would not expect the issue of Abimelech's capacity for divine communication to be of great concern. Yet, as indicated above, the king's fertility, and hence the continuation of his line, turns out to play a central role in the unfolding plot, and this too may be taken as evidence that Abimelech's dream is not quite the inappropriate literary production that Westermann envisages. The fact that the dreamer is royal, and that the dream concerns the

what is within the framework does not suit the frame. A legal process with its accusation, sentence and defense cannot be the matter of a dream. God's address to Abraham [Abimelech] in a dream is but a literary vesture just as is the dialog the literary vesture of the discussion of the question of guilt. The frame, the dream, merely enables the dialog between God and the Canaanite king to take place' (p. 321).

58. 'Dreams in the Old Testament', p. 157. Robinson notes that there are relatively few reports of rulers receiving symbolic dreams which required interpretation by a third person.

survival of Abimelech's line as well as the continuation of Abraham's, may indicate that the writer was working firmly within the tradition of royal dreams in the ancient Near East.

And God Came to Abimelech in a Dream of the Night

Von Rad and others have argued that ch. 20 represents the attempt of the more theologically sophisticated Elohist to address the question of why Pharaoh was punished when he was not guilty.[59] The Elohist's supposed preference for dream theophany[60] is, for him, explanation enough for the occurrence of Abimelech's extraordinary dream. A number of objections may, however, be raised against this reading of ch. 20 and the apparent willingness of its proponents to overlook the significance of the dream report.

First of all, the narrative does not succeed in fulfilling the role ascribed to it. While it is reasonable to suggest, as Y. Zakovitz does,[61] that a reader's knowledge of one text may sharpen his or her perceptions of another, the later narrative, even if it affects in hindsight our reading of the earlier one, cannot alter the facts presented there. Had the narrators been concerned about a possible miscarriage of justice, or important unanswered questions in ch. 12, they could surely have amended that account to emphasize Pharaoh's guilt or, alternatively, to show that he was compensated for his unfair treatment. The attempt to justify the repetition of this story with the addition of a dream revelation on the basis of theological refinement is simply not plausible, and we must look elsewhere for an explanation.

Whereas most of the structural elements that occur in all three versions of the wife-sister story are more or less identical, the means by which the king discovers Sarah's true identity are quite different in each case. In ch. 12 we are not told explicitly, but we can assume that the information is derived from the incidence of plague. In ch. 20 God informs Abimelech in the dream, and in ch. 26 Abimelech relies on

---

59. See *Genesis*, pp. 225-30.
60. See *Genesis*, pp. 26-27.
61. 'Reflection Story: Another Dimension of the Evaluation of Characters in Biblical Narrative', *Tarbiz* 54 (1985), pp. 165-76 (Hebrew). For an interesting application of this device see J.D. Safren, 'Balaam and Abraham', *VT* 38 (1988), pp. 105-28.

simple observation.[62] The dream marks the change from direct intervention in the form of autocratic punishment to naturalistic observation
arising from a more sympathetic view of the patriarch in which he is
accorded a respect that is heightened by the awareness that he is blessed
by God.

In ch. 26, then, the relationship between Isaac and Abimelech is
markedly different from the relationship implied between Abraham and
Pharaoh in ch. 12. This is partly a matter of human considerations.
Nachmanides, in his commentary on ch. 20, suggests that Abimelech
should have known to make proper inquiries about Sarah before taking
her, and that, specifically, he should have asked whether Sarah was
Abraham's wife as well as being his sister.[63] Without question, this
represents a desperate attempt to defend Abraham's virtue, but it does
reveal a characteristic of ch. 26 that is more or less absent in ch. 20 and
entirely absent in ch. 12. There is no suggestion that either Pharaoh or
the first Abimelech are inclined to treat Abraham with any respect, and
in Pharaoh's case this is summed up in his terse command (12.19),
'Now, here is your wife; take her and begone!' (קח אשתך הנה ועתה
ולך). In ch. 26, on the other hand, Abimelech is sufficiently aware of
Isaac to note that the relationship between him and Rebekah is unusual
in siblings, and, ultimately, he initiates the making of a covenant between himself and Isaac (v. 28). What explains this dramatic shift in
attitude? It is impossible to answer this question without consideration
of the changing relationship between God and the foreign king which is
evident in these three texts. In ch. 12 Pharaoh makes the entirely rational decision to return Sarah to Abraham once he makes the connection
between the plagues and the presence of the patriarch's wife in his
court, but there is no suggestion that he actually comes to fear God. The
two later narratives, on the other hand, indicate both that the relevant
foreign king has come to respect the patriarch in question, and that he
has come to fear his God. When, in ch. 20, Abimelech asks Abraham
why he lied about his relationship with Sarah, the patriarch offers two
explanations. The second, that she is indeed his sister, although the
child of a different mother, is something of an afterthought, and this has

---

62. One might, however, see the naturalistic means by which Abimelech makes
his discovery—he looks out of the *window* (חלון) and sees Isaac fondling Rebekah—
as a nod in the direction of the means by which he discovers the truth about Abraham and Sarah in ch. 20—through a *dream* (חלום).

63. *MG, ad loc.*, p. 264.

continued ever since to trouble exegetes worried about the violation of the incest laws. His primary reason, however, is that he thought there was no 'fear of God' (יראת אלהים) in Abimelech's land (20.11). The Sforno has an ingenious, though ultimately untenable, interpretation of this text in which he equates 'fear of God' with 'fear of government'.[64] In fact, of course, it does refer to God and Abraham is wrong; there is no question that Abimelech fears God.

Pharaoh, in confronting Abraham, is referring simply to the plagues when he asks, 'What is this you have done to me! Why did you not tell me that she was your wife?' (12.18). Abimelech's reproach, on the other hand, has a moral element, entirely lacking in Pharaoh's words, which sets it firmly in a theological context.[65]

מה עשית לנו ומה חטאתי לך כי הבאת עלי ועל ממלכתי
חטאה גדלה מעשים אשר לא יעשו עשית עמדי:

What have you done to us? What wrong have I done that you should bring so great a guilt upon me and my kingdom? You have done to me things that ought not to be done (20.9).

The explanation for this change is that God's dream revelation to Abimelech has set their relationship on a different footing. This is not to say that Abimelech is in any respect an Israelite, but merely that he has a special relationship, rather complicated to define, with Abraham's God. It is the very fact of his receiving a dream from God, whom he addresses in the course of the dream as אדני (O Lord), which initiates this new relationship. The relationship is maintained, and even deepened in ch. 26, where Abimelech shows that he is God-fearing without the help of a divine revelation (vv. 11-12), and that he wants to make a covenant with Isaac because he recognizes that God is with him (26.28).

The rabbinic commentaries, for their own theological reasons, attempt to make a distinction between dreams received by Israelites and those received by non-Israelites.[66] Here they base their distinction on the similarity between the announcements of the dreams received by

64. See *MG*, *ad loc*. This is based on the fact that the Philistines had officers instead of kings, but it is difficult to see how he can account for the fact that Abimelech is repeatedly called a king.

65. Sarna, *JPS Torah Commentary*, p. 142, points out that this verse marks a distinction between Israelite law, where adultery was an offence against divinely given moral standards, and ancient Near Eastern law codes, where it was merely a violation of the husband's proprietary rights.

66. See, for instance, *GR* on 20.3.

Abimelech and Laban. Abimelech's dream report begins (20.3), 'But God came to Abimelech in a dream by night' (ויבא אלהים אל אבימלך בחלום הלילה). This is almost identical to the announcement of Laban's dream (31.24), 'But God appeared to Laban the Aramean in a dream by night' (ויבא אלהים אל לבן הארמי בחלם הלילה). The commentaries focus on the use of 'He came' (ויבא) and 'in a dream by night' (בחלום הלילה). These are the only occasions in Genesis when God *comes* in a dream, and the rabbis suggest that this indicates an inferior form of revelation as compared, for instance, to God's presence before Jacob in 28.13, or his direct speech to Abraham in 15.1. Similarly, while the Pentateuch may specify that a particular vision occurs at night (cf. 15.1 and 46.2), it is usually assumed that a dream occurs during the night.[67] Once again, the rabbis take the allusion to night as an indication of the inferiority of non-Israelite dreams, suggesting that God comes to them only by night. While their motivation for emphasizing these distinctions is questionable, the general point cannot be dismissed out of hand; there are, indeed, respects in which Abimelech's dream is qualitatively different from the dreams received by the patriarchs.

The patriarchal dreams invariably involve divine speech accompanied by some form of visual imagery.[68] The visual element may be essentially symbolic (the ladder of 28.12); or relating to the dreamer's external environment (the starry skies of 15.5); or an allusion to the dream's subject matter (the mating flocks of 31.10). Abimelech's dream, on the other hand, is purely verbal. This qualitative difference may be merely a matter of reticence, but it may also be attributed to the different role ascribed to Abimelech's dream versus the patriarchal dreams. The latter are intended to be inspirational as well as instructive, providing evidence of God's commitment to his promises (ch. 15), or authorization for a certain course of action (ch. 28). Even Jacob's dream of the flocks in ch. 31, the least obviously inspirational of the patriarchal dreams, may have more symbolic import than outward appearances suggest. Abimelech's dream, on the other hand, is primarily a means of conveying important information, such as Sarah's true identity and Abraham's prophetic standing.

67. Oppenheim, 'The Interpretation of Dreams', p. 187, cites only one text in which it is explicitly stated that the dream occurred during the day (the dream of Pharaoh Thutmose IV).

68. Jacob's experience in 46.2 may be an exception to the rule here, but it is a 'vision of the night' rather than a dream.

Having said this, however, Abimelech's dream demonstrates beyond all doubt that divine intervention will not be limited to Israelites, and the fact that it is beneficial to the king and his people, as well as to Abraham and Sarah, is emphasized in several ways. First of all, the existence of two other versions of the story in which no dream occurs indicates that, in terms of patriarchal benefit, it was dispensable: one way or another, the patriarchs come out of each of the wife-sister episodes with great wealth and divine blessings. In real terms, Abraham is little affected by Abimelech's dream, although royal respect is, of course, accorded to him on account of God's declaration that he is a prophet. For Abimelech, on the other hand, the dream makes all the difference. He (and his kingdom) are spared the plagues with which God afflicted Pharaoh, and even death (v. 3) is averted when God gives the king a second chance. Ultimately, the dream enables Abimelech to take the necessary steps to ensure the safe continuation of his royal line (vv. 7, 17).

In ch. 20 the interest in Abimelech's relationship with God is also emphasized by the introduction of certain moral and theological elements which, as noted above, were absent from ch. 12. In the earlier account, God permits Pharaoh to sin against him and then punishes him accordingly. In ch. 20, on the other hand, the timely dream revelation saves Abimelech from Pharaoh's fate. Indeed, a slightly unorthodox reading of 20.6 suggests that, at some stage of the redaction, if not in the original text, this verse may have been taken as an explicit contrast of God's attitude towards Abimelech as opposed to Pharaoh:

ויאמר אליו האלהים בחלם גם אנכי ידעתי כי בתם לבבך עשית זאת
ואחשׂך גם אנכי אותך מחטו לי על כן לא נתתיך לנגע אליה:

And God said to him in the dream, 'I knew that you did this with a blameless heart, and so I kept you from sinning against me. That it why I did not let you touch her.

The replacement of the א (aleph) with a ו (waw) at the end of מחטו (from sinning) is usually explained as a scribal error. It seems possible, although admittedly unlikely, that the error arose from a reading of this word as the noun plus suffix מחטאו (from his sin), where the suffix would refer to Pharaoh (so I spared[69] you from *his* sin against me).[70] At

69. See BDB, 'חשׂך', which cites 2 Kgs 5.20 and, perhaps, 2 Sam. 18.16 as instances of חשׂך which justify the translation 'spared'.

70. For a discussion of a similar concept see R.P. Gordon, 'Aleph Apologeticum', *JQR* NS 59 (1979), pp. 112-16.

any rate, even without this reading, it is clear that God's treatment of
Abimelech is markedly different from his treatment of Pharaoh, and the
existence of the dream revelation is a powerful indication of this.

As will, by now, be obvious, this chapter has been based on the assumption that it is impossible to assess the significance of Abimelech's
dream without first setting ch. 20 in the context of the wife-sister
narratives. This initial analysis having been carried out, it is possible to
identify a development within the three texts in which Abimelech's
dream plays a pivotal role. In ch. 12 Abraham is a sojourner in the land
of Egypt. Aware that he is at the mercy of the foreign king, and fearful
for his survival, the patriarch takes the drastic course of allowing his
wife to reside in Pharaoh's court, with all that that entails. (Although
the text refrains from spelling it out, we have no reason to believe that
Pharaoh did not sleep with Sarah.) Abraham leaves Egypt a wealthy
man, but there is no hope of reconciliation between himself and Pharaoh. Subsequently this very wealth becomes a source of conflict between himself and Lot, with whom, however, he is ultimately able to
reach an agreement over the possession of the land. God's intervention
takes the form of a swift punishment of Pharaoh, and, when the patriarch is finally escorted out of Egypt, it seems as unlikely that Pharaoh
will revere God, who has after all cursed him, as that he will respect
Abraham.

At the beginning of ch. 26, Isaac is a sojourner in Gerar, but only
because God has commanded him to be there. He is dubious about
the existence of God-fearers in Gerar, and consequently lies about
Rebekah's identity, but, even though he resides there for a long time,
nothing happens to her (or to him on her account). Abimelech is sufficiently interested in Isaac to note that his behaviour with Rebekah
belies their stated relationship, and he immediately warns his people
against committing a great sin.[71] He needs no divine revelation in order
to recognize that God has been with Isaac (and has blessed him with

---

71. M. Weinfeld, 'Sarah and Abimelech (Genesis 20) Against the Background
of an Assyrian Law and the Genesis Apocryphon', *AOAT* (1985), pp. 431-36,
provides additional support for Cassuto's claim in *Commentary on the Book of
Genesis* (trans. I. Adams; Jerusalem: Magnes Press, 1974 [1964]), pp. 357-58, that
knowingly taking the wife of a man on a trade journey constituted an offence
against Assyrian law, but we can probably assume that the offence envisaged here
is against God.

great wealth), and ultimately the king makes a covenant with the patriarch, presumably because he hopes to gain benefit, and indeed blessing through association (cf. Gen. 39.2-5).

All the changes that occur between these two texts arise from Abimelech's dream in ch. 20. Abraham, identified within the dream as a prophet who can intercede on Abimelech's behalf, acquires respect in the monarch's eyes, and the money he receives, though not direct from God (cf. Isaac), is given to him because he is God's prophet. Abimelech, receiving a dream from God (as opposed to dire plagues whose origin is never made explicit to Pharaoh), reveals that he is, indeed, a God-fearing king, and despite some residual hostility between himself and Abraham (21.25-26), a covenant is made (21.27-32). While Abimelech is not exactly blessed through Abraham, it is because of the patriarch's prophetic intervention that God reverses the curse imposed upon the king and his house. Its role in transforming the relationship between Israelites, non-Israelites and God, and in clarifying the meaning of God's repeated promise that the nations (or families) of the earth will be blessed through Abraham and his descendants, sets Abimelech's dream at the heart of the wife-sister texts. Indeed, only by acknowledging the dream's pivotal role can one hope to approach something akin to an understanding of these intensely complex texts.

Thematic Links

As the following summary shows, the six themes outlined in the introduction find vivid expression in Genesis 20:

(1) *The dream is received during a period of anxiety or danger.*
It occurs at a time of potential crisis for both Abraham and Abimelech. Abraham believes that his life is at risk in a foreign country, and his wife is in the harem of a foreign king. Abimelech is in danger of being killed for the crime of taking Sarah.

(2) *The dream concerns descendants, immediate or eventual.*
Abraham has not yet had a child by Sarah; the birth of Isaac is announced (with Abraham's paternity strongly emphasized) immediately after the episode in Gerar. Abimelech's line is threatened because God has made his entire household barren, perhaps to protect Sarah.

(3)   *The dream signals a change in status.*
       The dream signals a change in Abimelech's status, identifying
       him as a God-fearer and as someone with whom God is will-
       ing to communicate. It also confirms that Abraham is a prophet
       with intercessory powers. The dream prepares the ground for
       the covenant between king and patriarch.

(4)   *The dream highlights divine involvement in human affairs.*
       The end of the narrative reveals that what had appeared to be a
       human decision was the product of divine necessity; God had
       intervened to prevent Abimelech from touching Sarah. The
       dream exemplifies the means by which God will protect the
       patriarchs in times of crisis.

(5)   *The dream concerns the relationship between Israelites and
       non-Israelites.*
       The text defines the relationship between the patriarch and the
       non-Israelite king. Within the wife-sister texts the dream func-
       tions to show how Israelite can ultimately live alongside non-
       Israelite without the need for divine protection, and how the
       nations or families of the earth will be blessed through Israel
       (here through intercessory powers and later through shared
       prosperity).

(6)   *The dream deals with absence from the land.*
       Abraham is in Gerar, perhaps to escape unmentioned famine.
       Gerar may function in the wife-sister texts as a physical and
       metaphorical half-way house to Egypt. Abraham's status as a
       sojourner is emphasized.

Chapter 2

JACOB'S DREAM AT BETHEL
(GENESIS 28.10-22)

Introduction

As bees around a honey-pot, exegetes and theologians have swarmed
over Jacob's ladder,[1] and the multiplicity of their interpretations is such
that an entire book could be devoted to recounting them. Yet scholars
have yet to offer a convincing reading of the dream which both makes
sense of its symbolism and accounts for its occurrence at precisely this
point in Jacob's life. The reasons for this will emerge in full during the
course of this chapter, but a brief summary at the outset should prove to
be useful.

The widely held belief that Gen. 28.10-22 seeks simultaneously to
discredit the Canaanite sanctuary formerly located at Bethel, and to
establish the patriarchal origins of the Israelite sanctuary that is presumed to have replaced it, has discouraged many scholars from further
investigation of the dream's significance.[2] I will argue here that,
although Genesis 28 may well reflect Bethel's long and complex history as a pre-Israelite and Israelite sanctuary, the sanctification of a
shrine is not a plausible goal of this narrative.

---

1.   Although what follows will indicate that 'tower' or 'ziggurat' may be more
appropriate than 'ladder' as translations of the biblical hapax legomenon סֻלָּם, it
seems simpler to follow custom when referring in English to the object of Jacob's
vision.

2.   Von Rad, *Genesis*, summarizes the narrative purpose of Gen. 28.10-12 as
follows: 'But above all, the purpose of the narrative becomes clear in this verse
[v. 18]: it intends to tell how Bethel, which was later so famous, became a cultic
centre and in what way the holiness of the place first became known. But there is
more: it intends to explain what were the circumstances connected with the stone at
Bethel. Jacob had erected it and dedicated it to God by pouring oil on it' (p. 285).

While much attention has been paid to ancient Near Eastern symbolism that parallels Bethel's ladder and gate of heaven,[3] no exegete has explored the possibility that the entire dream, rather than just certain aspects of it, may belong to a tradition that was not exclusively or even distinctively Israelite. A study of literature from surrounding cultures shows that dream reports were often used as a means of conferring status, or of confirming status that had been called in doubt. I see

Westermann, *Genesis 12–36*, emphasizes the Israelite assimilation of pagan traditions connected with Bethel: 'The story of the discovery of a sanctuary was narrated and handed on at this sanctuary at Bethel. Excavations have shown that the sanctuary existed long before the immigration of the Israelite tribes; hence the story was already being narrated and handed on long before their arrival. It contains, therefore, only such elements as are known from and widespread in the history of religions. J then takes up a story which arose and was handed on at a sanctuary and gives it new meaning in the context of the patriarchal story: it is Jacob who discovered the holy place on his flight from Esau. J's takeover of the pre-Israelite narrative presupposes the takeover of Bethel by the immigrant tribes whereby Jacob became the discoverer of the holy place' (p. 453). Gnuse, *The Dream Theophany of Samuel*, likewise emphasizes the official sanctification of Bethel: 'The legitimation of the shrine seems to be the point of the text by virtue of other motifs. The narrative is the closest parallel to a covenant in the epic tradition. Jacob promises to build a pillar for the cult of the god on his return, and this may refer to a pilgrimage that may have linked the two sanctuaries of Shechem and Bethel together during the days of the divided monarchy. The Elohist may have recounted a tradition in order to legitimate a different sanctuary than the one at which calf worship was advocated, for he is reluctant to localise the sanctuary as the Yahwist did in Genesis 12:8' (p. 68).

3.   Gnuse, *The Dream Theophany of Samuel*, offers a useful summary of ancient Near Eastern parallels which have been observed in Gen. 28: 'What is the ladder observed by Jacob? It may have been suggested by the stones piled upon each other in this old Middle Bronze sanctuary. The word for ladder *sll* is a *hapax legomenon*, which may mean "to heap up". In Egyptian texts there is a celestial ladder which deceased pharaohs are said to ascend, and the image may reflect strong influence of a solar religion in Egypt, for the rays of the sun suggest such a ladder. When Jacob calls the place the gate to heaven, he may have been using Egyptian terminology. However, there is an Akkadian word, *simmiltu*, which means "stairway", and it is a cognate of *slm*, which may mean "step, slab". Sumerian mythology has a gate of heaven in the story of "Nergal and Ereshkigal", where the viziers of the great gods ascend and descend the long stairway of heaven between the realm of the underworld and the gate of Anu, Enlil, and Ea. Unlike the ladder in Egypt upon which men could travel, the Sumerian ladder permitted passage only of gods, which is more comparable to the ladder in Genesis 28, where the celestial messengers of God travel to all the peoples of the earth' (p. 68).

this as a central concern of Jacob's dream, which provides the requisite divine validation of his dubiously acquired birthright and blessing. Finally, although certain types of temple imagery have been identified in Jacob's dream, so that the ladder, for instance, is often described as a ziggurat,[4] scholars have been reluctant to acknowledge that the temple-building motif may not be restricted to the dream's symbolism. This reluctance is not altogether surprising; it is not easy to explain how a dream that occurs in Bethel,[5] and in which there is no mention of Jerusalem, can be centrally concerned with the building of a temple. Once again, however, a glance at surrounding cultures is instructive; temple-building dreams were reported throughout the ancient Near East as evidence that a king was favoured by the gods. The dream at Bethel may well belong to that class of dreams in which a king (here a patriarch) receives divine authorization for the construction of a temple, thus confirming that he is held in high esteem by the gods.

As elsewhere in this study, I will analyse the text at the level of final redaction, making no attempt to account for the various strands of which Gen. 28.10-22 may be comprised. I will examine the dream initially in its immediate narrative context, with the aim of explaining its role in Jacob's own life. Subsequently, I will try to gauge its possible significance for readers contemporary to its final redaction. This latter line of enquiry will inevitably demand an assumption concerning when the Pentateuch reached its final form. While it must be acknowledged that the date cannot be established beyond dispute, and that Bible scholars have been unable to reach a consensus on this point, I will follow the general trend of recent scholarship in assuming an exilic background for the Pentateuch's final redaction.[6]

---

4. Sarna, *Understanding Genesis*, p. 193.

5. Bethel was reviled by later prophets, especially Hosea, who called it 'Beth-aven', 'House of Delusion' (see NJPS, Hos. 4.15 *ad loc.*), on account of the bull-worship practised there during the reign of Jeroboam (cf. 1 Kgs 12.27-31). The sanctuary was ultimately abolished during the Josianic reform. It seems to me unlikely that Gen. 28.10-22 achieved its present form when Bethel was a focus of great hostility, and one might well ask whether it would have survived such hostility had it been known at the time of Josiah's reforms. I think it most plausible that the temple building elements I will discuss here were incorporated into an older narrative about Bethel long after it ceased to be a controversial rival to Jerusalem.

6. D.J.A. Clines, *The Theme of the Pentateuch* (JSOTSup, 10; Sheffield: JSOT

The Significance of the Dream for Jacob

In certain important respects, the dream at Bethel functions in Jacob's life as the Covenant of the Pieces does in Abraham's, both being pivotal events in the spiritual development of the patriarch, occurring at a time of personal crisis.[7] A comparison of Gen. 15.1-21 and 28.10-22 which examines both the differences and the similarities between these two events may thus be helpful.

It is clear that Abraham's dream-vision in Genesis 15, like many dreams reported in ancient Near Eastern literature, came in response to uncertainty.[8] The source of Abraham's need for reassurance is self-evident: God has failed to act upon his earlier promises of descendants and land (12.2, 7). The enactment of the covenant ritual is, among other things, God's sign that these promises will be fulfilled. In view of evidence offered elsewhere in Genesis of Abraham's prowess as a negotiator,[9] it is not surprising that Genesis 15 should convey a strong impression of the patriarch's active role in bringing about the events reported in vv. 17-21. Offered a great reward, Abraham looks the gift-horse in

Press, 1978), makes the following claim: 'The question of historical function demands an answer to a prior literary-critical question: at what period was the Pentateuch in its final shape brought into being? The answer that has long been popular is that the Pentateuch as a whole (and not only some part of it) provided the basis for Ezra's reform and was probably brought by him from Babylonia, though of course that event is variously dated as 458 or 398 BCE or sometime between those dates. Some have recently called into question this consensus view, alleging that the Ezra narrative is nothing but a piece of "edificatory 'church history'", but this appears to me an unnecessarily sceptical view of the Ezra material, and the evidence that the law invoked by Ezra and Nehemiah contained not only P but also at least J and D seems conclusive enough to affirm that the Pentateuch was in existence by the end of the fifth century. If that is the case, and if, as is generally assumed, the redaction of the Pentateuch took place in Babylonia, the crucial point about the historical setting of the Pentateuch is that it is the product of the Babylonian exile' (p. 97).

7. In *PRE, ad loc.* both the Covenant of the Pieces and the vision of the ladder are said to signify the four kingdoms, their dominion and their downfall.

8. For a discussion of dreams sought in response to illness, for instance, or the lack of an heir, see Jeffers, 'Divination by Dreams', esp. pp. 168-70.

9. Abraham's interaction with God at Sodom and Gomorrah provides the best evidence of his skill in this respect, but, even when he sends someone else to negotiate on his behalf (his servant in search of a wife for Isaac in ch. 24), he makes a shrewd choice.

the mouth with an unflinching gaze, and is satisfied only when he receives an incontrovertible sign that God will keep his word.

The source of Jacob's insecurity, though equally obvious, is rather more complex. It is derived from three separate causes for concern. Will God approve the stolen blessing? Will he accompany Jacob in exile? Will Jacob find a suitable wife? That Jacob is given no credit for bringing about the remarkable sign at Bethel is not altogether surprising. Unlike Abraham, Jacob is no smooth negotiator, his success in acquiring his brother's birthright and his father's blessing being largely attributable to the fortuitous combination of a stupid brother, a smart mother and a self-deluding father. Left entirely to his own devices, and pitted against a more equally-matched opponent, Jacob's attempts at striking bargains are dogged by failure and confusion; seven years of service are rewarded by a wife he does not love, and only divine intervention subverts Laban's plan to take advantage of his son-in-law by reneging on the terms of their agreed division of the flocks.[10]

The contrast between Abraham's active pursuit of a sign from God and Jacob's total passivity in this respect is not only the result of their different personalities. Whereas Abraham's relationship with God is firmly established when the Covenant of the Pieces occurs, Jacob's interaction with God at Bethel is his first, and it is only appropriate that their behaviour should reflect this difference. Abraham, having already been promised offspring and land, is entitled to the feelings of impatience and insecurity evident in his request for confirmation in ch. 15. Jacob, on the other hand, has no reason to assume that God will be with him when he leaves his father's house; on the contrary, he has every reason to fear that he has been banished alone and must fend for himself. In this situation, he has little choice but to wait and hope for a sign of God's approval, which is, indeed, forthcoming in the vision of the ladder.

Since Jacob, unlike Abraham (15.2-3, 8), neither takes active measures to bring about the vision of the ladder,[11] nor voices any concerns or anxieties out of which we can be certain it grew, the significance of

---

10. While Laban's deception of Jacob is a clear example of the biblical interest in justice and symmetry—the patriarch deceives and is in turn deceived—Jacob, deceptive or not, is portrayed as naive and, with the striking exception of his dealings with Esau, not inclined to take the initiative.

11. Most scholars have rejected the possibility that Jacob took positive steps to bring about this dream by performing a dream incubation ritual.

his dream at Bethel must be inferred from its context. The process of deduction is hardly challenging. Following Jacob's deception of Esau and Isaac, his expulsion from Isaac's house and the command to find a wife, the revelation is exquisitely timed, and, in this respect, an examination of the dream in its narrative context is crucial. It is, without doubt, the product of the sequence of events that preceded it.[12]

For the purposes of this discussion, we need not distinguish between Jacob's separate deceptions of Esau and Isaac; they are merely stages in the process that culminates with God's promises to Jacob in 28.13-15. We cannot assume from the outset, however, that the validity of birthright and blessing in God's eyes were unaffected by the dubious means by which they were acquired. The dream is the first confirmation that Jacob has met with God's approval; the magnificent vision would hardly have been accorded to him otherwise.

And Behold a Ladder

It is no accident that the silent image of a ladder with ascending and descending angels which towers over all subsequent interactions between God and Jacob occurs at the very beginning of Jacob's first divine encounter. Whereas Abraham's symbolic vision of the smoking oven and flaming torch provides a dramatic confirmation of the promises God has *already made*, the ladder and angels guide Jacob towards an appropriate interpretation of the promises that God is *about to make*. The significance of the fact that the most dramatic element of 28.10-22 comes almost immediately (v. 12) is clearly worth considering, particularly in view of the contrast with Genesis 15, where the build-up to the theophany is slow and full of suspense.

J. Fokkelman is among the few commentators to have shown any interest in the order of events in Genesis 28. At the outset he seems dismissive about the vision:

> Consequently, when the ladder and the angels have accomplished their task, they do not occur again, just as Moses' burning bush was also a mere eye-catcher. The attention has been fixed and from the primary

12. If this seems like an anachronistically psychological reading of Jacob's dream, see, once again, Jeffers, 'Divination by Dreams', for a discussion of the role of anxiety in promoting the use of dream incubation rituals. Oppenheim, 'The Interpretation of Dreams', also links dream reports with personal or political uncertainties.

sensory perception, seeing, the story now proceeds to the hearing of
God's promise. Not till the end of the vision does the theophany proper
start. But—is it not strange that precisely this vision, a mere eye-catcher,
is the only part of the story which has been put in a different perspective
and is presented as taking place now? Is it justifiable? We shall say more
about this presently, with v. 18.[13]

The reader might well suspect a little artifice here; Fokkelman feigns
surprise at the narrator's decision to emphasize the vision, the 'mere
eye-catcher', only to reveal its central importance in his discussion of
v. 18. Yet it transpires that he is sincere:

> Just as a dull drop of dew is turned into a bright brilliant by the beams of
> the morning sun, so, by the theophany, the unimportant trivial action of
> Jacob is transformed into a historical example in the dialogue of man
> and his God.[14]

For Fokkelman, the vision of the ladder is reported primarily to highlight the raising of the stone. Since ladder and stone are undoubtedly
connected, it is not difficult to see how this interpretation took shape,
but the claim that the ladder serves to draw attention to the stone, when
the stone seems so obviously intended to commemorate the vision of
the ladder, fails to convince. We must surely look elsewhere for explanations of their role in the text and their relationship to each other.

Dreams and Divine Approval

Although Jacob's extraordinary vision of ladder and angels leaves little
doubt about the validity of his stolen birthright-blessing, the narrator is
careful to reiterate God's approval in several other ways. Verbal confirmation that Jacob is Isaac's rightful heir is offered with God's opening
words in v. 13, 'I am the LORD, the God of your father Abraham and
the God of Isaac' (אני יהוה אלהי אברהם אביך ואלהי יצחק). The fact that
Abraham, and not Isaac, is called 'your father' is, at first glance, puz-
zling. While the Hebrew 'your father' (אביך) may certainly be translated
as 'your ancestor',[15] the terminology is confusing in a verse which has
occasion to use the term in its far more familiar sense. It is possible that

---

13. *Narrative Art in Genesis*, pp. 54-55.
14. *Narrative Art in Genesis*, p. 73.
15. The term is used throughout the Bible with reference to the patriarchs or to
the exodus generation. This is, however, the only occasion on which it refers to a
grandfather when a father is mentioned in the same verse.

'your father Abraham' was a formulaic phrase already known, and chosen here for its power to reassure, and evidence for this reading might be found in God's reassurance to Isaac in time of famine that he will be with him and bless him, 'fulfilling the oath that I swore to your *father Abraham*' (26.3). Although Abraham really is Isaac's father, this use of the term implies a lasting security that transcends their biological relationship.

Alternatively, the description in 28.13 of Abraham as Jacob's father may represent a subtle slight of Isaac; the emphasis on Abraham hints at divine displeasure with Isaac for favouring Esau over Jacob. The wording of God's promise to Jacob in 28.14, with its obvious parallels to 13.14-15 (both passages contain directional references and the analogy between dust and descendants), likewise underlines a direct connection between Jacob and Abraham in which Isaac is quietly overlooked. Admittedly, Isaac is, in certain respects, the least developed of the patriarchal figures, and it is not surprising that he stands in his father's shadow. Nevertheless, the narrator's failure to emphasize Isaac's link in the transmission of God's blessing, highlighting instead the connection between Jacob and Abraham, may imply a criticism of Isaac for his difference of opinion with God over which son should be blessed. In thus lowering Isaac in the reader's estimation the narrator may have intended a corresponding elevation in her assessment of Jacob.

Jacob's lineage having been approved, it remains to be seen how his relationship with God will unfold. Returning to the parallel between Genesis 15 and 28, we might expect to find a prophetic element in God's words to Jacob, comparable to his prediction (15.13-15) that, although troubles are in store for Abraham's descendants, the patriarch himself will return to his fathers in peace. A prophecy concerning Jacob and his descendants does, indeed, ensue, but the differences between this and its parallel in ch. 15 are striking. While God's prediction to Abraham in 15.13-15 makes a sharp distinction between the patriarch's peaceful death at a ripe old age and the years of oppression in store for his offspring, the prophecy to Jacob (28.13-14) is pointedly ambiguous:

הארץ אשר אתה שכב עליה לך אתננה ולזרעך: והיה זרעך כעפר...
הארץ ופרצת ימה וקדמה וצפנה ונגבה ונברכו בך כל משפחת
האדמה ובזרעך:

... the ground on which you are lying I will assign to you and your off-spring. *Your descendants* shall be as the dust of the earth; *you* shall spread out to the west and to the east, to the north and to the south. All

the families of the earth shall bless themselves by *you and your descen-*
dants.

Verse 14 reports that Jacob's *offspring* will be as numerous as the dust
of the earth, that *Jacob* ('you' singular in Hebrew) will spread out, and
that the families of the earth will be blessed through *both Jacob and his*
offspring, and the references to the patriarch and his descendants are
grammatically intertwined in such a way that Jacob's fate is not easily
distinguished from that of his descendants.

That 28.14 fails to separate patriarch from descendants in the clear-
cut manner in which Abraham is distinguished from his offspring in
15.13-15 is beyond dispute. Likewise, there is little doubt that what
God promises Abraham, namely return to his fathers in peace at a ripe
old age, is regarded as a favourable prediction, while the prediction that
his offspring will spend 400 years in thrall to a foreign power is unambiguously negative. By contrast, it is difficult to be sure about precisely
how 28.14-15 should be read. Are Jacob's descendants implicitly included in the prediction that he will spread out to the four corners of the
earth, and is this prediction for Jacob and/or his descendants regarded
positively or negatively?

We may assume at the outset that God's promise that Jacob will
spread out in all four directions is not limited to the confines of the
land. A comparison with the similar promise to Abraham in 13.14-15 is
illuminating. The repeated emphasis on what is visible to Abraham
from his present vantage point suggests rather strongly that the four
directional references refer to the land immediately surrounding him.
God is simply promising that the patriarch, and his descendants after
him, will inherit all his eye can see. In 28.14, on the other hand, the
prediction that Jacob will be brought back to 'this land' makes little
sense if his spreading out is envisaged within its borders. Moreover,
God's promise that he will remain with Jacob and protect him on his
journey, not abandoning him until he has kept his word, would seem
overstated in the context of the land. Finally, we should note that, at its
most basic level, the prophecy of 28.14 is fulfilled in 30.43. Jacob has,
indeed, spread out *outside the land*.

ויפרץ האיש מאד מאד ויהי לו צאן רבות ושפחות ועבדים וגמלים וחמרים:
So the man grew exceedingly prosperous, and came to own large flocks,
maidservants and menservants, camels and asses.

And at least one family of the earth has been blessed through him:

ויאמר אליו לבן אם נא מצאתי חן בעיניך נחשתי ויברכני יהוה בגללך:

But Laban said to him, 'If you will indulge me, I have learned by
divination that the LORD has blessed me on your account' (30.27).

Yet it remains to be seen whether this prediction should be understood
positively or negatively; was Jacob's spreading out to the four corners
of the earth an ideal, or a situation to be remedied at the first possible
opportunity?

Even if we see this promise in terms of personal increase for Jacob,
fulfilled in 30.43 as cited above, the promise of expansion still turns out
to be something of a double-edged sword. Jacob does spread out, but in
a foreign land while in service to a cheating father-in-law, and even
prosperity has its problems. The very announcement of his good fortune is followed immediately by accusations (made more menacing still
by being overheard) from Laban's sons concerning its origins (31.1).
As is so often the case in biblical narrative, the acquisition of wealth
proves to be a mixed blessing.[16]

If the promise that Jacob will spread out in all directions appears, at
first glance, to be a welcome turn of events, the words immediately
following it indicate otherwise.

והנה אנכי עמך ושמרתיך בכל אשר תלך והשבתיך אל האדמה הזאת
כי לא אעזבך עד אשר אם עשיתי את אשר דברתי לך:

Remember, I am with you: I will protect you wherever you go and will
bring you back to this land. I will not leave you until I have done what I
have promised you (28.15).

Even for readers who do not make use of the privileged information
that Jacob's own spreading out will occur in a foreign land while in service to a duplicitous employer whose sons resent him, the words of
God's promise contain ample evidence that all will not be well. The
offer of protection would be strange in a context in which none was
required, and its very expression implies that the time when Jacob will
need God's help is close at hand, as indeed it is. Jacob could not have
outwitted Laban without divine intervention, and his eventual escape
from bondage in the house of his father-in-law is the result of God's
protection and encouragement. It is, moreover, difficult to comprehend

16. This is one of several occasions where the acquisition of wealth brings its
own problems: Abraham and Lot, finding that the land cannot support them both on
account of their great wealth, must separate to avoid strife (13.1-12), and the
Philistines drive Isaac away because of his great wealth (26.12-16).

God's emphatic assurance that he will return Jacob to 'this land' if inhabiting the four corners of the earth is an unambiguously desirable end in itself.[17] In particular, the promise that God will not *forsake* Jacob during this period suggests that the spreading out is a stage in the fulfilment of God's promise that does not necessarily constitute a straightforward blessing.[18]

Another indication that the promise of expansion is, in the first instance, a personal prediction to Jacob himself and that it is not entirely positive comes in the form of Jacob's vow. Although M. Sternberg does not include Genesis 28 in his discussion of the structure of repetition in biblical narrative,[19] his observations may be applied to it with good effect. Of the many classes of repetition Sternberg examines, the category of deliberate variation best fits the vow:

> As well as being a distinctive constant of the narrator's practice, indispensable to the coherence of the narrative as artifact, deliberateness in variation is an option available to the whole *dramatis personae* as reporters. Of course, the narrator's motives will remain purer—aesthetic or communicative rather than worldly—and his control surer. In principle, however, a character intent on slanting or embroidering his report may (if caught) be punished after the fact, but no more prevented than one who misreports for lack of wit or knowledge. It follows that *every* structure of repetition is *throughout* a product not of two but three axes: the axis of the object ('verbal vs. non-verbal'), the axis of equivalence

---

17. A. Gottlieb Zornberg, *Genesis: The Beginning of Desire* (Philadelphia: Jewish Publication Society, 1995), captures well the ambiguity inherent in the term ‎ופרצת‎ (you shall spread out): 'The very terms in which God blesses him, in the dream at Beth-El, are expansive and even violent in their resonance: "You shall spread out [*u-faratzta*] to the west and to the east, to the north and to the south" (28.14). This, it is true, will lead to blessing for the whole world ("All the families of the earth shall bless themselves by you"). But the word *u-faratzta* ("You shall spread out"), which Rashi reads as an indication of strength, does have explosive, even destructive implications. It often suggests the breaking of structures; indeed, the midrash specifically interprets "One who makes a breach [*ha-poretz*] goes before them" (Mic. 2.13) as a reference to Jacob, in whose merit God breaks open the Red Sea for his descendants' (p. 184).

18. God's promise that he will not forsake Jacob until he has fulfilled his promise has interesting parallels in 1 Kgs 6.12-13, where God reassures Solomon about his presence in the Temple, and in 1 Chron. 28.20, where David assures Solomon that God will not forsake him until the work on the Temple is complete.

19. *The Poetics of Biblical Narrative*, pp. 365-440.

('verbatim vs. variant') and the axis of motivation ('deliberate vs. non-deliberate').[20]

The promise in v. 15 contains four separate elements: God will be with Jacob, guard him wherever he goes, return him to this land, and will not abandon him until his word has been fulfilled. The vow (vv. 20-22) comes close to being a restatement of the promise, with the addition of a request for food and clothes. Although this addition may seem trivial at first glance, it serves to drive home the crucial point that Jacob has his own distinctive understanding of God's promise.

God's assurance that he will 'be with' Jacob may be interpreted in several different ways, but the vow makes it clear that what Jacob has in mind is a divine presence of the most tangible and concrete kind. In this regard, Jacob's request for clothes and food is sometimes taken as an inappropriate response to the vision he has been accorded. Scholarly disapproval has likewise been provoked by Jacob's seeming presumptuousness in making what appears at first glance to be a conditional acceptance of God:[21]

וידר יעקב נדר לאמר אם יהיה אלהים עמדי ושמרני בדרך
הזה אשר אנכי הולך ונתן לי לחם לאכל ובגד ללבש: ושבתי בשלום
אל בית אבי והיה יהוה לי לאלהים: והאבן הזאת אשר שמתי מצבה
יהיה בית אלהים וכל אשר תתן לי עשר אעשרנו לך:

Jacob then made a vow, saying, 'If God remains with me, if he protects me on this journey that I am making, and gives me bread to eat and clothing to wear, and if I can return safe to my father's house—the LORD shall be my God. And this stone, which I have set up as a pillar, shall be God's abode; and of all that you give me, I will set aside a tithe for you (28.20-22).

The thought that, if this were indeed a conditional acceptance of God, it would be the only one of its kind in the Bible[22] has deterred few translators from concluding the protasis with בית אבי, so that Jacob's acceptance of the LORD as his God, the stone becoming an abode of God,

---

20. *The Poetics of Biblical Narrative*, p. 419.

21. J. Skinner, *Genesis* (ICC; Edinburgh: T. & T. Clark, 1980 [1910]), p. 379, suggests that only the separation of sources 'relieves Jacob from the suspicion of questioning the sincerity of an explicit divine promise'.

22. Even unconditional acceptances of God are rare in the Bible. Ruth 1.16, with its declaration that Naomi's God will be Ruth's, may appear to provide a counter-example, but, in fact, this concerns conversion to another religion, and thus does not belong in the same category as Jacob's vow. A particularly interesting

and Jacob's promise to tithe are all part of the apodosis. Yet the accepted translation, followed by *JPS* as cited here, constitutes a highly counter-intuitive reading, both grammatically and theologically.

The grammatical construction suggests that the shift from 'if' to 'then' should take place not half way through v. 21 as above, but rather at the beginning of v. 22. The initial אם יהיה אלהים עמדי (if God will be with me) is followed by four waw consecutives in which the verb precedes the noun. Verse 22, in contrast, opens with a noun, האבן הזאת (this stone), while the verb, יהיה (will be) is in the imperfect. This grammatical change may well mark the shift from protasis to apodosis.[23]

Yet exegetes usually resist reading the second half of v. 21 as a summary of the protasis—if God will be with me, and protect me and provide for me, and return me to my fathers; *if the LORD really will be my God*. Their reasons are complex, but revolve around difficulties with בית אלהים, translated above as 'abode of God'. This translation implies that, if God keeps his side of the vow, then the stone will become a dwelling place for him. Yet, quite apart from the lack of biblical precedence for an association of this kind between God and stones, it hardly

example, for our purposes, of a divine declaration of this type occurs in 1 Chron. 28.6:

ויאמר לי שלמה בנך הוא יבנה ביתי וחצרותי כי בחרתי לו לי
לבן ואני אהיה לו לאב:

He said to me, 'It will be your son Solomon who will build My house and My courts, for I have chosen him to be a son to me, and I will be a father to him.'

Elsewhere, God frequently promises that the Israelites will be his people and that he will be their God (cf. Exod. 6.7; Lev. 26.12; Num. 15.41), but the Israelites do not usually make this statement in reverse. A possible exception is in Deut. 26.17-18:

את יהוה האמרת היום להיות לך לאלהים ...:
ויהוה האמירך היום להיות לו לעם סגלה ...

You have affirmed this day that the Lord is your God...
And the lord has affirmed this day that you are His treasured people...

Yet this is by no means a straightforward reversal of the usual declaration, and it is probably significant that it takes the form of an affirmation of an existing state rather than initial acceptance.

23. This is Rashi's assumption. See Rashi's commentary on the Torah, *MG, ad loc.*

constitutes an enticing offer on Jacob's part. The stone is there as a potential abode for God, and no action of Jacob's will make it more or less inhabitable. If, however, we translate בית אלהים not as 'abode of God' but as 'house of God', then we have at least solved the problem of how Jacob intends to deal with the stone. Provided God keeps his promises, Jacob will use the stone in the construction of a temple at Bethel, which fits well with his secondary promise to tithe there.

Moving now to the theological perspective, the inclusion of 'and the LORD will be my God' (והיה יהוה לי לאלהים) in the apodosis assumes a relationship that is particularly out of place in the Bethel narrative; Jacob is hardly likely to have responded to the confirmation that God will accept him by implying that he may not accept God. Perhaps it is the extraordinarily low esteem in which Jacob is held by many commentators that has made them satisfied with a reading that would be jarring in almost any biblical context.[24]

As well as criticizing Jacob for the supposedly conditional nature of his vow, exegetes have worried about the lack of trust in God that it implies. Yet, as indicated by the addition of a request for food and clothes, the vow is not a mere repetition, but rather a restatement in which Jacob expresses his personal need. This is consistent with the relationship described between God and the patriarchs elsewhere in Genesis; Jacob is no more culpable for demanding reassurance than is Abraham for seeking a sign to confirm God's sincerity (15.8). Indeed, he may be rather less at fault. Whereas Abraham is motivated, at least in part, by the fear that God may not keep his word, Jacob is unlikely to have worried about such an eventuality only moments after the promise had been uttered. When Jacob restates the divine promise in the context of his vow it is not because he doubts that God will keep it, but because

24. Von Rad, *Genesis*, offers an extreme but not unusual condemnation of the patriarch: 'As for Jacob and his human nature, i.e., any worthiness that he may perhaps possess: no art of empathy can succeed in understanding the incomprehensible, namely, that the fleeing deceiver received such a word of grace' (p. 287). More recently T.W. Cartledge, *Vows in the Hebrew Bible and the Ancient Near East* (JSOTSup, 147; Sheffield: JSOT Press, 1992), has made the following assessment: 'The content of Jacob's vow underscores not only Jacob's distrust but also his reputedly selfish nature. Although the promises in vv. 13-15 are all of a part and derived from the same source (J), Jacob seems to have tunnel vision when recalling them ... [The vow] adds colour to the author's portrayal of Jacob's character. He is distrustful (even of God), he is selfish, and he is determined to gain the upper hand in every transaction' (pp. 169-74).

he wants to clarify precisely how it will be fulfilled. And if the patriarch can be criticized for emphasizing its most down-to-earth aspect, what ensues shows either that he has understood it correctly, or that God does indeed follow his interpretation. For the account of life in Laban's house provides a graphic illustration of active divine intervention in Jacob's daily affairs.

In the following chapter I will discuss in some detail God's involve-. ment in the choice of Rachel. For the moment it is enough to say that the narrative contains several indications of the role of divine providence in the match, and, in this respect, the dream's position between Jacob's setting out to find a wife and his meeting with Rachel is far from coincidental. The patriarch makes it clear in his vow that he hopes for tangible support, and here, at once, it is forthcoming.

The intimate connection between the dream and Jacob's discovery of Rachel was observed by many rabbinic commentators, and *Genesis Rabbah's* interpretations of 28.10 commence with some reflections on the difficulty of finding a wife. Most memorable may be the interaction between Rabbi Yosi bar Halafta and the Roman matron who finds it hard to believe that, since creating the world, God has spent his time making matches. Only her disastrous attempt to pair off her numerous male and female slaves convinces the matron that this activity does, indeed, require divine assistance.[25] Another midrash on the same verse emphasizes the absence of paternal support, contrasting Jacob's situation with that of Isaac, whose father sent a clever servant bearing gifts in search of a wife for his son.[26] This observation is not simply a product of the rabbinic imagination; Jacob's utter isolation as he sets out for Haran is a crucial element of the biblical narrative. Once again, the lack of human support or material sustenance heralds divine intervention, and Isaac's withdrawal is doubtlessly connected with God's intensified presence in Jacob's life.

It is not surprising that the rabbis should have connected the dream at Bethel with Jacob's search for a wife; dreams were sought to confirm the choice of a spouse long after the biblical period.[27] Indeed, it is this connection that led some commentators to speculate about the presence of an incubation ritual in Genesis 28.[28] As noted above, ancient Near

25. *GR, ad loc.*
26. *GR, ad loc.*
27. *b. Ber.* 55b.
28. Ehrlich, *Der Traum im Alten Testament*, ultimately rejects the idea that

Eastern dream incubation is often associated with the lack of a wife or an heir,[29] and the presence in ch. 28 of several elements of incubation (namely sleep in a holy place with the intention of summoning a dream in response to uncertainty) lends it the appearance of an incubated dream report. Recent scholars have rejected this possibility, largely because, assuming that Jacob was unaware of Bethel's holiness when he fell asleep, he failed to meet all requirements of dream incubation.[30] Attempts to overcome this objection by recourse to a sub-category of incubation called 'unintentional incubation' are, as Gnuse has shown, misguided.

This author is critical of the endeavour to call this (1 Sam. 3) or any experience an unintentional incubation dream, as though that were a formal category in itself. The label is our creation, which is placed upon experiences that do not explicitly mention an incubation process. The phrase is a contradiction in terms, for incubation implies purpose, unintentional incubation is accidental; therefore unintentional incubation is the same as no incubation at all.[31]

Jacob's dream may have been incubated, but he nevertheless discusses it under the general heading of 'Incubation Dreams' (p. 27). With regard to incubation in Gen. 28, Gnuse, *The Dream Theophany of Samuel*, suggests: 'The Israelite narrator may have masked that aspect of the tradition, and Jacob's surprise at the dream experience is meant to remove any suspicion of deliberate incubation' (pp. 67-68). For a brief discussion of biblical dream incubation texts, see also McAlpine, *Sleep, Divine and Human*, pp. 158-59.

29. For a discussion of situations typically preceding dream incubation, see again, Jeffers, 'Divination by Dreams', esp. pp. 175-83.

30. McAlpine dismisses the possibility of incubation at Bethel because Gen. 28 'narrates, at most, Jacob's discovery, rather than his use of, a holy place' (*Sleep, Divine and Human*, p. 159). Against this, however, one might note the use of the verb לִין (which occurs in Num. 22.8 where Balaam tells the officers of Moab to '*stay overnight*' so that he can report God's words to them), in Isa. 65.4, where God rebukes people who sit in tombs and spend the night in secret places, and in Ps. 91.1, with reference to those who dwell in the shadow of the Almighty. A. Caquot, 'Le Psaume XCI', *Semitica* 8 (1958), pp. 21-37, sees in this latter example a possible allusion to dream incubation practices, and posits that the verb לִין may sometimes be paraphrased 'spending the night for a purpose of securing a divine revelation' (p. 25).

31. *The Dream Theophany of Samuel*, p. 151.

Plausible as it seems that Genesis 28 preserves the memory of incubation rituals conducted at Bethel, it must be admitted that, at the level of final redaction, incubation is no more than a fleeting glimpse.[32]

Thus far, I have considered the dream's function of validating Jacob's newly and duplicitously acquired status, and its role in confirming that God will help Jacob with practical matters such as the search for a wife. There is, however, a third concern that it must address: will God accompany Jacob when he leaves his paternal home and, more to the point, his native land? This question may be examined on several different levels. Once again, the contrast between this account of Jacob's solitary search for a wife and the description of Abraham's active involvement in procuring a wife for Isaac is revealing. Of particular interest is Abraham's insistence that Isaac should not leave the land (24.6-8). It is difficult to know whether he was afraid that Isaac's right of possession would be compromised if he left the land, or whether he feared that his son's interest in possessing it might wane, but, in either case, there is a striking contrast between Abraham's protectiveness of Isaac, and Isaac's own readiness to expel Jacob in markedly similar circumstances.

Von Rad believes that God's promise to be with Jacob (28.15) arises from the question of where he can be worshipped:

> Israel always thought that YHWH could be worshipped only in Canaan but that his sovereign realm also included all foreign lands. That is strange, because ancient Israel never considered the gods of the nations only as 'nothings' but attributed to them a relative sphere of power and cult (Judg. 11.24; 1 Sam. 26.19f.). Our Genesis narrators, to be sure, show no further evidence of such ideas.[33]

For rather different reasons, rabbinic commentators also saw God's presence outside the land as an issue here: Rashi, following midrash, claimed that the angels who descended the ladder at Bethel were those whose tour of duty began only when the patriarch went into exile.[34]

---

32. M. Oliva, *Jacob en Betel: Visión y voto* (Madrid: Universidad Pontificia Comillas, 1975), draws attention to one such possible fleeting glimpse by relating Jacob's words to his wives in 35.3, 'Come, let us go up to Bethel, and I will build an altar there to the God who answered me when I was in distress', to certain Psalms of individual lamentation (20.2; 69.18; 86.7; 91.15; 102.3; 120.1) which may request consolation in the form of a vision (p. 46).

33. *Genesis*, p. 285.

34. Rashi's commentary, *MG, ad loc.*

While this association of angels and exile may seem fanciful, it cannot be ruled out. Their prominence in Jacob's life may well result from his tenure outside the land, and Abraham's insistence that an angel accompany his servant when he sets out to find a wife for Isaac (24.7) may likewise indicate that angels were associated with exile, or at least with difficult travel before the land was successfully conquered.[35] Some additional links between Bethel and the theme of exile will be discussed in detail below. In the meantime, I will explore the significance of Jacob's dream in the light of ancient Near Eastern texts which have not previously been brought to bear upon Genesis 28.

Kingship, Dreams and Temples in the Ancient Near East

As a result, perhaps, of a world view in which kings were the channel through which gods bestowed their favour upon people, the relationship between the two was of paramount importance. In *Kingship and the Gods*, H. Frankfort offers the following brief account.

> The king's duties were threefold: the interpretation of the will of the gods; the representation of his people before the gods; and the administration of the realm. This division is somewhat artificial, for the king, as representative of the people, interpreted the will of the gods.[36]

According to Frankfort, the gods could communicate with kings by three methods—signs, oracles and dreams[37]—and, of these, dreams were the most direct and least easily disputed. Kings who did not receive divine communications were unlikely to have been regarded as effective leaders of the people, and for this reason alone it is not surprising that so many royal dream reports have survived. Indeed, as M. Robinson has pointed out, the immense importance attached to the royal dreams makes it probable that many were essentially literary products, recorded for the purpose of maintaining a king's status in the eyes of his people.[38] Although dreams could be used to convey both good news and bad, the complete withholding from a king of dream messages could

35. See Exod. 23.20, 33.2, Num. 20.16 for similar examples of angels accompanying Israel in difficult circumstances.

36. *Kingship and the Gods: A Study of Ancient Near Eastern Religion as the Integration of Society and Nature* (Chicago: University of Chicago Press, 1978 [1948]), p. 252.

37. *Kingship and the Gods*, p. 252.

38. 'Dreams in the Old Testament', p. 169.

signify little but divine disapproval. As is evident from Frankfort's summary of the situation, kings were utterly dependent upon information from the gods, particularly in spheres such as temple building, where men could not operate without divine authorization.

It was not merely the case that temples were built by men who had been authorized by the gods to do so; they were also constructed according to divinely approved plans which had to be communicated to the builder. Thus temple building was a popular theme of royal dreams.[39] Among the most illuminating of these temple-building dream reports is the account of the three dreams received by Gudea of Lagash relating to the construction of the temple that established Lagash as a city-state. According to V. Hurowitz,[40] the account of Gudea's temple building is an unusually detailed and complete example of a pattern that was followed throughout the ancient world.[41] Most pertinently for the purposes of this discussion, Hurowitz sees extensive parallels between the Gudea account and 1 Kgs 5.15–9.25.[42] His observations are based on structural

39. Robinson, *Dreams in the Old Testament*, states: 'Dream reports relating to temple building probably form the single largest category of dreams recorded in Ancient Near Eastern literature and are to be found in virtually every region over a wide timespan. This situation is, no doubt, partly to be explained by the fact that dream reports contained in building inscriptions are more likely to survive than other types of dream report, but it is also probably a fairly accurate indication of the importance attached to this particular royal activity' (p. 169).

40. *I Have Built You an Exalted House*. See pp. 31-57 for a detailed discussion of the Gudea Cylinders.

41. *I Have Built You an Exalted House*, pp. 143-49, provides a brief survey of other ancient Near Eastern temple-building accounts in which dreams are the means by which the gods reveal their demands. Hurowitz notes that dreams are especially prominent in building reports concerning Assurbanipal, king of Assyria and Nabonidus, king of Babylon (pp. 147-48).

42. Hurowitz, *I Have Built You an Exalted House*, provides the following structural outline of the Gudea Cylinders:

Cyl. A
(1) The divine decision to build Eninnu, and notification of the decision to Gudea.
(2) Clarification of the divine command by Gudea—revelation of the temple's spiritual dimensions.
(3) The preparations of the building project—clarification continued, the form revealed.
(4) The construction process and description of the structure and its furnishings.

similarities between the two accounts, and he notes the speculative nature of the suggestion, made by A.S. Kapelrud and M. Weinfeld respectively,[43] that the dream in which Solomon was promised wisdom (1 Kgs 3) may have replaced an earlier report, subsequently deleted by the Deuteronomist for being theologically unsound, of an incubated dream containing God's command to build the Temple.[44]

If Hurowitz is correct about the overall structural parallels between biblical and extra-biblical building accounts, so that biblical narrators were, indeed, familiar with the pattern exemplified by the Gudea Cylinders, it is more than reasonable to explore the possibility that Jacob's dream at Bethel may have been based on this model. Although many commentators have recognized in Genesis 28 allusions to a temple or sanctuary, few have seen temple building as a central concern of the text, and even fewer, if any, have related it to the temple building accounts treated by Hurowitz.[45] Those who regard the ladder as a temple tower or ziggurat see it as a symbol of Bethel's holiness rather than as a component of an actual temple, and the pillar is likewise regarded simply as a standing stone commemorating Jacob's experience there.[46] The

Cyl. B
(5) The gods assemble in the temple.
(6) Ningirsu is brought to the new temple.
(7) Presentation of gifts and appointment of temple personnel.
(8) Determining destinies for the seven day human and divine celebrations—revelations to Gudea.

He notes 'the great similarity between the structure of the Gudea Cylinders and the structure of the story about building the Temple in Jerusalem by Solomon as found in 1 Kgs 5.15–9.25' (p. 56).

43. This suggestion is discussed by A. Kapelrud, 'Temple Building: A Task for Gods and Kings', *Or* 32 (1963), pp. 56-62; and by M. Weinfeld, *Deuteronomy and the Deuteronomic School* (Oxford: Clarendon Press, 1983 [1972]). See pp. 248-54 for this discussion.

44. *I Have Built You an Exalted House*, pp. 165-66.

45. In *I Have Built You an Exalted House*. This includes Hurowitz himself, whose book includes no reference to Gen. 28.

46. G.J. Griffiths, 'The Celestial Ladder and the Gate of Heaven in Egyptian Ritual', *ExpTim* 78 (1966), pp. 54-55; and A.R. Millard, 'The Celestial Ladder and the Gate of Heaven (Gen. 28:12, 17)', *ExpTim* 78 (1966), pp. 85-87, note various ancient Near Eastern parallels to the imagery of Jacob's dream. For a comprehensive summary of interpretations of both ladder and standing stone see C. Houtman, 'What did Jacob See in his Dream at Bethel?: Some Remarks on Genesis 28:10-22', *VT* 27 (1977), pp. 337-51.

reasons for this are fairly obvious. Most importantly, the dream occurs in Bethel rather than Jerusalem, and, in any case, Jacob does not actually build a temple.[47] Secondly, the ladder has many plausible interpretations relating to God's accessibility to Jacob and his willingness to communicate with him, and there has been no obvious reason to explore further. Finally, the pillar, functioning here as a stone commemorating an event, does not appear to require a special explanation.

In fact, however, it seems likely that the pillar may well require a special explanation. Genesis has only eight occurrences of the word מצבה (standing stone/pillar), all in texts featuring Jacob.[48] Elsewhere, with rare exceptions such as Exod. 24.4 where 12 pillars are erected by Moses at the foot of Mount Sinai to signify the 12 tribes, and Isa. 19.19, where a standing stone is raised at the Egyptian border, apparently as a focus for Egyptian worship of the God of Israel, the references to these pillars are almost exclusively negative, and with strong pagan associations.[49] In what follows I will explore the possibility that Genesis 28 is, in fact, a dream authorizing Jacob to build a temple, and that the vision of the ladder and the raising of the standing stone correspond closely to traditional elements of the ancient Near Eastern temple building dreams exemplified by the Gudea reports.

Much attention has been devoted to explaining exactly what Jacob saw when he looked at the ladder (28.12). The image of a ladder has been immortalized in popular thought, but, as noted above, some exegetes have argued that a ziggurat or temple tower may have been intended. While we are entitled to be sceptical about the rejection of

47. He does go on to build an altar at Bethel (35.1-8), but this does not seem to represent the fulfilment of his promise in 28.20-22. First of all, 35.1 reports an independent command by God to build an altar. Secondly, it makes no mention of the standing stone (contrary to 31.13, which mentions the pillar but no altar). Thirdly, Jacob subsequently raises another at Bethel (35.14-15), which also commemorates the naming of the place, but seems to have no connection with the earlier pillar. It seems most likely that these were originally separate traditions, each with its own standing stone, about the naming of Bethel, just as 35.9-10 appears to reflect a tradition about Jacob's renaming which has no connection with the one in 32.23-33.

48. 28.18, 22; 31.13, 45, 51, 52; 35.14, 20.

49. See, for instance, Lev. 26.1; Deut. 7.5; 12.3, 16.22; 2 Kgs 18.4. Van Seters, 'The Religion of the Patriarchs in Genesis', *Biblica* 61 (1980), pp. 220-33, emphasizes that the standing stone in Genesis is used as a memorial and not as an object of worship and suggests that, in any case, the redactors would not have been concerned about pillars which clearly predated the Deuteronomic ban (p. 232).

'ladder' by scholars who cannot envisage 'messengers going up and
down in a steady stream'[50] (these are angels not window-cleaners), we
must probably concede that Jacob's סלם is more likely to be a tower
than a ladder.

Hurowitz provides an extensive selection of texts, from the Bible and
elsewhere, in which the cosmic dimensions of temples are described
using what must have been a standard ancient Near Eastern reference to
heaven and earth:

The epilogue to the Hammurabi law monument says that the stele
was erected:

> *In Babylon*
> *The city which Anum and Ellil*
> *raised up his head,*
> *in Esagila*
> *the temple which like heaven and earth*
> *its foundations are firm.*

In a Neo-Assyrian 'city-hymn' the city of Arba-ilu is depicted:

1.2   *Arba-ilu is the unrivaled heaven,*
1.14 *Arba-ilu lies like the heavens.*
1.15 *Its foundations are firm like those [of the earth]*
1.16 The head of Arba-ilu is lofty
       it rivals the heavens …

In the Papulegara hymn:

> *The head of the temple is lofty*
> *Below its roots touch the netherworld*
> *The head of the Kesh temple is lofty*
> *Below its roots touch the netherworld*
> *Above may its … rival heaven*
> *Below its roots touch the netherworld.*

In a temple hymn to Ezida in Barsippa we read:

1   *Barsippa resembles heaven*
2   *Rivaling Esarra, is lofty Ezida*
5   *Its foliage reaches the clouds,*
6   *Its roots are founded piercing the netherworld.*

---

50. Houtman, 'What did Jacob See', p. 340, and E.A. Speiser, *Genesis* (New
York: Doubleday, 1986 [1962]), p. 218. Von Rad makes a similar objection in *Genesis*: 'When we think of the 'ladder to heaven', however, we should not think of an
actual ladder, for such a simultaneous mounting and descending of wingless divine
messengers on it would not be easily conceivable' (p. 284).

In a description of Esarhaddon discussed above, the temple of Assur is described:

> *I raised the top of Esharra to heaven*
> *Above, to heaven I elevated its top.*
> *Below in the netherworld*
> *I made firm its foundations.*[51]

Hurowitz offers additional examples (from *Nabopolassar* no. 1 col. 1 ll. 36-39, *Nebuchadnezzar* no. 1 col. 1 ll. 31-32, and no. 20 col. 1 ll. 68), but, for present purposes, it is unnecessary to cite these in full. It is clear that the description of a structure reaching from earth to heaven would inevitably have evoked for ancient readers the image of a temple, and there is no obvious reason why Gen. 28.12 should have represented an exception to this rule, particularly in view of the subsequent occurrence of the term בית אלהים (house of God) in vv. 17 and 22.

There are many reasons for assuming a link of some sort between the ladder and the standing stone. Thinking linguistically, Fokkelman argues for a connection between the top of the ladder (v. 12) and the top of the stone (v. 18).[52] Archaeologically-inspired exegetes have suggested that the stones mentioned in v. 11 grow into a tower linking heaven and earth and that Jacob erects the standing stone as a symbol of this tower.[53] As Houtman points out, though, there is little evidence elsewhere in the Bible for this function of a standing stone, and he concludes that the stone is related not to the ladder but to the description of God standing by Jacob:

> It is particularly attractive to presuppose such a relation, if one is inclined to agree with De Groot in considering the *massebah* in vv. 16-18 as a representative of YHWH. In v. 22 the stone apparently indicates the whole place, which had received in the massebah a characteristic cult object.[54]

While the standing stone in mentioned in Isa. 19.19-20 may possibly be understood as representing the Lord in some way, Genesis offers no evidence that it was thus conceived. On the contrary, other occurrences suggest that it was regarded as more of a marker than a symbol.[55]

---

51. *I Have Built You an Exalted House*, pp. 335-36.
52. *Narrative Art in Genesis*, pp. 66-67.
53. Gnuse, *The Dream Theophany of Samuel*, p. 68.
54. 'What did Jacob See', p. 343.
55. In 31.44-54 the stone both marks the border between Laban and Jacob, and

Houtman's interpretation of the standing stone also fails to account for the delay implied in v. 22, where Jacob's words suggest it will *become* a 'house of God'. Why should the stone function as a symbol of God's presence only upon Jacob's safe return to Bethel? Even if Houtman's explanation of the stone is correct, it is difficult to envisage a convincing explanation for the delay.

If we return now to the Gudea Cylinders, a more plausible explanation of the significance of the standing stone, as well as of its connection to the ladder, should quickly suggest itself. Gudea Cylinder A provides an account of three dreams received by Gudea of Lagash, one seemingly spontaneous and two incubated, authorizing him to build a temple and providing him with a blueprint for its design. Cylinder B deals primarily with the dedication of the temple and the entry of the god for whom it was built. The first dream, which is reported at length by Gudea to Nanshe, the dream interpretess, is highly symbolic:

> In the dream, the first man—like the heaven was his
> surpassing (size),
> like the earth was his surpassing (size),
> (according) to his (horn-crowned[?]) he was a god,
> (according) to his wings he was Imdugud (the
> bird of the Weather-god),
> (according) to his lower parts (?) he was the Storm-flood,
> lions were lying to his right and left—
> commanded me to build his house;
> but I do not know what he had in mind.
> Daylight rose for me on the horizon.
> The first woman—whoever she may have been—
> coming out ahead (?) did ...
> a ... stylus she held in her hand,
> a tablet of (?) heavenly stars she put on (her) knees,
> consulting it.
> The second (man) was a warrior,
> he ..., a tablet of lapis lazuli he held in (his) hand,
> set down (thereon[?]) the plan of the temple.
> Before me stood a pure carrying pad,

acts as a witness lest they should cross it with evil intent. In 35.14 it once again marks the place where God spoke to Jacob at Bethel, and in 35.20 it marks Rachel's grave. Elsewhere in the Bible the standing stone is mentioned almost exclusively in conjunction with pagan altars and sacred pillars (e.g. Exod. 23.24; Lev. 26.1; Deut. 12.3; 2 Kgs 17.10).

a pure brick-mold was lined up (?),
a brick, determined as to (its) nature was placed in
the mold for me ... [56]

Nanshe's interpretation follows immediately: the monstrous figure is her brother Ningirsu, for whom the temple will be built; the woman with the stylus is her sister Nisaba, announcing the pure star which determines the building; the man is the god Nindub, copying the plan of the house; and the brick is the pure brick (foundation stone) of the temple.[57]

Setting aside the man and woman, both of whom are explanatory additions, two central images remain: the figure of the god extending from earth to heaven and the brick-mould. The fact that Oppenheim did not attempt a translation into grammatical English makes it difficult to know precisely what to envisage in 'like the heaven was his surpassing size', and 'like the earth his surpassing size', but fortunately he elaborates elsewhere:

> On the optic plane, the impact of the apparition, be it a deity or his substitute or messenger, etc., is, in Near Eastern dream-reports, sometimes expressed by a reference to his towering size. This is an essential feature of the famous dream of Gudea, ensi of the Sumerian city of Lagash, in which he reports seeing a divine figure reaching from earth to heaven.[58]

That the image of a figure reaching from earth to heaven belongs to the class of traditional temple descriptions cited by Hurowitz is hardly surprising: Gudea's dream deals explicitly with this subject. Moreover, it seems that the enormous figure must represent the plan for the temple, as well as the building authorization. The man who appears in Gudea's vision is said to be *copying* the plan, and, since it has not been conveyed verbally, we must assume that it was visible in some symbolic sense, most probably through the details of the figure itself.

The significance of the other central image of Gudea's first dream, the brick-mould, becomes apparent in the third dream report in Cylinder A. By this time Gudea has assembled the materials required to build the temple, and he falls asleep, at the very place where construction will commence the following day, in order to incubate the dream which will

56. Oppenheim, 'The Interpretation of Dreams', p. 245.
57. Oppenheim, 'The Interpretation of Dreams', claims that the first brick corresponded in Mesopotamian practice to the Israelite corner-stone (p. 212).
58. 'The Interpretation of Dreams', p. 189.

88

Revisions of the Night

provide the precise details of the architectural plan. The plan having
been successfully transmitted to the king, one final step will remain: the
moulding of the first brick. Frankfort describes the great symbolic significance of this final act:

> When at last the production of bricks for the new temple could be
> taken in hand, the mood of the celebrations changed completely. The
> tentative questioning of the gods, the mournful occupation with the
> relics of past misfortune or neglect were left behind; and all attention
> was centred on the positive achievement of rebuilding. However, this
> happy change required that the first brick for the new building be well
> and truly formed, and the nature of the material makes the extraction of a
> perfect brick from its mold by no means a foregone conclusion. Conse-
> quently, the successful molding of the first brick assumed the signifi-
> cance of a last ordeal, the final answer to the question whether the gods
> would accept the labor of their servant.[59]

The dream which Gudea receives immediately following the moulding
of the brick is, in some respects, the most important of the three, for in
it the temple is finally revealed in its entirety.

The parallels with Genesis 28 should, by now, have emerged, revealing a possible explanation of the significance of Jacob's standing stone
and its relationship to the ladder. In Gudea's dream the vision of the
towering figure provides the divine plan and building authorization,
while the brick-mould represents the king's own contribution to the
construction of the temple. I believe that ladder and stone function in
similar ways in Jacob's dream; the vision of the ladder provides God's
authorization to build a temple, as well as the blueprint for its design,
while the pillar is the foundation stone, representing Jacob's commitment to fulfilling God's command.[60] The presence in Genesis 28 of
these two distinctive elements of ancient Near Eastern temple building,
followed by explicit promises that the stone will become a 'house of
God', and that Jacob will tithe there, make it extremely difficult to deny
that we are dealing here with some form of temple building dream
report.

Thus Gudea prepares the first brick, and is subsequently rewarded
by a dream in which the plan for the temple is revealed in full. When

59. *Kingship and the Gods*, p. 272.
60. 1 Chron. 28.11-19, Exod. 25.9 and Num. 8.4 provide biblical examples in
which buildings or ritual objects are constructed according to a divine plan.

he wakes from the dream, construction may begin.[61] Similarly, Jacob selects a significant stone (v. 11), receives a dream in which he sees a structure that strongly evokes a temple tower, anoints the stone and names the place Bethel (28.16-19). If Oppenheim is correct in his assertion that the first brick is simply the Mesopotamian equivalent of a foundation stone, then it seems entirely reasonable to regard Jacob's anointing of the stone as the structural equivalent of Gudea's setting of the first brick.

Jacob's anointing of the stone, particularly in view of its occurrence in conjunction with Jacob's allusions to the house of God and the gate of heaven, recalls another ancient Near Eastern temple ritual. In an excursus on 'Oil, Scents, and Doors in Dedication Rites', Hurowitz describes the ritual oiling of gates as a means of enticing the gods to enter temples built in their names:

> In Nabonidus's description of the dedication of Shamash's temple Ebabbar, we read
>
> *The door posts, locks, bolts, and door leaves*
> *I drenched with oil*
> *and for the entry of their exalted divinity*
> *I made the contents of the temple full of sweet fragrance.*
> *The Temple, for the entry of Shamash my lord,*
> *its gates were wide open*
> *and it was full of joy.*[62]

In addition to this report of a dedication ceremony, Hurowitz cites other texts which feature the anointing of temple gates (the Nabu-apla-iddinna inscription, and an Esarhaddon text describing the introduction of Ishtar of Uruk into her temple Enirgalanna, as well as biblical references to the anointing of the tabernacle), noting possible echoes in Ezek. 43.1-9 and perhaps 44.1-4 and in Psalm 24. Of particular interest is the view of C. Meyers that the pillars Jachin and Boaz (2 Chron. 3.17) may have

---

61. Hurowitz, *I Have Built You an Exalted House*, describes the progress of events as follows: 'Gudea is depicted as zealous and eager in all he does, and there are no preparatory activities in which he does not participate personally. He measures the building site, molds the first brick amidst a glorious festive ritual, and sets it in its place. At this point, he lies down, and, as promised, is granted a third dream in which the Enninu temple is revealed to him. The remainder of the first cylinder details the building process and describes the edifice itself' (p. 40).

62. *I Have Built You an Exalted House*, p. 278.

been monuments to God's entry into the new Jerusalem Temple.[63] While none of this establishes beyond dispute that Jacob's standing stone should be understood as a door pillar, or that the oil which he poured upon it was, in part, an invitation to God to enter the future temple, possible ancient Near Eastern parallels cannot be dismissed out of hand.

In this respect, the image of the gate of heaven (28.17) is also worth examining in some detail. Houtman has the following to say:

> If the *massebah* is the representative of YHWH, who had revealed himself to the sleeping Jacob by standing in his proximity, then that place really can be called 'the/a house of God' (v. 17). But can it also be called 'the gate of heaven' (v. 17)? Certainly, for YHWH is there. It is important, in view of the question under consideration, that v. 17 presupposes that Jacob was sleeping *in* the gate of heaven.[64]

A minor difficulty is the notion that Jacob had fallen asleep in the gate of heaven. More troubling is the fact that this analysis does not account for the small but significant word in v. 17:

וירא ויאמר מה נורא המקום הזה אין זה כי אם בית אלהים
וזה שער השמים:

Shaken, he said, 'How awesome is *this* place! *This* is none other than the abode of God *and this* is the gateway to heaven.[65]

If it was Jacob's intention to describe the place both as a house of God and as the gate of heaven, the use of 'and this' (וזה), with its suggestion that two distinct locations are being denoted, is out of place.[66] While it is not impossible that all three occurrences of 'this' (זה) in v. 17 have the same point of reference, it seems more likely that Jacob is referring to two different locations, namely the two ends of the ladder. His exclamation might then read: 'How awesome is this (entire) place; this (the

63. 'Jachin and Boaz in Religious and Political Perspective', *CBQ* 45 (1983), pp. 167-78.

64. 'What did Jacob See', p. 343.

65. *JPS* actually uses 'this... and that', but I diverge from them slightly to reflect the Hebrew, upon which my discussion is based.

66. Admittedly, 'this ... and this' (זה ... וזה) occasionally has the same point of reference, as in Exod. 3.15, 'This shall be my name forever, this my appellation for all eternity' (זה שמי לעלם וזה זכרי לדר דר). More often, though, it is used in the sense of 'this... and that', as in Job 1.16, 'This one was still speaking when another one came and said ...' (עוד זה מדבר וזה בא ויאמר ...) or 1 Kgs 22.20, 'Then one said thus and another said thus' (ויאמר זה בכה וזה אמר בכה).

base of the ladder) is nothing but a house of God, and this (the head of the ladder) is the gate of heaven'. Houtman objects to this reading:

> In any case the story does not tell us that Jacob saw a staircase, starting from the place where he was sleeping, with its end at the gate of the heavenly palace. Jacob is not lying at the place of the deity's revelation, which is to be distinguished from the deity's real abode at the end of the *sullam*, but Jacob is *in* the gate of heaven, at the place which gives entry to heaven, at the place where the abode, the house of God, *is*.[67]

Yet his objection is odd, both because the narrative *does* tell us about a structure extending from earth to heaven (v. 12) which, we may most plausibly imagine, begins at the very place where Jacob is sleeping, and because Jacob must be lying on the ground, not at the top of the ladder. The confusion may arise from Houtman's interpretation of בית אלהים as 'abode of God'; if his image is replaced by a picture in which the ladder's base is seen as the temple where God will be worshipped, and its top as the house where he dwells, then the interpretative problems quickly evaporate.[68]

The occurrence of several important elements from the typology of ancient Near Eastern temple building does not, of course, prove beyond all doubt that Jacob's dream at Bethel should be understood as a dream authorizing him to build a temple. Yet its images of the structure reaching from earth to heaven, the gate of heaven, and the house of God,

---

67. 'What did Jacob See', p. 344.

68. Evidence from elsewhere in the Bible indicates that God is envisaged as dwelling above the earthly Temple, not in it. See especially 2 Chron. 6.18-21. According to von Rad, *Genesis*, there was a general distinction in the ancient Near East between the place where the gods dwelt and the place where they were worshipped: 'To understand the whole, however, one must know that in the ancient Orient a rather general distinction was made between the earthly place of a god's appearing and his actual (heavenly) dwelling place. Thus on the gigantic Babylonian temple towers, the dwelling place is symbolized by the uppermost chamber, while below on earth there is a temple where the god appears; and from top to bottom, as the characteristic mark of this cultic building, there runs a long ramp. Thus Jacob too makes a distinction in this sense: this is a house of God, i.e., the place where God appears, which is to become a cultic centre with a cultic building, "and this is the gate of heaven" (v. 17)' (p. 284). This is compatible with A. Parrot's account of the ziggurat, 'E-temen-anki' (the House of the Foundation-stone of Heaven and Earth), which stood next to Marduk's temple, Esagila. At the summit of the ziggurat was a small temple faced with blue enamelled bricks. See *Babylon and the Old Testament* (trans. B. Hooke; London: SCM Press, 1958), pp. 43-59.

seen in conjunction with the anointing of the stone, begin to present
a rather plausible picture. To this list we might add Jacob's promise
to tithe (v. 22), which, although it could have been made in reference to
a location other than the Temple (cf. 14.20) certainly evokes temple
practice, and his naming of Bethel, which may reflect the tradition of
renaming cities and temples to denote a change in status.[69] Even the
notorious request for food and clothes may preserve an aspect of ancient Near Eastern temple building that emphasizes the material welfare
of the builders.[70] Naturally, objections may be raised to each individual
component of the picture presented here. The question is, though, how
persuasive are they when viewed as a whole? To answer this question,
it may be helpful to move away from Genesis 28 itself in order to
assess the impression it conveyed to readers closer to its own time.

Some Evidence from Post-biblical Readings of Genesis 28

The Temple Scroll from Qumran makes an interesting and explicit connection between Jacob's dream and the Temple:

> I will accept them, and they will be my people and I will be theirs for-
> ever, and I will be present among them forever after and I will sanctify
> my temple with my Majesty by causing my Majesty to be present over it
> until the day of blessing when I myself will create my temple so that it
> be established for me all the days, according to the covenant which I
> made with Jacob at Bethel.[71]

---

69. Cf. 2 Sam. 5.9, where David occupies the Jebusite stronghold and names it
'City of David'.

70. Hurowitz, *I Have Built You an Exalted House*, cites a passage from the
report of Nabonidus's building of Ebabbar in Sippar, which describes the use of oil:

> So as not to cause within it
> anger, curse and sin
> and not to place in the mouth
> of the builders doing its work—
> (but instead) to place in
> their mouths good blessings—
> loaves, beer, meat and wine ... (p. 278).

71. Col. 29.8-10. Cited by Hurowitz, *I Have Built You an Exalted House*,
p. 332.

Y. Yadin in *The Temple Scroll*[72] considers whether this statement refers to the Temple or, alternatively, to an eschatological temple, but, in either case, its author cannot have had in mind a cultic site of the sort envisaged by recent scholars. Indeed, the notion of an eschatological temple may represent an ingenious attempt at an interpretative solution to a problem posed by the Genesis text: if the temple is eschatological rather than actual, the earthly location of the dream is no longer a cause for concern. At any rate, it is clear that the author of the Temple Scroll saw a temple of some kind as an explicit subject of Jacob's dream at Bethel.

Yadin makes an interesting observation about the date given in the book of *Jubilees* for Jacob's experience at Bethel:

> It is possible that some connection with the Temple is reflected in Jacob's *first* arrival at Bethel, which, according to the *Book of Jubilees*, took place on the first day of the first month (27:19), on which day Jacob dreamt of the ladder; that day is linked with the building of the Tabernacle. Significantly, the Septuagint translation of Ezek. 40:1—'in the first month', instead of 'at the beginning of the year'—may point to a tradition 'which associates the month of Nisan with the time when the vision of the Temple was revealed to Ezekiel, perhaps based on the then current exegesis'; S. Abramsky, '*Rosh ha-Shanah* and *Pesah* in Ezekiel', *Beer Sheva*, I, Jerusalem (1973), p. 57.[73]

Although *Jubilees* provides what is essentially a midrashic reading of Genesis, no more authoritative than *Genesis Rabbah* with regard to the text's original meaning, it nevertheless represents an ancient interpretation well worth considering. Moreover, since its author's agenda, the incorporation of Jewish law into patriarchal history, is easily identifiable, it is a relatively straightforward matter to distinguish elements that reflect this aim from those which attempt to resolve inconsistencies in the original biblical account.

Jubilees 27.19-27 is, with a few exceptions, fairly faithful in its rendering of Gen. 28.10-22. The possible significance of the specification

72. Jerusalem: Israel Exploration Society, 1983, I. See especially pp. 182-87 for a discussion of this issue.

73. Yadin explores the possible connection between the Feast of Booths and the covenant at Bethel (comments to col. 29.10). He also lists other events that supposedly occurred on the first day of the first month: the construction of the tabernacle (Exod. 40.2), the beginning of the journey up from Babylon (Ezra 7.9), and the completion of the case against the exiles who returned with foreign wives (Ezra 10.17) (p. 90).

of the date of the dream's occurrence has been noted above. Far
more informative is a seemingly minor change in the announcement of
Jacob's arrival at the place where he is to spend the night:

> And Jacob went from the Well of the Oath to Haran on the first year of
> the second week in the forty-fourth jubilee, and he came to Luz on the
> mountains, that is, Bethel, on the new moon of the first month of this
> week, and he came to the place at even and turned away to the west of
> the road that night: and he slept there; for the sun had set.[74]

The telling insertion of 'that is, Bethel' provides strong evidence that
the author of *Jubilees* saw neither the discovery of Bethel's holiness
nor its transformation from a pagan to an Israelite holy place as central
concerns of Genesis 28. From a literary perspective it seems inconceivable that a version of the narrative that sought to assert that Bethel
became holy *because of* Jacob's experience there would begin by using
the name supposedly given to it by Jacob as a result of his experience.

The strongest evidence for how Genesis 28 was understood by the
author of *Jubilees* comes later, though, in an account that has no parallel in the biblical narrative. Here Jacob, who has resolved to build a
temple at Bethel in accordance with his own interpretation of his
dream, is visited by an angel carrying the seven tablets that outline the
destiny of the patriarch and his descendants. The angel shows them to
Jacob and issues a spoken warning against building a temple at Bethel:
...'Do not build this place, and do not make it an eternal sanctuary, and
do not dwell here; for this is not the place.'[75] Since this addition does
not serve the purpose of bringing the actions of the patriarchs in line
with Jewish law, we may assume that it was inserted to resolve what its
author regarded as a troubling inconsistency in the original account:
Jacob promises to build a temple at Bethel, but no temple is built.
Where the Temple Scroll implies that the temple of Jacob's dream may
have been an eschatological construction, *Jubilees* suggests that it was
not built simply because God had in mind another location. Genesis
22.11-12 provides an obvious precedent for angelic intervention to
change a previously issued divine command, and also shows that the

---

74. R.H. Charles (ed.), *The Apocrypha and Pseudepigrapha of the Old Testament in English* 2 (Oxford: Clarendon Press, 1913). *OTP*, II in an almost identical
translation, replaces 'that is, Bethel' with 'i.e., Bethel'.

75. *Jub.* 32.22.

Jubilees version is no more likely to reflect a misunderstanding by Jacob than a perceived change of heart by God.[76]

In an article dealing explicitly with the representation of Bethel in the book of *Jubilees*, J. Schwartz suggests that the *Jubilees* version of Genesis 28 may have been written during the period when the Maccabees were hiding in the hills, reflecting their wish to change the location of the now inaccessible Temple from Jerusalem to Bethel.[77] Given that his interest in *Jubilees* is more historical than literary, it is not surprising that Schwartz looks to history for an explanation of the angelic intervention in *Jub.* 32.22. Yet, from a literary perspective, an author interested in demonstrating the superiority of Bethel over Jerusalem would have been better served by the original Genesis text. It is difficult to reconcile the idea that Bethel may, after all, be an appropriate location for the temple with the unambiguous command that it should not be built there; a writer wishing to keep the options open as far as Bethel was concerned would surely have favoured 'this is not the time', or 'you are not the builder' over 'this is not the place'.[78]

Another indication that the author of *Jubilees* associated Bethel with the Jerusalem Temple is his report of an additional dream at Bethel, the dream of Levi and his election to the priesthood (*Jub.* 32.1-9). Schwartz notes that the tradition linking Levi and Bethel is also reflected in the Greek Testament of Levi, although not in the Aramaic Testament.[79] Once again, he is inclined to look for an explanation for Levi's dream in the historical circumstances of Bethel:

> Bethel takes on a tremendous amount of cultic importance. In accordance with his vow in Gen. 28:20-22, Jacob sets up an altar and pillar at this site. It is true that this is also the case in the biblical account. In *Jubilees*, however, Jacob begins a series of offerings corresponding to those offered on the Feast of Tabernacles or Succoth. Jacob also seeks to fulfil the vow concerning the tithing of his possessions (which the Bible does not discuss) and *Jubilees* subsequently discusses not only the laws

76. 2 Sam. 7.1-16, with its specific reference to temple building, is also interesting in this respect, but does not represent as close a parallel. In this case the LORD intervenes to correct what may previously have been no more than a false impression on Nathan's part (v. 3): God has not authorised David to build a temple.

77. 'Jubilees, Bethel and the Temple of Jacob', *HUCA* 56 (1985), pp. 63-85.

78. Once again, see 2 Sam. 7.12-13, where David is told that not he but his son will build a house for God.

79. 'Jubilees, Bethel', pp. 66-68.

of the first tithe, but also the laws of the second tithe. Levi is appointed
as high priest to officiate at these events.[80]

In seeking to identify the Succoth offerings with Jacob, the author of
Jubilees is merely pursuing his general interest in back-dating Jewish
law. More to the point, however, Schwartz is surely wrong to identify
Levi with the cult at Bethel as opposed to the Temple in Jerusalem. It
seems far more likely that Levi is said to have dreamt at Bethel because
the author of *Jubilees* associated Jacob's dream there with the Jerusalem Temple, in addition to which his association of Levi and Jacob here
may have been influenced by the notion, established in later tradition,
that Jacob's tithe in Gen. 28.22 has in mind the Levitical priesthood.[81]

Schwartz also perceives Bethel's cultic history behind the rabbinic
commentaries linking Bethel and Jerusalem, but, once again, the plausibility of this view is highly questionable. The rabbis were far more
likely to have been motivated by a desire to resolve textual inconsistencies in Genesis than by a dim recollection of practices at Bethel and
Succoth which, even Schwartz must admit, were unlikely to have survived in their memories in any distinct form. Since Schwartz believes
that Jacob's announcement of his intention to build a temple at Bethel
reflects historical developments in the Maccabean period, rather than an
interpretation of the Genesis text, it is not surprising that he finds in the
rabbinic commentaries on Genesis 28 an attempt to 'play down the
cultic role of Bethel, whether as a conscious response to the cultic pretensions of that place or as an unconscious reflex mechanism to defend
the sanctity and primacy of Jerusalem'. Yet even he recognises the
implausibility of this view:

> It is certainly unlikely that any of these [cultic pretensions] survived the
> destruction of the Second Temple and especially the difficult situation
> after the Bar-Kochba Revolt. Any Jewish settlement which may have
> existed there until 135 CE ceased to exist after the revolt and no Jewish
> settlement existed there throughout the remainder of the Roman-Byzan-
> tine period.[82]

Bethel's cultic past would have been of little interest to the rabbis, and
it is doubtful that they were responding in this sense to the texts that

80. 'Jubilees, Bethel', p. 67.
81. See, for example, an interchange between a certain Cuthean and Rabbi Meir
in *GR, ad loc.*
82. 'Jubilees, Bethel', p. 81.

fuelled its cultic pretensions, Gen. 28.10-22 and 35.1-8. Once again, it is far more likely that they were struggling with the paradox of why Genesis 28 seems to allude to a temple that Jacob would build at Bethel when the only Temple was destined to be built in Jerusalem.

The association of Jacob's dream at Bethel with the Jerusalem Temple was not, of course, the idiosyncratic view of a few rabbis, but an idea that pervades almost every rabbinic commentary on this text. The predominance of this view is illustrated vividly by *Bereishis: A New Translation with a Commentary Anthologized from Talmudic, Midrashic and Rabbinic Sources*,[83] which reflects a traditional reading of the Bible based heavily upon rabbinic writings. Throughout its lengthy commentary on Genesis 28, the location of Jacob's dream is described as 'Bethel/Moriah', and sceptical readers are chided for being so tightly bound to physical reality as to be incapable of conceiving of a world in which such an event can take place.[84]

Not surprisingly, particularly in view of the later use of מקום (place) as a name of God, the threefold repetition of this word in 28.10-11 attracted a great deal of attention from rabbinic commentators. Rashi argues that במקום (in the place) must indicate a place already designated by that name, and this, he claims, is Mount Moriah.[85] (In Genesis 22.2 God tells Abraham to go to the land of Moriah, which is subsequently called המקום [the place] in vv. 3, 4 and 14.) Ralbag likewise notes the repeated designation in Deuteronomy of the future location of the Temple as 'the place', and, like Rashi, infers a connection between the two.[86] The idea that 'the place' suggests a randomly chosen place is quite alien to the rabbinic writers, and Nachmanides goes as far as to claim that the sun set prematurely to ensure that Jacob would spend the night at Bethel.[87] At any rate, the use of 'place' is taken as the first sign that Jacob's dream at Bethel alludes in some sense or other to the construction of the Jerusalem Temple.

Several rabbinic commentators use the ladder as a mechanism for establishing the link between Bethel and Jerusalem; Rabbi Elazar in the name of Rabbi Yosi ben Zimra claims that the ladder has its foot in

83. (Artscroll Tanakh Series; New York: Mesorah Publications, 1989 [1977]).
84. *Bereishis*, II, p. 1181.
85. Rashi's Commentary on the Torah, *MG, ad loc.*
86. Ralbag's Commentary on the Torah, *MG, ad loc.*
87. Ramban's Commentary on the Torah, *MG, ad loc.*

Beer Sheba, its head over Bethel and its mid-point over the Temple,[88] while Rabbi Yehudah claims that the ladder extended from Jerusalem to Bethel.[89] In other cases, the connection is established through the stone. Rabbi Eliezer identifies the stones mentioned in v. 11 as 12 of the stones from the altar upon which Abraham almost sacrificed Isaac. These 12 stones later merged into one, the foundation stone, and the Temple was built upon it.[90] For some exegetes, the dream itself, as opposed to its symbolism, effects the crucial transition from Bethel to Jerusalem. The expression 'he came upon' or 'he struck upon' (ויפגע במקום) is taken by Rashi to refer to the talmudic notion,[91] oddly reminiscent of Hardy's lines on the convergence of the iceberg and the Titanic,[92] that the earth 'sprang', transporting Jacob and Jerusalem towards each other. Of particular interest here is the suggestion that Luz and Bethel are not proper names, but allude rather to the 'perverse estrangement from God' (נילוז ומליז) which prevailed there before Jacob's dream required that its name be changed to 'house of God'.[93] A place that was formerly devious and crooked[94] became, by virtue of God's revealed presence there, a house of God. It may well be the case that the significance of the name far outweighed the importance of the place for the redactors of Genesis 28.

While it may sometimes seem that rabbinic interpretations of Genesis 28 have little interest in the text's original meaning, they are, in this case, highly revealing. In view of their commitment to the idea of one Temple in Jerusalem, one might have expected the rabbis to overlook altogether any temple associations in a narrative about Bethel. That the temple allusions are not only acknowledged but actually expanded suggests that they were too powerful to be ignored, and that the only viable alternative was to shape them into a form which was theologically consistent with the 'one Temple' view.

88. *GR, ad loc.*

89. *GR, ad loc.*

90. *PRE, ad loc.*

91. *b. Ḥul* 91b.

92. 'The Convergence of the Twain: Lines on the Loss of the Titanic', in *The Complete Poems of Thomas Hardy* (ed. J. Gibson; London: Macmillan, 1983 [1976]), pp. 306-307.

93. *Midrash HaGadol* ([ed.] S. Schechter; Cambridge: Cambridge University Press, 1902), *ad loc.*

94. BDB, 'לוז', *ad loc.*

Bethel and Babel: The View from Another Tower

Having now examined some post-biblical evidence in support of the view that Jacob's dream at Bethel concerned the construction of a temple in Jerusalem, we might now look to the Bible itself. Sarna and others have observed that the ladder is closely related to the tower (מגדל) in Genesis 11, as a kind of ziggurat,[95] and Parrot has suggested some theological links,[96] but it is worth exploring other points of contact between these two texts.

The most obvious connection is semantic. The builders say (11.4), 'Come, let us build a city, and a tower with its top in the sky' (הבה נבנה לנו עיר ומגדל וראשו בשמים) and Jacob sees (28.12) a stairway that 'was set on the ground and its top reached to the sky' (סלם מצב ארצה וראשו מגיע השמימה). The image of a tower with its head in the heavens is a standard ancient Near Eastern description of a temple building, but for those sceptical about its application to the ladder, its occurrence in a context in which a temple tower is unambiguously intended should prove reassuring.

As A. Berlin shows in her caution against mistaking hermeneutics for poetics, interpretations based on semantic similarities have the potential to mislead,[97] and cannot be taken as incontrovertible proof that the texts in which they occur are actually related. Whilst keeping this in mind, an attempt will be made here to show that Genesis 11 and 28 may be usefully read as 'reflection stories', as the idea is characterized by Y. Zakowitz,[98] and applied and developed by J.D. Safren.[99]

F. Greenspahn claims that the Genesis account of the building of Babel does not actually specify that the building of the tower is a

---

95. Sarna, *Understanding Genesis*, p. 193.

96. *The Tower of Babel* (trans. E. Hudson; London: SCM Press, 1955). It is Parrot's view that Babel and Bethel cannot be interpreted independently, and that the origins of both may be traced to the Mesopotamian concept of a structure which permitted human access to the gods and divine access to earth.

97. 'Literary Exegesis of Biblical Narrative: Between Poetics and Hermeneutics', in J. Rosenblatt and J. Sitterson (eds.), *'Not in Heaven': Coherence and Complexity in Biblical Narrative* (Bloomington: Indiana University Press, 1991), pp. 120-28.

98. 'Reflection Story'. See also *idem*, 'Through the Looking Glass: Reflections/ Inversions of Genesis Stories in the Bible', *BibInt* 1 (1993), pp. 139-52.

99. 'Balaam and Abraham'.

crime.[100] While this may be correct in a literal sense, it is difficult to conceive of a plausible reading of the Babel narrative in which it is not some aspect of the construction that angers God. Yet it remains to be demonstrated as to precisely which aspect was the cause of divine wrath. Greenspahn mentions the traditional view that God was angered by the people's failure to be fruitful and multiply, but unless we see building the tower as an ancient equivalent of driving a Ferrari, then it is not obvious how the two are related. He is, however, more interested in the crime of desiring immortality:

> However unrealistic one may consider human efforts to reach God, there is no reason to assume that the tower builders would have agreed. The Bible provides ample evidence that heaven was conceived as the dwelling place of God, who is once explicitly identified as the God of heaven (Gen. 24:7) and often presented as speaking from the sky or descending to the earth. This concept underlies Psalm 82, where a sentence of mortality results in the denizens of the divine council falling from heaven to die *like man* (v. 7). Here, heaven and immortality are joined in a now familiar juxtaposition as characteristics of the divine. By trying to reach heaven, the tower builders sought to accomplish the opposite of what had been experienced by the divine beings in Psalm 82 (p. 36).[101]

While this is certainly an interesting reading of Genesis 11, Greenspahn may be on the wrong track; in 11.4 the tower builders say their intention in building Babel is to make a name for themselves lest they be scattered all over the world (ונעשה לנו שם פן נפוץ על פני כל הארץ). It is easy to see why Greenspahn reached the conclusion that this is a text about man's longing to live forever; the desire to make a name for oneself is, after all, the desire for a form of immortality. Yet there is an important distinction to be made between these two aspects of the same concept, as Woody Allen made exquisitely clear in his expressed wish to achieve immortality not through his work, but by living forever. The

---

100. 'A Mesopotamian Proverb and its Biblical Reverberations', *JAOS* 114 (1994), pp. 33-38. On pp. 35-36 Greenspahn claims: 'In fact, the project is never identified as a sin nor God's response as a punishment; the scattering of the participants and the disruption of their language are presented only as efforts to prevent the unacceptable consequence of a united undertaking (v. 6). Interpreters since the time of Josephus have, therefore, proposed that it was not the tower itself that angered God so much as its builders' failure to carry out his mandate to be fruitful, multiply, and fill the earth (Gen. 9:1)'.

101. 'A Mesopotamian Proverb', p. 36.

tragedy of Ozymandias was not that he died, but that his works crumbled and thus he was forgotten.[102]

The idea that the builders of ancient temples were interested in a form of immortality that did not involve living forever is further supported by some of the temple inscriptions cited by Hurowitz. The following prayer from *Nebuchadnezzar* no. 23, Col. 1 10ff concerning the restoration of Ebabarra illustrates this point well.

> O Shamash, great lord!
> Upon my good works
> look joyfully!
> Life, long days,
> ripe old age,
> stability of throne and
> longevity of reign
> grant me as a gift.
> Truly accept the uplifting of my hands!
> By your exalted command,
> the work done by my hands
> may I cause to become eternally ancient.
> May my descendants flourish constantly in kingship,
> May it (my kingship) be stable in the land.[103]

Unless the king was attempting to deceive the gods about his intentions in rebuilding the temple, his emphasis on descendants (typical in these texts) does not sit well with a desire to live forever. The king's hope that his *work* will endure is, on the other hand, perfectly compatible with the notion that the builder saw his temple as a means of being remembered forever, and not as an instrument of assault upon heaven.

If, at first, it is not clear what aspect of man's interest in being remembered after his death might have provoked God's anger, a further examination of Hurowitz's work is revealing. The problem is that the temple should have been constructed for the purpose of immortalizing God's name, and not for immortalizing the name of its builders. The fact that the builders of Babel were concerned with their own lasting reputations is made explicit in the intentionally pointed 'let us make a name *for ourselves*'. Fokkelman provides a detailed discussion, based largely on sound associations, of the connection between שם (name)

---

102. P.B. Shelley, *Poetical Works* (London: F. Warne, n.d.), p. 553.
103. *I Have Built you an Exalted House*, p. 298.

and שָׁמַיִם (heavens) in Genesis 11.[104] To this one might add that else-where in the Bible שֵׁם (name) has explicitly established divine connotations, especially in the context of the tabernacle and the Temple.[105] The crime of the builders of Babel was to try to build a name for themselves when they should have been building a house for God's name.

Yet it was not only the intentions of the builders that were at fault. Equally problematic was their failure to seek the divine authorization requisite for temple builders throughout the ancient Near East. Hurowitz has the following to say about men who built unauthorized temples:

> A man who starts building a temple without the express consent of the gods places himself in a dangerous situation. He might receive a signal of approval after the fact, but he is equally liable to receive a message of disapproval, and if this is the case he will have to abandon a project which he has already started. This is all the more serious if building a new temple entails first demolishing an old temple, for the god will be left homeless. The king who builds a temple without permission is courting disaster—either he will not complete the project successfully, or the completed building will not stand, and may collapse after completion.[106]

The Babel narrative employs an especially ingenious means of emphasizing this crucial oversight:

וַיֵּרֶד יְהוָה לִרְאֹת אֶת־הָעִיר וְאֶת־הַמִּגְדָּל אֲשֶׁר בָּנוּ בְּנֵי הָאָדָם:

The LORD came down to look at the city and tower that mortals had built (11.5)

There are few other occasions in the Bible when God's presence is reported as anthropomorphically as this, and perhaps it is no coincidence that another rare example occurs in 3.8, when people have like-

---

104. In *Narrative Art in Genesis* Fokkelman suggests that the alliteration of *šem*—*šamayim* communicates in sounds more or less the following idea: 'What they want to attain, *šem* = make a name, they make conditional on the *šamayim*, the abode of God. Implicitly they want, perhaps as yet unconsciously, to make impossible the salvation history, which according to the biblical message is essentially the thrilling dialogue between God and man. Implicitly they want to penetrate the strictly divine and become divine themselves. What drives them is hubris. We see how, in a nutshell, the narrator conveys in language the idea that hubris has not only a "positive" component, megalomania, wanting-to-be-like-God, but also a negative one, fear, the fear of being scattered abroad, of having to live without safety and existential security, of being lonely and vulnerable' (p. 17).

105. Cf. Gen. 32.30; Deut. 16.11; Judg. 13.17.

106. *I Have Built You an Exalted House*, p. 137.

wise acted without divine authorization. In both cases the anthropomorphism creates a scene reminiscent of a man's returning home to discover his children hosting a wild party for 50 of their closest friends. 'What is going on here?' really means 'Why was my permission not sought?' Similarly, God goes down to Babel, not to get a better view, but to drive home the point that he was not consulted.

Thus the builders of Babel were building a temple for the wrong reason and, more to the point, they commenced without even seeking, let alone obtaining, God's approval. It is in response to this that God comes down as a physical presence and punishes the builders by scattering them over the face of the earth. It need hardly be said that Gen. 28.10-22 features elements almost identical to those contained in the Babel narrative: a structure reaching from earth to heaven, God's physical presence, the scattering of the people, and the naming of the place. Before dismissing all this as a matter of coincidence, it is worth exploring the extent to which Genesis 11 succeeds in highlighting the central concerns of Genesis 28.

Jacob's need for divine validation as he approaches Bethel is considerably greater than that of either Abraham or Isaac. For Abraham, the possibility that God might have chosen someone else simply does not arise, while Isaac, though less secure than Abraham, is nevertheless the only son of his father's first and favourite wife. Furthermore, the events resulting in the choice of Isaac instead of Ishmael as Abraham's heir are initiated by Sarah, with God's support, when Isaac is still a child. This makes a stark contrast with the situation for Jacob, whose father prefers Esau, and who is forced to steal both birthright and blessing without any sign of approval or encouragement from God. While one might argue that there is no sense in which the vision at Bethel can be seen as anything but an overwhelming indication that God has chosen Jacob, this is not altogether true. The response of commentators throughout the ages makes it abundantly clear that almost nothing that could have occurred at Bethel would have validated Jacob in their eyes, and, more to the point, the fact that Jacob's expansion occurs outside the land means that, in its biblical context, it is, at the very least, a mixed blessing.

The contrast between Babel and Bethel succeeds brilliantly in emphasizing both that the vision of the ladder was an unambiguous sign of God's approval, and that the scattering to the corners of the earth in Genesis 28 is not a punishment, but a stage in the divine plan. In

Genesis 11, God comes down to see a towering structure that the people of Babel have built *for themselves*, and expressly without his approval. In Genesis 28, God shows Jacob a vision of a structure that does not merely have its head in the heavens, but has actually reached them. Because they did not seek planning permission for their tower, the people of Babel are scattered with no sign that they will ever return or be reunited. The vision of Jacob's tower represents both the planning permission and the sign that his offspring will return and be reunited.[107]

The Significance of 'The Place'

J.M. Husser regards the founding of Bethel as the first of three stages that mark Jacob's development as a patriarch: the acquisiton of a sanctuary identified with him, a blessing for his 'house' and a new name for his 'clan'.[108] He is clearly on the right track in connecting Jacob's experience at Bethel with his coming of age as a patriarch, and his point that what he calls the three requisites of patriarchy—cultic centre, dynasty and new name—are acquired during nocturnal encounters with God is well-taken.[109] Yet evidence from the ancient Near East suggests that the dream itself, rather than the discovery of a cultic centre, is the means by which Jacob's patriarchal status is acquired. Nevertheless, the role of Bethel in this text clearly merits further investigation.

Exegetes have differed greatly in their characterization of the role of chance or destiny in Jacob's arrival at Bethel. Von Rad envisages a less than walk-on part, with Jacob alighting upon Bethel almost by accident:

> The narrative begins by letting the lonely traveler rest at a place that has something emphatically coincidental about it. The sun had just gone down and had forced him into an improvised camp.[110]

---

107. M. Hilton, 'Babel Reversed—Daniel Chapter 5', *JSOT* 66 (1995), pp. 99-122, sees the Babel narrative reflected in Dan. 5. In this connection, it is interesting to note that rabbinic commentaries link Jacob's dream directly with the dreams of Nebuchadnezzar through word-play based on the similarity between סלם (ladder) and סמל (image). See, for instance, *GR*, on Gen. 28.12 *ad loc.*

108. *Le songe et la parole*, p. 124.

109. A similar point is made by A. de Pury, *Promesse divine et légende cultuelle dans le cycle de Jacob* 2 (Paris: J. Gabalda, 1975), p. 368. De Pury, however, is primarily interested in the relationship between these themes and the various sources to which he ascribes Gen. 28.

110. *Genesis*, p. 283.

J. Skinner, on the other hand, puts providence at centre stage:

> In v. 11 the rendering 'a certain place' would be grammatically correct
> (G-K 126 *r*); but it destroys the point of the sentence, which is that night
> overtook the patriarch just at the sacred spot (see Ex. 3:5).[111]

It is not surprising that von Rad, convinced that the discovery of
Bethel's holiness is at the centre of this narrative,[112] is inclined to
emphasize the random nature of Jacob's decision to sleep there. Along
with Westermann and many others, he perceives a gradual build-up to
the climactic:

וייךא ויאמר מה נורא המקום הזה אין זה כי אם בית אלהים
וזה שער השמים: וישכם יעקב בבקר ויקח את האבן אשר שם
מראשתיו וישם אתה מצבה ויצק שמן על ראשה:

> Shaken, he said, 'How awesome is this place! This is none other than the
> abode of God and that is the gateway to heaven.' Early in the morning,
> Jacob took the stone that he had put under his head and set it up as a
> pillar and poured oil on the top of it (28.17-18).

Certainly, the text is at pains to show that the discovery of Bethel's
holiness comes as a complete surprise to Jacob (28.16), but this is by
no means inconsistent with Skinner's claim, cited above, that Bethel's
holiness preceded Jacob's experience there, and was simply unrecog-
nized by him.[113] Nor does it provide conclusive proof against the notion
that the revelation is, at least in part, a response to Jacob's physical and
psychological condition at the time.

---

111. *Genesis*, p. 376. See also *Gesenius' Hebrew Grammar* (E. Kautzsch [ed.],
2nd English edn by A.E. Cowley; New York: Oxford University Press, 1990
[1909]): 'Bamakom Gen. 28:11, according to Dillman, upon *the* place suitable for
passing the night, or the right place, but it may also refer to the sanctuary of Bethel,
afterwards so sacred and celebrated' (126.r.).

112. In *Genesis*, von Rad emphasizes Jacob's correct identification of Bethel's
holiness over the dream's personal significance for him: 'The experience of this
night was much more than an inner consolation for Jacob. Something had happened, a revelation of God had occurred that would affect the spatial and the material. Accordingly the two statements in which the weakened man reacts to what he
has experienced are much more than an echo of his emotional experience. They are
concerned, rather, with the realistic statement of an objective fact, namely, with the
correct understanding of a place. The statement, "The LORD is in this place", here
has a very definite and exclusive local meaning' (p. 285).

113. I am grateful to Professor R.P. Gordon for suggesting that the fact that the
angels are reported as ascending before they descend (i.e. they were there before
Jacob) may provide additional evidence of Bethel's prior holiness.

There are other compelling reasons against accepting the view of Fokkelman and others that Genesis 28 is part of a campaign to transform a Canaanite sanctuary, Luz, into an Israelite one, Bethel.[114] To begin with, it is not easy to see why this would have been regarded as a central function of the text by the time it was finally redacted. Writers for whom Bethel had already been discredited as an Israelite sanctuary were unlikely to care one way or another about its possible pagan origins, and the use of one of the Bible's most spectacular visions to transform an obsolete Canaanite sanctuary into what was by then an obsolete Israelite sanctuary would be the literary equivalent of bringing nuclear arms to a playground scuffle. Furthermore, the Bible's insistence upon preserving the name Luz in conjunction with Bethel[115] would be inexplicable if readers at the time had understood the denial of Luz's very existence as being a central aim of the text.[116] At any rate, Skinner's view that the sanctuary and the city were never intended to be understood as one place is highly plausible:

> 19b is usually considered a gloss. From Jos. 16:2 (18:13) it appears that Luz was really distinct from Bethel, but was overshadowed by the more famous sanctuary in the neighbourhood.[117]

114. Fokkelman, *Narrative Art in Genesis*, describes thus the fate of Luz: 'Canaanite Luz does not stand a chance of existing, not even for a moment! Actually, it is a place without identity, without local colour, a place which has been named Bethel before it has been able to represent itself as an important Canaanite town' (p. 68). H.J. Kraus, *Worship In Israel* (trans. G. Buswell; Oxford: Basil Blackwell, 1966), p. 146, makes the following claim: 'Bethel was not an Israelite foundation, but was originally a Canaanite cultic centre. The place was formerly called Luz, then the designation of the sacred place that was situated to the east displaced the name-place Luz, and so Luz became Bethel'; cited by M.G. Glenn, 'The Word לוז in Genesis 28:19 in the LXX and in Midrash', *JQR* 59 (1968–69), pp. 73-76 (74).

115. Cf. Gen. 35.6, 48.3; Josh. 18.13; Judg. 1.23.

116. It should be noted in this context that several scholars have identified Temple Menorah with the almond tree (לוז) which may have grown next to the Canaanite sanctuary at Bethel. See, for instance, L. Yarden, 'Aaron, Bethel, and the Priestly Menorah', *JJS* 26 (1975), pp. 39-47 and J. Taylor, 'The Asherah, the Menorah and the Sacred Tree', *JSOT* 66 (1995), pp. 29-54. Unfortunately, it is not possible to pursue this interesting connection here.

117. Skinner, *Genesis*, p. 378.

Finally, the naming of the place does not represent the narrative climax, any more than Abraham's designation of Mount Moriah as Adonai-yireh can properly be understood as the climax of Genesis 22.[118]

The claim that Genesis 28 was intended to promote Bethel as an alternative to Jerusalem as the centre of Israelite worship is less easily countered.[119] As M. Haran has shown in his discussion of the subject, Bethel had a complicated history, and we can be by no means confident that the 'place' (מקום) of Deuteronomy was universally regarded as Jerusalem.[120] Yet if the subtext of Genesis 28 is taken to be a claim for the superiority of Bethel over Jerusalem, then we must ask why the narrative would have been preserved in this form in a document unambiguously committed to the latter.

The strongest argument against centralizing the discovery of Bethel's holiness may well be literary. In the first place, the general agreement of scholars in locating the final redaction of the Pentateuch in the exilic period should undermine confidence in the claim that the repetition of 'place' in 28.10 asserts the emphatically coincidental nature of the location. The editors could hardly fail to be aware of the associations of holiness acquired by 'place' through its repeated use in Deuteronomy to denote God's chosen site for the Temple,[121] and it seems unlikely that they would have used the same word with the aim of producing precisely the opposite effect.

---

118. Wyatt, 'Where Did Jacob Dream his Dream?', raises an additional objection: '... Jacob does not in the body of the narrative name the place Bethel (בית אל), but calls it בית אלהים (v. 17). Had his exclamation been the moment of naming the place, he would surely have used the same name as occurs in v. 19' (p. 44). As the comparison with Gen. 22.1-19 suggests, however, an exact correspondence between the name used in the body of the narrative and that used in the final designation is not inevitable.

119. M. White, in 'The Elohistic Depiction of Aaron: A Study in the Levite-Zadokite Controversy', in J.A. Emerton (ed.), *Studies in the Pentateuch* (VTSup, 30; Leiden: E.J. Brill, 1990), pp. 149-59, connects the treatment of Bethel in Genesis, especially ch. 35, with an Elohistic interest in discrediting Aaron as a means of promoting the Levitical priesthood. This line of inquiry is, however, too far removed from the direct concerns of this study to be pursued here.

120. M. Haran, *Temples and Temple Service in Ancient Israel: An Inquiry into the Cult Phenomenon and the Historical Setting of the Priestly School* (Oxford: Clarendon Press, 1978), pp. 28-31.

121. See Deut. 16.11 for an example typical of many such uses of 'place'.

Indeed, even if it could be demonstrated beyond all doubt that 'place' did *not* imply 'a holy place' at any stage in the transmission of Genesis 28, its three-fold repetition in the introductory verse can hardly be said to convey an impression of chance. On the contrary, it suggests rather strongly that, holy or not, the place was already in some sense special. To this, one might object that the narrator is simply preparing the ground for the momentous event which is about to occur, but a comparison with the similar usage in Genesis 22 suggests that this is not the case. Here, God's first reference to the location of the 'sacrifice' is carefully non-specific.

ולך לך אל ארץ המריה והעלהו שם לעלה על אחד ההרים ...
אשר אמר אליך:

... and go to the land of Moriah, and offer him there as a burnt offering on one of the heights that I will point out to you (22.2).

We must think only in terms of 'one of the mountains' until v. 9 reports Abraham's arrival at the exact site, 'And Abraham arrived at the place of which God had told him' (ויבאו אל המקום אשר אמר לו האלהים). Now that he is actually there, however, the place which God had chosen from the outset is identified as 'the place' (המקום), and this is reconfirmed in v. 14 when Abraham names it, 'And Abraham named that site Adonai-yireh' (ויקרא אברהם שם המקום ההוא יהוה יראה). No commentator would suggest that Moriah became holy because of Abraham's experience there; it is clear all along that God has guided Abraham to Moriah so that his experience will occur in a holy place. The repetition of 'place' in Genesis 28 indicates that God's intentions for Jacob were similar.

If Bethel was in some sense special prior to Jacob's dream, and if it is indeed the case that God guided Jacob there in order that the dream take place in the significant location of Bethel, then we must inquire further as to what made it an appropriate place for Jacob's dream. There are several possible avenues of exploration, but it seems sensible to begin with allusions to Bethel outside Genesis 28.

Immediately before descending into Egypt, Abraham stops near Bethel, builds an altar and invokes the name of the Lord (12.8). Upon re-entering the land, he returns to the same place and calls to the Lord once more (13.3-4). Thus, at either end of his sojourn outside the land, Abraham visits a place near Bethel, identified twice in vv. 3 and 4 as 'the place', and invokes God's name.

This account contains some striking parallels, in terms of both itinerary and actions, to the description of Jacob's experience at either end of his exile from the land (28.10-22 and 35.6-7). For Jacob too, Bethel is a stopping-point on the journey out of and into the land, and he too builds an altar at Bethel, and this raises the possibility that Jacob's experience at 'the place' may be a deliberate echo of Abraham's. The Talmud assumes that Jacob knew his ancestors had prayed at Bethel,[122] a view whose plausibility is supported by the observation that what occurs quite casually in Abraham's case is highly orchestrated in the case of Jacob. For although it is often claimed that Jacob stopped at Bethel by chance, a reading of 28.10-11 in which the choice of Bethel is anything but random cannot be dismissed out of hand. At any rate, it is certainly not by chance that Jacob returns to Bethel on his way home: God pointedly reminds him of his experience there (31.10-13), and finally instructs him explicitly to go back and build an altar (35.1). The fact that Jacob performs the same actions as Abraham, in the same context and in the same place, suggests that the narrator may have been attempting to create a link between the two patriarchs. Yet it also suggests that a typology of exile and re-entry may have been intended, in which Bethel functions as the point where God's protection is sought on the way out of the land, and where he is thanked for this protection on the way in.[123]

Evidence for an association between Bethel and exile may be gleaned from the description of ritual purification in 35.1-3. In preparation to visit Bethel, Jacob rids himself of the trappings of exile, banishing foreign gods in readiness to re-encounter God in the land.[124] An interesting

122. *b. Ḥul* 91b.

123. The parallels between the experiences of Abraham and Jacob at Bethel may provide additional evidence contrary to the view that 28.10-22 is primarily a device for transforming a pagan sanctuary into an Israelite one. Typological emphasis of this kind is hardly compatible with the claim that the sanctuary was not holy before Jacob's experience there.

124. A. Soggin, 'Jacob in Shechem and in Bethel (Genesis 35:1-7)', in M. Fishbane and E. Tov (eds.), *Sha'arei Talmon: Studies in the Bible, Qumran, and the Ancient Near East Presented to Shemaryahu Talmon* (Winona Lake, IN: Eisenbrauns, 1992), pp. 195-98, cites the view of A. Alt ('Die Wallfahrt von Sichem nach Bethel', *idem, Kleine Schriften zur Geschichte des Volkes Israel*, I [Munich: C.H. Beck, 1953]), 79-88, that this reflects an ancient pilgrimage ritual. Soggin rejects this notion, placing the text in 'the second half of the sixth century BCE, maybe already in late preexilic times', and connecting it with 'the elimination of

solution to the Bethel paradox has been proposed by N. Wyatt in his imaginative article 'Where did Jacob Dream his Dream?'. In summary, Wyatt's answer to his own question is that Genesis 28 was written in Babylon as a message of hope for the Jewish exiles, but it is worth quoting a more detailed version:

> On the literary plane, the picture seems at first confusing. But that is per-haps because we bring to it a spatial logic which tends to compart-mentalise: either it is here, or it is there. But in the figurative terms of literature, both are possible, and a slide from one to the other is perfectly feasible. Hence on a literary plane one may speak, as I did above, of the reaction of Jacob on waking. He is at Jerusalem when he dreams, and it is of Jerusalem that he dreams. But on waking he is brought back with a jolt to another less secure world of exile. Is he really at Jerusalem? No, he is far away in Babylon. Did he really dream of Jerusalem? No, he dreamt of Babylon with *its* stairway to heaven, but for one wonderful moment confused the two locations, and in that apparent confusion intu-ited the greatest hope he could offer his age: that even in remote and curs-ed Babylon YHWH revealed himself to those with receptive hearts.[125]

Although Wyatt is right to connect Bethel with Babylon, his sugges-tion that Jacob was actually dreaming in Babylon, possibly, it appears, of the Tower of Babel itself, is not entirely convincing. One might argue that Genesis 28 would function most effectively as a message of hope and inspiration to the exiles by creating a parallel between their own experience and that of the patriarchs. According to Wyatt's ver-sion of events, the dream should properly have occurred during Jacob's tenure with Laban, when, in fact, it is only recalled then. On the con-trary, the dream at Bethel is emphatically the product of the land itself, being dreamt by Jacob on his way into exile; God's unconditional prom-ise of protection on the journey and return to 'this place' makes sense

---

Canaanite polytheism from Judah's faith and ritual, in favour of monotheism' (p. 198). He claims that the reference to Bethel where one might have expected Jerusalem may be explained by Judah's adoption of a northern custom after 720 BCE (p. 197). Another text, not mentioned by Soggin, which offers an interesting comparison to Gen. 35.1-7 is Ezra 10.9-11, which reports the priest's injunction against Israelites who had acquired foreign wives in exile. Jacob purifies himself of foreign elements before going to Bethel, and the exiles must purge themselves of foreign women, who are inclined to bring their gods with them (cf. Ezra 9.1-3, and 1 Kgs 11.1-8), when they return to Jerusalem.

125. N. Wyatt, 'Where Did Jacob Dream his Dream?', *SJOT* 2 (1990), pp. 44-57 (55).

only if it was made while Jacob was still in the land. Wyatt's attempt to find a semantic link between Jerusalem and Babylon based on Jacob's exclamation that he has seen the 'gate of heaven' is ingenious:

> That Jerusalem was the gate of heaven, the place where YHWH communicated with man through the king and the temple cultus was self-evident. But to call Babylon, hated symbol of oppression and the destruction of the state, the gate of heaven, was to a Jewish mind either a monstrous parody or a theological breakthrough of extraordinary courage and profundity.[126]

Yet neither the idea of a monstrous parody nor the concept of a theological breakthrough rings quite true; it would be a cruel twist if Jacob's ladder turned out to be nothing more than the Tower of Babel.

It was not among Wyatt's aims in his article to consider the dream in its narrative context, but, ultimately, an understanding of the relationship between Bethel and Babylon may depend upon connections that do not arise explicitly in the dream report itself. The points of contact between Jacob's situation preceding and subsequent to the dream at Bethel and the situation of the exiles in Babylon are obvious; both are expelled from their native lands, both enter service to a foreign power, both have brothers who remain at home, and both return in a position of superiority. The extent to which these parallels would have reassured the exiled Jews need hardly be spelled out. Once Jacob has received the dream at Bethel, there remains no remote possibility that Jacob's exile from his father's house will adversely affect his relationship with God or jeopardize his illicitly-won precedence over Esau. The dream confirms both that the time spent in service to Laban is part of God's plan for Jacob, and, still more to the point, that Jacob's destiny will be shared by his descendants.

In his influential study of the Jacob Cycle, M. Fishbane has explored the question of historical influences on the composition of the stories about Jacob, basing his work on the premise that the epic Genesis narratives took shape during the United Monarchy.[127] Now that scholars

---

126. Wyatt, 'Where Did Jacob Dream his Dream?', p. 54.

127. 'Composition and Structure in the Jacob Cycle (Gen. 25:19–35:22)', *JJS* 26 (1975), pp. 15-38. See pp. 15-17 for Fishbane's assessment of the influence upon the Genesis narrative of historical episodes in the national life of Israel and Edom. B. Dicou has offered a detailed analysis of this subject in *Edom, Israel's Brother and Antagonist: The Role of Edom in Biblical Prophecy and Story* (JSOTSup, 169; Sheffield: Sheffield Academic Press, 1994).

have come increasingly to place the final redaction of Genesis in the exilic period,[128] the questions posed by Fishbane may be asked again with reference to the many connections that may be observed between the life of Jacob the patriarch and the situation of Israel in exile. This typological reading may, at first, sound rather rabbinic, and, indeed, the rabbis did regard Jacob as representing the closest parallel to Israel in this respect.[129] Yet the prophetic writers clearly interpreted Israel's history according to the experiences of her forefathers (admittedly, they appeal more often to the exodus story than to the patriarchal narratives), and Deutero-Isaiah contains several indications either that its author was influenced by a Genesis prototype of the image of exile, or that the Genesis redactor was influenced by Deutero-Isaiah's representation. The prophet's description in 43.5-7 (cited also by Wyatt in this context) of the return of the exiles to Jerusalem is almost a mirror image of Gen. 28.14, while Isa. 43.5 may also be linked to the reassurances offered to Jacob in Gen. 28.15 and later in 46.3-4. It can hardly be a matter of mere coincidence that all deal in one way or another with the subject of 'exile'.

The following account captures well the unequal distribution of power, both political and religious, between the returning exiles and the Judean remnant:

> The fate of the Jewish exiles in Babylon would probably be of little concern to us were it not for the fact that the restoration of the Jewish state in the late sixth–early fifth century was the work of Jewish leaders who came from Babylonia. It was they who led the initial return to Jerusalem, the subsequent rebuilding of the Temple under Sheshbazzar and Zerubbabel, and finally the cultic/national reforms and rebuilding of the city under Ezra and Nehemiah. In the books of Ezra and Nehemiah, the local Judean population (who had not been exiled) is regarded with contempt; the only citizens who seem to matter (and the only Temple personnel allowed to function) are those with proper genealogical records brought from Babylonia.[130]

It would be surprising indeed if this situation had arisen without effort on the part of those exiled in Babylon to establish their superiority over

128. For an account of the Abraham narratives based on this dating see Van Seters, *Abraham in History and Tradition*.
129. *GR* on Gen. 28.10-22 includes several allusions to the Babylonian Exile.
130. H. Shanks (ed.), *Ancient Israel: A Short History from Abraham to the Roman Destruction of the Temple* (London: SPCK, 1989), p. 162.

the remnant in Jerusalem, and, in particular, to demonstrate their claim
to oversee the rebuilding of the Temple. The research presented in this
chapter suggests that the redacted form of Gen. 28.10-22 may well be
an example of such political efforts in this direction. The dream at
Bethel confirmed that, despite being the exiled brother, Jacob was the
chosen son, and it also provided a form of typological confirmation that
the Jewish exiles would return from Babylon in a position of superiority over the remnant who stayed behind. The fortuitous occurrence of
Jacob's dream at a place that means 'House of God' offered an opportunity for an extended allusion to the Temple, while the skilful use of a
traditional ancient Near Eastern dream type, namely the temple building
authorization dream, created a device that functioned in its immediate
narrative context as a divine validation of Jacob the patriarch, and, in
the long term, as a prophetic authorization of the exiles to undertake the
rebuilding of the Jerusalem Temple.

Thematic Links

There is a sense in which the thematic links outlined in my introduction
are manifested most vividly when Jacob's two dreams are examined as
a unit. As the following summary indicates, however, the six themes
are present even when the dream report contained in Gen. 28.10-22 is
treated separately.

(1)   *The dream is received during a period of anxiety or danger.*
       Jacob's dream occurs when he has been expelled, presumably
       empty-handed, from his father's house and his native land.
       Esau is angry enough over the stolen blessing to harm him,
       and, without parental support, he has been ordered to find a
       wife.

(2)   *The dream concerns descendants, immediate or eventual.*
       God promises offspring as numerous as the dust of the earth,
       but at a time when Jacob does not even have a wife.

(3)   *The dream signals a change in status.*
       It confirms God's approval of his acquisition of the birthright
       and blessing of his first-born brother.

(4)   *The dream highlights divine involvement in human affairs.*
       The preceding narrative offers two different explanations for
       Jacob's flight; his mother sends him away to escape Esau's
       wrath, and his father dispatches him to get a wife. The dream

confirms that God has determined both Jacob's departure and his eventual return.

(5) *The dream concerns the relationship between Israelites and non-Israelites.*

It occurs as Jacob is en route to his non-Israelite uncle, and includes God's promise, fulfilled in a limited way with Laban, that the families of the earth will be blessed through Jacob.

(6) *The dream deals with absence from the land.*

Jacob dreams as he is about to enter personal exile in Paddan Aram.

Chapter 3

JACOB AND THE SPECKLED FLOCKS
(GENESIS 31.10-13)

Jacob's dream of the flocks may well be the most obscure of the biblical dreams. The narrative in which it appears is extraordinarily detailed,
and the additional information which the dream supplies about Jacob's
dealings with the sheep and goats[1] is confusingly inconsistent with what
has preceded it.[2] This may explain why the dream and the narrative
immediately surrounding it have received scant attention from commentators on the patriarchal narratives in general, and even from those
concerned specifically with the Jacob cycle.[3] Indeed, even S. Sherwood,
who deals exclusively with Gen. 29.1–32.2 in his recent book,[4]
discusses the dream only summarily in its role as a 'gap-filler'.

1. It would be convenient to speak of 'geep' or 'shoats', especially since the
distinction between the two types of animal appears to be unimportant. Unless
specified otherwise, however, 'sheep' or 'flock' will be used as an inclusive term
for both, and it will be assumed that shepherds shepherded goats as well as sheep.
2. Precise details of this inconsistency will be provided later in the chapter.
Briefly stated, however, the dream suggests that Jacob's decision to leave Laban's
house was the result of a divine command, when, in fact, the announcement of his
departure (30.25) preceded the command (31.3). Furthermore, the dream implies
that God was responsible for the success of Jacob's flocks, when 30.37-43 has
attributed it to Jacob's own manoeuvering.
3. It is not constructive to enumerate here the commentators who have *failed*
to consider in detail Gen. 30.25–31.54, but, in a telling example, Fishbane, in
'Composition and Structure in the Jacob Cycle', focuses almost exclusively on
Laban's role in 'continuing the *Leitmotif* of familial strife and deception' (p. 30).
Certainly, Fishbane's representation of the various deceptions in Paddan Aram as
counterpoints to the earlier deceptions involving Esau and Isaac is convincing, but
he considers neither Laban's contribution as a character in his own right, nor themes
(such as servitude versus service) which are raised for the first time in connection
with Jacob and Laban. He does not mention the dream at all.
4. *'Had God Not Been on my Side': An Examination of the Narrative Tech-*

The dream of the flocks has, of course, been considered more carefully by scholars for whom dreams are a primary interest. Gnuse believes that by this means the so-called Elohist 'sanctions the trickery of Jacob by giving it divine origin in a dream'.[5] Ehrlich classifies it as an 'occupation' (*Wirklichkeit*) dream, arising from Jacob's shepherd-craft.[6] Oppenheim cites other examples of this type of dream, some of which relate to temple building and the construction of sacred artifacts.[7] Yet there are respects in which each of these interpretations represents an over-simplification of the text, and here Husser may be nearer the mark in characterizing Gen. 31.10-13 as a case of 'onirisme prophétique', part exilic and part postexilic, dependent on the visions of Proto-Zechariah, introduced to link the patriarch, Moses and the Babylonian Exile.[8] Not surprisingly, Husser's connection between Gen. 31.10-13 and the visions of Proto-Zechariah is based largely on the figure of the interpreting angel.

Although angels are mentioned several times elsewhere in Genesis (18.2; 19.1; 22.11), they feature more prominently in Jacob's life than in the lives of the other patriarchs. Rashi associated them with the period of Jacob's exile, regarding them as a protective force (akin perhaps to the Shekhinah) which travelled with the patriarch outside the land.[9] This idea may be less midrashic than it sounds, since angels appear in the dream at Bethel, which comes at the beginning of Jacob's period of exile, and again in the dream of the flocks, when an angel reveals to Jacob, immediately before his return to his native land, that God has been protecting him during his 20 years of service to Laban. To this picture may be added the angels of God who meet Jacob at

---

nique of the Story of Jacob and Laban. Genesis 29:1–32:2 (Frankfurt: Peter Lang, 1990). The dream of the flocks is discussed on pp. 297-302.

5.   *The Dream Theophany of Samuel*, p. 69.

6.   *Der Traum im Alten Testament*, p. 122. In another example, Ehrlich designates Pharaoh's dreams as 'occupation' dreams, because they refer to matters of Egyptian state-craft.

7.   'The Interpretation of Dreams', pp. 179-353. Oppenheim describes 31.10-13 as an inspirational dream regarding shepherd-lore, equating it with what he understands as a temple-building dream report in 1 Chron. 28.11-19 (pp. 193-94).

8.   *Le songe et la parole*, p. 129. See pp. 129-37 for a discussion of the dream of the flocks.

9.   See *MG* at 28.12. Rashi envisages two different sets of angels: the ascending angels who were not permitted to leave the land of Israel and thus returned to heaven, and the descending angels who came to accompany Jacob outside the land.

Mahanaim (32.2), and the figure (אִישׁ) with whom he wrestles immediately before being reunited with Esau (32.25), which, although it
is not explicitly called an angel, was already known as such by Hosea
(12.5). The angel of 31.10-13 may thus represent nothing more complicated than the narrator's desire to give a high profile to Jacob's
guardian angels during his absence from the land. Yet this reading does
not take account of the facts that this is the only Genesis dream to be
mediated by an angel, and that the angel performs a particular function
which distinguishes it from the other Genesis angels: it is what might
be described as an *angelus interpres*.

Husser is not alone in noting a resemblance between Gen. 31.10-13
and the visions of Proto-Zechariah. Yet where he assumes that Jacob's
dream was dependent on the postexilic prophet, J. Tollington, in her
monograph on Haggai and Proto-Zechariah, speculates that the prophet
may have been influenced by the Genesis narrative.[10] It is difficult to
dismiss as coincidental the similarities between the dream of the flocks
and Zechariah's visions; both describe an angelic figure who draws
attention to an object and explains its significance, and they share a distinctive terminology in which the respective encounters are reported. In
Gen. 31.11-12 the angel of God summons Jacob and instructs him to
look at the sheep:

> ויאמר אלי מלאך האלהים בחלום יעקב ואמר הנני:
> ויאמר שא נא עיניך וראה כל העתדים העלים על הצאן עקדים
> נקדים וברדים כי ראיתי את כל אשר לבן עשה לך:

And in the dream an angel of God said to me, 'Jacob!'. 'Here', I answered. And he said, 'Raise your eyes and look at that all the he-goats
which are mating with the flocks are streaked, speckled, and mottled; for
I have noted all that Laban has been doing to you.

This is reminiscent of the language of Zech. 5.5-6:

> ויצא המלאך הדבר בי ויאמר אלי שא נא עיניך וראה מה היוצאת הזאת:
> ואמר מה היא ויאמר זאת האיפה היוצאת ויאמר זאת עינם בכל הארץ:

Then the angel who talked with me came forward and said, 'Raise your
eyes and see what is approaching.' I asked, 'What is it?' And he said,
'This tub that is approaching—this,' said he, 'is their eye in all the land.'

---

10. J. Tollington, *Tradition and Innovation in Haggai and Zechariah 1–8*
(JSOTSup, 150; Sheffield: Sheffield Academic Press, 1993): 'It may be that Zechariah knew this passage and although there is no evidence that his concept of an
interpreting angel depends directly upon it, it may have influenced his thought as he
formulated his ideas' (p. 99).

In both cases the angel's order ('raise your eyes and look') is followed by an explanation of what Jacob and Zechariah, respectively, will see when they comply. Yet, striking as these similarities are,[11] it is difficult to determine whether Jacob's dream or Zechariah's vision came first. In either case, however, it seems reasonable to hope that Zechariah may cast some light on the Genesis text.

Zechariah's angel, unlike many of its narratively earlier counterparts, must clearly be regarded as an independent entity, as opposed to an aspect or manifestation of God. Elsewhere in Genesis it is not easy to ascertain whether or not angels were envisaged as having an independent existence. On the one hand, they are more than divine messengers who merely voice, without addition or subtraction, the words of God; thus the angel in 22.12 contradicts God's command. Yet, on the other hand, they show a disturbing tendency to speak in a voice that is at one moment quite distinct from God's, and at the next indistinguishable from it. Even the angel who stills Abraham's hand as he is poised to sacrifice his son in accordance with God's command speaks in the divine first-person in the last clause of v. 12, '... since you have not witheld your son from me' (ולא חשכת את בנך את יחידך ממני). The angel of 31.11-12 is even more ambiguous in this respect, and by the middle of v. 12 its voice has become inseparable from God's, 'for I have noted all that Laban has been doing to you (כי ראיתי את כל אשר לבן עשה לך). Yet, despite this ambiguity, the angels of Gen. 22.12 and 31.12 seem to have an identity which is separate from God's, and, in the latter case, evidence for this may be derived from what appears to be a parallel occurrence in Zechariah of a distinctly independent angelic figure.

Additional evidence concerning the intended function of both Jacob's and Zechariah's angels may be gleaned from other ancient Near Eastern texts, where the use of an interpreter of dreams and visions, distinct from the dream's actual sender, is widely attested. Oppenheim's discussion of dream interpreters focuses on a special class of priests and priestesses whose job it was to interpret symbolic dreams for therapeutic purposes.[12] Yet the priest or priestess may be a divine figure, as is the case in the Sumerian dream report of Gudea of Lagash, whose

---

11. For an additional coincidence, see ברדים (mottled), which occurs only with reference to Jacob's sheep (Gen. 31.10, 12) and Zechariah's horses (Zech. 6.3, 6).

12. See Oppenheim, 'The Interpretation of Dreams', pp. 217-25.

dream is interpreted by the sister of the god who sent it (p. 221).[13] It is possible that either Genesis or Zechariah (or both) owed the idea of an *angelus interpres* to an ancient Near Eastern antecedent.[14]

Tollington's claim that Zechariah was familiar with Gen. 31.10-13 is based partly on the occurrence in both texts of an idiom concerning the raising of the eyes.[15] Once again, regardless of which came first, I hope that a brief examination of this idiom will be illuminating. Its usage elsewhere often signals the imminent solution to a problem: in 22.13 Abraham raises his eyes and notices, for the first time, the ram which will replace Isaac as a sacrificial offering, and in 37.25 the brothers raise their eyes and see the Ishmaelites who will participate (indirectly) in Joseph's journey down to Egypt. Alternatively, it may direct attention to a subject of particular importance, as in 13.14, where God addresses Abraham about the land. The flocks have, of course, played a highly visible role in preceding events, and, unlike the ram or the Ishmaelites, they can hardly be regarded as a narrative turning point. Likewise, it is difficult to see Jacob's sheep and goats in the same vein as God's promise of the land to Abraham. Yet in each case the idiom suggests that the protagonist should re-evaluate the object in question. Thus the ram ceases to become a trapped animal and becomes a substitute for Isaac; the land is no longer dusty grazing ground but the

13. P. 221. For a more detailed discussion of Gudea's dream and its interpretation see Oppenheim, 'The Interpretation of Dreams', pp. 211-13.

14. Many scholars have emphasised the dream-like quality of Zechariah's visions. M. Fishbane, 'The Qumran Pesher and Trails of Ancient Exegesis', *Proceedings of the 7th World Congress of Jewish Studies* (Jerusalem: World Union of Jewish Studies, 1981 [1977]), pp. 97-114 (especially pp. 107-108), applies to the visions standard techniques of dream interpretation. C.L. and E.M. Meyers, 'Jerusalem and Zion after the Exile: The Evidence of First Zechariah', in M. Fishbane and E. Tov (eds), *Sha'arei Talmon: Studies in the Bible, Qumran, and the Ancient Near East Presented to Shemaryahu Talmon* (Winona Lake, IN: Eisenbrauns, 1992), pp. 121-35, see a close link between Zechariah's medium and his message: 'The visionary mode involves a presentation of the prophet's experience that arises from reality and yet is distinct from the mundane. The vision as a form of prophetic experience is like a dream: supernatural yet built upon the natural. The use of this mode is magnificently appropriate to what it presents, namely, the temple and Zion, which are composed of matter within time and yet have eternal and transcendant dimensions' (p. 133).

15. J.E. Miller, 'Dreams and Prophetic Visions', *Biblica* 71 (1990), pp. 401-404, also observes that 'lifted his eyes' is 'terminology usually reserved for prophetic visions' (p. 403).

focus of God's promise to Abraham and his descendants; the Ish-maelites are transformed from travelling merchants to the means by which the brothers can preserve Joseph's life and profit from it; and the flocks are no mere grazing animals, but the symbol of God's presence in Jacob's life. With this in mind, we should surely join S.C. Reif in resisting the diminishing 'Look!' or 'I looked' as an appropriate English rendition of the idiom.[16] The apparent duplication inherent in transla-tions such as 'raise your eyes and look!' or 'I raised my eyes and looked' is far from redundant. Rather, it helps to convey the sense of looking deeply or beneath the surface which so often accompanies the use of this idiom, and which is particularly evocative when used with reference to images seen in the context of a dream.

The participation of the interpreting angel is not the only respect in which the dream of the flocks differs from the other Genesis dreams. It is also the only one which is not reported by the narrator, both refer-ences to the activity of dreaming coming from the dreamer himself (31.10, 11). The absence of narrative confirmation must influence a close reading of this dream report, and it is interesting to examine the ways in which this omission affects the text. To begin with, it lends a rather casual air to the dream report; Jacob mentions the dream as if the memory of it occurred to him quite by chance. This represents a strik-ing contrast to other Genesis dream reports, which invariably demand our immediate attention. In 15.1 it is established at the outset that Abraham is about to receive a message from God, and likewise, the report of Abimelech's dream opens with the announcement that God came to him. Chapter 28 adopts a rather different tactic, engaging in some atmospheric scene-setting before God is mentioned. Yet, with its description of the setting sun and the resonant repetition of 'the place', the reader would have every right to feel cheated if no momentous event ensued.

By contrast, 31.10-13 makes no attempt to create an atmosphere ap-propriate to divine revelation, and, although the narrator is immediately informative about the dream's visual content, it is not clear at first that it constitutes a message from God. Indeed, as noted above, God's mes-sage is initially mediated by the angel, and the fact that Jacob reports the angel's command to raise his eyes (v. 12) after he has reported his

16. 'A Root to Look Up: A Study of the Hebrew *ns' 'ayn'* (VTSup, 36; Leiden: E.J. Brill, 1985), pp. 230-44.

own complicity (v. 10) is more than mildly confusing. Far from creating an atmosphere of anticipation or foreboding, this dream report is reminiscent of an ineptly told joke.

In Jacob's telling, then, the dream of the flocks does not sound especially inspirational, and certainly it lacks the inspiring qualities of his dream at Bethel. One explanation for the very different impressions conveyed by these two dream reports may be a simple matter of imagery; a ladder or staircase reaching from earth to heaven, complete with ascending and descending angels, is intrinsically more impressive than mating sheep. Equally worthy of attention, however, are the strikingly different roles played by these two dreams in the narrative. The dream at Bethel is an interaction between God and Jacob of which the latter is the sole direct beneficiary. The value of the dream of the flocks, on the other hand, lies as much in being reported as in being received. It both enables Jacob to see that God has been with him and provides him with the crucial 'evidence' required to convince Rachel and Leah that their place is with him as opposed to Laban.

The Dream as Rhetoric

The rhetorical, or persuasive, function of the dream of the flocks invites comparison with the dreams of the Joseph narrative. Three different mechanisms serve to demonstrate God's involvement in Joseph's life: the narrator reports that God is with Joseph; he prospers and those whom he serves prosper with him; and he both receives dreams and has the ability to interpret the dreams of others. While dream interpretation plays no part in the Jacob narrative, it is Jacob's dreams, his prosperity and God's explicit promise to be with him (made and confirmed in the two dream-revelations) which combine to confirm Jacob's relationship to God. As we see in the Joseph story, however, it is not enough that the protagonist himself be aware of his special relationship with God; it is crucial that those around him are also aware of it. Indeed, this is a feature of the patriarchal narratives in general, as the wife-sister texts, for instance, make abundantly clear. In chs. 12 and 20 God does not simply withdraw Abraham from an awkward situation, but intervenes in such a way that Pharaoh, and later Abimelech, together with their entire households, can scarcely fail to be aware that God is protecting the patriarch. The third wife-sister text operates rather differently, but there too Abimelech's recognition that the Lord is with Isaac (26.28) signals the all-important transition from hostility between the patriarch and the local residents to peaceful coexistence.

The dream of the flocks, like Joseph's dreams and his ability to interpret the dreams of others, serves to demonstrate that God is with Jacob, and this sets it firmly in the ancient Near Eastern tradition of politically useful dream reports. The predominance of royal dream reports among surviving ancient Near Eastern texts is only partly attributable to the importance of the dreamer. Certainly, a king's dream was more likely to be reported and preserved than was the dream of a peasant, but, in fact, few of the reports available to us appear to be based on actual dream experiences. On the contrary, most are highly stylized and are ultimately concerned with validating a particular claim or action of the dreamer.[17] A temple constructed without divine approval was deemed unacceptable in many ancient cultures, and the dream was a convenient means of providing it.[18] Likewise, claims to the throne were often contested, and a timely dream from the gods could smooth the path considerably.[19] In other words, we have so many royal dream reports partly because a king's *need* for 'divinely-sent' revelations was so much greater than the need of the average peasant.

Jacob's position presents several obvious parallels to that of royal figures in other ancient Near Eastern societies, and his needs were more or less identical. In the first instance he needed to establish superiority over his brother, and the dream at Bethel came at precisely the right moment to confirm divine approval of the blessing which, at least in the human scheme of things, belonged to Esau. Later on he needed to establish his right to leave Laban's house and start his own, and the dream of the flocks provides divine support for what was, after all, orig-

---

17. The 'political' value of the dream as a means of bestowing divine endorsement upon human actions was recognised throughout the ancient Near East. Indeed, it almost certainly accounted for the profusion of formulaic dream reports which had no basis in experience. See Robinson, 'Dreams in the Old Testament', pp. 159-63, for a discussion of the dream as a legitimising device in the ancient Near East.

18. See Hurowitz, *I Have Built You an Exalted House*: 'The best-known (to us) way for the god to deliver a message to the king was by means of a dream. In a dream the god would reveal, either explicitly through words or symbolically through visual means, what was demanded' (p. 143).

19. See, for example, Robinson's discussion of the election of the Hittite king Hattusilis, 'Dreams in the Old Testament', pp. 159-60.

inally Jacob's own decision. In addition, and just as importantly, it convinces the wives that they and their children should go with him.[20]

Support for considerable emphasis on the rhetorical element in the dream of the flocks may be derived from an analysis of the text immediately around it. This reveals that ch. 31 abounds with rhetorical devices designed to convince Rachel and Leah that their loyalties should be with their husband and not their father. The chapter opens with a catalogue of items in support of Jacob's decision to leave; Laban's sons resent his success (v. 1); Laban is no longer favourably disposed towards him (v. 2); and God has commanded him to return to his native land (v. 3). These three factors, we may assume, are justification enough for Jacob to leave, taking his wives and animals with him. Yet when he summons his wives to inform them of their imminent departure, Jacob presents the issues somewhat differently. For reasons which are not clear, he fails to mention Laban's sons at all, expanding instead the second and third motivating factors. Not only has Laban's manner towards Jacob recently changed for the worse, but, it transpires, he has been systematically cheating him for some time (31.7). Even if we count Laban's various underhanded dealings with the sheep, such as agreeing to Jacob's request for the speckled, spotted and dark-coloured sheep and then promptly entrusting all such animals into the care of his sons, we have heard nothing to suggest deception on the scale indicated by Jacob here.[21] In the end it seems most likely that Jacob is simply engaging in the rhetorical device of hyperbole. Having emphasized both the dedication with which he served Laban and the duplicity with which he was rewarded for his efforts, Jacob proceeds to a third level of argumentation (31.9):

ויצל אלהים את מקנה אביכם ויתן לי:

God has taken away your father's livestock and given it to me.

This is persuasive on several counts. First of all Jacob confirms that God has, indeed, been with him, and, more to the point, he successfully reassures his wives on the point of their material welfare. Jacob's claim

---

20. It is certainly possible that the fact that Israel is named for Jacob, and that the tribes are peopled by the offspring of his sons, made the constant affirmation of divine approval more crucial in his case than in the cases of Abraham and Isaac.

21. Some commentators are sceptical even about these instances. N. Leibowitz, for instance, *New Studies in Bereshit* (trans. A. Newman; Jerusalem: World Zionist Organization, 1972), p. 342, claims that the only allusions to altered wages are in 31.7 and 31.41. For her, at least, Laban's blatant sheep-juggling does not count.

on his share of Laban's flocks was of considerable importance, since he could not hope to maintain an independent household without them. Indeed, vv. 6-9, with their belt and braces style of argumentation, reflect the great value of these animals; Jacob earned the sheep and, if that fails to convince, God gave them to him anyway.

It is possible that additional rhetorical force is derived here from the use of the verb נצל (take away, redeem) which occurs first in v. 9, and is, significantly, reiterated by the wives in v. 16. Elsewhere in Genesis, this verb is used in potentially life-threatening situations (32.12, 32; 37.21, 22), suggesting deliverance of a kind not usually associated with sheep. In many respects, however, Exod. 12.36 represents a closer and more interesting parallel:

ויהוה נתן את חן העם בעיני מצרים וישאלום וינצלו את מצרים:

And the Lord had disposed the Egyptians favourably toward the people, and they let them have their request; thus they stripped the Egyptians.

One might argue that, after years of slavery in Egypt, the Israelites were entitled to a few pieces of jewellery on their way out, but it is only God's involvement that makes it impossible to define this act as theft or extortion. Similarly, Jacob, after 20 years of service in Laban's house (six of which were unpaid, while half of the remaining 14 were rewarded by a wife he did not want), has earned his portion of the flock, but the uncomfortable fact remains that he clearly hopes to leave with rather more than he has legitimately earned. It is not altruism that makes him reject what we may assume is Laban's offer of a conventional wage (30.31) in favour of the chance to manipulate the breeding patterns of his flocks. On the contrary, he hopes that this arrangement will ultimately be more profitable for him than Laban can anticipate. The following question may then arise: if Jacob multiplied his flocks by means of a deception, did he really earn them, and can he take them with him when he goes? God's involvement, as reported here to Rachel and Leah, guarantees a positive response, and there can be little doubt that it is this winning combination of divine protection and material reward (31.16) that convinces the wives to leave their father's house.

The reporting of the dream of the flocks underlines in another way the dream's rhetorical value. It is invariably the case in Genesis dream reports that the response of the dreamer and, indeed, of anyone to whom the dream is recounted, is strikingly 'on the mark'. Abimelech's courtiers are terrified (20.8), Jacob is fearful but impressed (28.17),

Joseph's brothers hate him more (37.8), Jacob is concerned (37.10), and Pharaoh is disturbed (41.8). In each case the dream elicits a reaction which, based on the impression conveyed by the original report and on its role in the narrative, turns out to be absolutely appropriate. Abimelech's courtiers are right to fear the possible repercussions of God's message to their king, Jacob correctly interprets the dream at Bethel as a major turning-point in his life,[22] Joseph's dream does provide additional confirmation of his superior status, and Jacob's concern about relations between his sons is entirely justified. It is safe to assume, then, that the response of Rachel and Leah to the dream of the flocks is similarly appropriate, and that they have interpreted its significance correctly.

The range of emotions that is usually displayed in response to dream revelations—fear, awe, amazement and concern—has been replaced here by a surprisingly matter-of-fact, and even legalistic, reaction on the part of the wives:

ותען רחל ולאה ותאמרנה לו העוד לנו חלק ונחלה בבית אבינו:
הלוא נכריות נחשבנו לו כי מכרנו ויאכל גם אכול את כספנו:
כי כל העשר אשר הציל אלהים מאבינו לנו הוא ולבנינו ועתה כל אשר
אמר אלהים אליך עשה:

> Then Rachel and Leah answered him, saying, 'Have we still a share in
> the inheritance of our father's house? Surely, he regards us as outsiders,
> now that he has sold us and used up our purchase price. Truly, all the
> wealth that God has taken away from our father belongs to us and to our
> children. Now then, do just as God has told you' (31.14-16).

The reference to their hereditary portion, their position as outsiders, and their used-up purchase price makes it clear that Rachel and Leah have construed this dream as confirmation that their father does not deserve their loyalty, and that they should have no qualms about taking a portion of his wealth when they leave with Jacob. The text gives us no cause to doubt that the wives are correct in their assessment of the significance of Jacob's dream, and, as noted above, a comparison with other dream reports indicates that we should accept their interpretation

---

22. H. Cooper, 'Connecting Heaven and Earth: Biblical and Psychological Perspectives on Jacob's Dream', a lecture delivered at Leo Baeck College, 8 June 1994 claimed that Jacob's vow in 28.20-22 shows that the patriarch had misunderstood his dream at Bethel, but this reading has already been contested in the previous chapter.

at face value. Once again, we are dealing with a reading of the dream of the flocks whose emphasis is, above all, rhetorical.

Additional support for this reading may be derived from the observation that none of the Genesis dreams is reported to a third party *unnecessarily*. Abraham's vision (15.1-21) and Jacob's dream (28.12-22) are not reported at all, perhaps because they provide a combination of inspiration and reassurance which is relevant only to their dreamers. Abimelech's dream, by contrast, has wider repercussions, and he reports it to his servants upon waking. First of all, it was generally assumed in the ancient Near East that the dreams of kings affected the general populace as well as their royal dreamer,[23] and in many respects the fate of people was inextricably bound up with that of the monarch. (Abimelech makes this quite clear when, in 20.9, he summons Abraham and voices his complaint.) Secondly, we may assume that the king was far from being the only citizen capable of committing adultery with Sarah, a point that is made explicit in the third version of the story (26.10). The combination of these two factors made it necessary for Abimelech to inform his household of his dream.

In the Joseph narrative, of course, all the dreams are reported, but none needlessly. On the contrary, the dreams are recounted on what might be described as a 'need to know' basis: the brothers need to hear Joseph's dreams, since these act as a catalyst for the jealousy and hatred which ultimately result in his being sold into Egypt; Joseph needs to hear the dreams of the butler and baker in order to establish his reputation for dream interpretation; the baker needs to hear the butler's dream, since its favourable interpretation encourages him to tell his own dream; and the butler needs to hear the baker's dream so that he can commend Joseph to Pharaoh with confidence (the fact that Joseph has interpreted *two* dreams correctly is a telling confirmation of his ability in the context of this narrative); the magicians need to hear Pharaoh's dreams so that Joseph's ability to interpret can be set against their failure, and so it continues. These comparisons indicate that Jacob would not have reported the dream of the flocks to his wives unless so doing was necessary, and that the wives' response is an important component of the dream report.

This emphasis on the rhetorical or persuasive element in the dream of the flocks fits well with the tendency of recent scholars to perceive oppositions between various characters in the Jacob narrative. Fishbane

23. See Robinson, 'Dreams in the Old Testament', p. 157.

focuses on the opposition between Jacob and Esau, which he takes to be at the core of the Jacob Cycle,[24] while A. Berlin emphasizes the extent to which this opposition is reflected in the subsequent rivalry between Rachel and Leah where, once again, the younger sibling assumes the rightful place of the older.[25] R. Hendel, in his endeavour to find parallels between Jacob and Rachel, also emphasizes the opposition between Rachel and Leah. His view that Rachel's theft of the teraphim from Laban mirrors Jacob's theft of the blessing from Isaac inevitably creates a parallel between Esau and Leah, both of whom are victims of their younger siblings.[26] R. Alter makes a similar point in his treatment of Gen. 30.1-4 as a brief case study in literary analysis of the Hebrew Bible:

> One might note that Leah is not mentioned by name here (v. 1): what is brought to the fore is the primary fact of her identity as sister, and hence the smouldering rivalry for progeny and love between these two daughters of Laban. That rivalry in turn is linked through analogy with the whole series of struggles between younger and elder brothers in Genesis, and the repeated drive of the secondborn to displace the firstborn, as Jacob himself had contrived to displace Esau.[27]

This is quite plausible. Yet, having announced the birth of Joseph, the narrative appears to lose interest in the tension between Rachel and Leah, and focuses instead on the opposition between Jacob and Laban. Admittedly, Hendel's analysis of the theft of the teraphim contrives to

24. See 'Composition and Structure in The Jacob Cycle': 'Because Jacob was Israel, every reading of the particular life history of Jacob could be deepened by a national reading of the same contents. Thus for later biblical traditions the original relations between Jacob-Israel and his brother Esau-Edom were but the surface level of numerous layers of allegorical possibilities. But it would seem that this later apprehension of a national dimension to the Jacob Cycle is, actually, a primary motivational feature of the narrative' (p. 15).

25. Berlin, 'Literary Exegesis of Biblical Narrative', emphasizes this aspect of the narrative when she refers to the 'younger sister motif, whereby these biblical Cinderellas [Rachel and Michal] end up married to a future patriarch and a future king, both of whom are younger brothers...' (p. 121). See also F. Greenspahn, *When Brothers Dwell Together: The Preeminence of Younger Siblings in the Hebrew Bible* (New York: Oxford University Press, 1994), especially pp. 94-96.

26. R.S. Hendel, *The Epic of the Patriarch: The Jacob Cycle and the Narrative Traditions of Canaan and Israel* (HSM, 42; Atlanta: Scholars Press, 1987), pp. 94-98.

27. *The Art of Biblical Narrative* (London: George Allen & Unwin, 1981), p. 186.

keep alive the rivalry between the two sisters for somewhat longer, but M. Greenberg's suggestion that Rachel's theft of the teraphim is a sign of her loyalty to her husband in preference to her father is ultimately more convincing, despite being based partly on a subsequently discredited comparison with Nuzi customs.[28] The opposition between Jacob and Laban remains unresolved until the pact at Mizpah (31.44), and is thus a live issue throughout most of chs. 30 and 31. Moreover, the narrator heightens the tension between the two by withholding until the eleventh hour (v. 43) Laban's grudging and somewhat back-handed agreement that Jacob can take his wives, children and flocks with him when he goes. Fokkelman refers briefly to a fourth opposition in the Jacob cycle; Laban versus God.[29] This subject deserves a more detailed consideration since it conforms in interesting ways to patterns that arise repeatedly in connection with the relationship between the Israelites and God. In his vow at Bethel (28.20-22), Jacob expresses the hope that God will feed and clothe him, and generally act as a protective force during his sojourning outside the land. Yet in the early stages of ch. 30 it appears that this role has been performed not by God but by Laban. As the narrative unfolds, however, we discover that, far from supporting and protecting Jacob, Laban has been exploiting and deceiving him, and that, in fact, God's intervention has been required to protect Jacob from Laban. This is a familiar turn of events in the patriarchal narratives. Abraham goes to Egypt to escape famine, thus making himself dependent upon Pharaoh rather than God. All too soon, however, God is forced to intervene to save Abraham from the very person from whom he has sought help. In some respects, the third wife-sister text represents an even closer parallel. Isaac goes to Gerar for sustenance during the famine (26.1), but he encounters difficulties, both potential (v. 10) and actual (vv. 15-20), with the local residents, and these are resolved only when Abimelech recognizes that the LORD is with Isaac. Here, as in the Jacob/Laban account, danger is averted only when the foreigner, having seen that the patriarch is blessed and protected by God, asks to make a pact with him.

28. M. Greenberg, 'Another Look at Rachel's Theft of the Teraphim', *JBL* 81 (1962), pp. 239-49.

29. In *Narrative Art in Genesis* Fokkelman contrasts the use of the preposition עִם (with) in Gen. 31.2 and 31.3 respectively: 'The two powers surrounding Jacob have been placed with that one preposition, but how far apart! Laban is by no means "with him" (31.2), but fortunately YHWH is then "with him" (v.3)' (p. 152).

As well as belonging to that group of narratives which confirm that Israel should never rely on the kindness of strangers, the Jacob/Laban episode conforms to another pattern that often occurs in Israelite history: before becoming a proper servant of God, Jacob must endure a period of servitude to an outsider. A similar structure may be perceived in the Joseph story, where Joseph is a slave to Potiphar and a servant to Pharaoh before securing some level of independence for his family and himself. It is manifested most clearly, however, in the Exodus narrative, where the Israelites are freed from slavery to Pharaoh to become servants of the LORD. It is interesting to note the extent to which this opposition between God and the powerful foreigner is reflected in the precise wording of Jacob's dream; the patriarch's prosperity is thanks to God, and no thanks to Laban (31.12). Laban's trickery is implicitly contrasted with God's steadfastness, and Jacob is left in no doubt about whom it is preferable to serve.

It has been argued here that the dream of the flocks serves a function that is rhetorical and even quasi-political. Regardless of the precise nature of the experience that its narrator envisaged behind it, its power in the text is primarily persuasive. Is it possible, however, that the narrator intended us to doubt that this report was based on an authentic dream experience, and that the lack of narratorial confirmation signals the possibility that Jacob had simply fabricated a dream revelation? This is a notion one is inclined to resist, yet this inclination may well be based on a certain reverence for the truth that would have been out of place in the ancient Near East.

It may be helpful to draw a present-day analogy. In certain situations, in the context of a courtroom, for instance, or a written business contract, lying is regarded as absolutely unacceptable and liars are punished accordingly. In other situations, such as political campaigns, lies are acceptable rhetoric; if most promises regarding taxes are lies, and liars are unfit for office, then most politicians should find themselves unemployed. It appears that ancient Near Eastern society was even more tolerant than twentieth-century Britain of fabrication for political advancement. It is difficult to imagine that the dreams that various royal figures claimed to have received, particularly the highly stylized examples, were taken at face value by those who heard them. Yet the recognition that they were not based on actual dream experiences did not diminish their value. The announcement of a divinely sent dream was simply one element of a formula (which may also have included founding a city and building a temple) designed to confer status upon royal figures. Thus, the question of whether or not Jacob's dream is to be understood as having actually occurred is unlikely to have been the cause of much insomnia in the ancient world; the narrator was merely utilizing a standard, and thoroughly acceptable, rhetorical device. Yet this leaves us with the considerable problem posed by the allusion to Bethel. Is it possible that the narrator would have described what he saw as Jacob's invention of a dream, and then proceeded to validate it by reference to his sacred experience at Bethel? A reasonable solution may be to separate these two components of the dream report, and claim that what Jacob fabricated was not the distinct experiences upon which each was based but merely the dream as a single entity which he reports in vv. 10-13. Indeed, it will now be argued that, for different reasons, this division of the dream of the flocks is ultimately unavoidable.

The Passage of Time

The period of the Jacob/Laban narrative that commences with Jacob's announcement that the time has come for him to leave Laban's house and return to his own land (30.25) presents an unusually distorted and compressed picture of the passage of time. In some respects this is true of all the patriarchal narratives; it is difficult to envisage the Isaac whom Abraham leads up Mount Moriah as a 37-year-old man. Yet the case in chs. 30 and 31 is quite different. Whereas the artificial representation of time elsewhere in the patriarchal narrative seems to be an unintended consequence of the emphasis on key events, here it conveys the impression of a literary contrivance. The portrayal in 30.25-43 of the events of six years (cf. 31.41) as though they occurred in one season[30] gives this text the flavour of a parable rather than a would-be historical account.[31]

30. Speiser, *Genesis*, p. 239, notes that 31.38 suggests that Jacob served Laban for an additional six years after the fourteen years he worked for his wives. This period of time, he claims, would have been sufficient for Jacob to amass the wealth indicated in 30.43. Speiser does not, however, take into account the fact that Jacob does not attempt to accumulate his own wealth until after the birth of Joseph, which may not have occurred within the 14 years of service.

31. In other respects, however, the narrator seems to have sought an aura of authenticity in his account of the dealings between Jacob and Laban. J.N. Postgate, 'Some Old Babylonian Shepherds and their Flocks', *JSS* 20 (1975), pp. 1-21,

Against this background of compressed time, the dream report is the cause of further chronological disorientation. Not least unsettling is the search for a reading of the text in which Jacob could have dreamt both parts of the dream in one night. The first part must have occurred prior to Jacob's amassing the wealth that is the stated source of his unpopularity (30.43–31.2). Indeed, it fits well between 30.36, which shows how far Laban is willing to go in breach of his agreement with Jacob, and 30.37, where Jacob embarks on the manipulation of breeding patterns by which means he outwits Laban. God's announcement that he has seen what Laban has done to Jacob (31.12) may thus be seen as an allusion to the events of 30.24-36, where Laban removes the type of animals specified by Jacob and places them in a separate flock to be shepherded by his sons. Finally, Jacob does actually state that he dreamt this dream at the time of the mating of the flocks (31.10), and 30.37-43 is the only part of the narrative that deals explicitly with a mating season.

The part of the dream that refers to Bethel, on the other hand, cannot have occurred at this point (30.36). Unlike the first part of the dream, it is not concerned with the creation of wealth, but rather with God's instruction to Jacob that he should leave Laban's house, presumably once he has gathered enough wealth to go. Most plausibly, the revelation referred to in 31.13 occurred at the beginning of ch. 31, in conjunction with v. 3:

ויאמר יהוה אל יעקב שוב אל ארץ אבותיך ולמולדתך ואהיה עמך:
Then the Lord said to Jacob, 'Return to the land of your fathers where you were born, and I will be with you.'

In chronological terms, then, it is possible that a period of six years elapsed between the dream of the sheep (vv. 10-12) and God's command that Jacob should return to his native land (v. 13).

This is by no means the only case in which an oral message (v. 13) is combined with a visual image (v.10), despite the fact that they were unlikely to have occurred at the same time. The dream at Bethel (28.12-15) provides what is probably the most extensively discussed example of this. Yet the parallel is not as close as it initially appears. First of all,

presents a view of the relationship between sheep-owner and shepherd which fits well with Gen. 30 and 31: 'The shepherd accepted personal liability for the flock and was remunerated in proportion to the growth of the flock and the amount of its produce' (p. 2).

the image of sheep, unlike the ladder, has an oral message which was clearly written to accompany it. Secondly, and more importantly, whereas the visual and oral components of the dream at Bethel fit together perfectly well, their counterparts in the dream of the flocks are fundamentally incompatible. Whereas the visual and oral elements of the dream at Bethel may have been *unlikely* to have occurred at the same time, the two components of the dream of the flocks *cannot* have occurred in one night.

This could, of course, be attributed to inferior redaction, but a more interesting explanation brings us back to the issue of persuasion versus inspiration. By combining two patently incompatible elements, the narrator may have provided yet another subtle indication about the rhetorical function of this dream report.[32] Not only has no attempt been made to convey a convincing impression of an actual dream experience, but, on the contrary, the account is written in such a way as to make it impossible to read it as such. The issue, for both the narrator and the reader, must surely be when, how, and to whom Jacob chose to report the dream of the flocks, and not whether such a dream actually occurred.

Another issue involving time which arises in connection with this dream concerns what Sternberg calls 'temporal discontinuity'.[33] With respect to its representation of time, the Jacob/Laban narrative bears a marked resemblance to the story of Abraham and Abimelech (20.1-18). As Sternberg shows in his analysis of ch. 20, events are reported not in order of occurrence, but as they are required to explain other events, or to revise a prior impression, and this narrative style significantly alters our perception of events that have already occurred. When a similar analysis is applied to the dream of the flocks it becomes evident that the timing of the dream report crucially affects the way it is read. Had it been reported at the point in the narrative when it presumably occurred (i.e. between 30.36 and 30.37), the reader might have assumed that its purpose was merely to inspire Jacob to experiment with creative breeding techniques, or perhaps to reassure him that God was still with him. As it stands, however, these elements, while they are still present, must take a back seat. Whether or not Jacob is inspired or reassured ceases to be a primary concern, and the reader focuses instead on the effect that

32. This follows the reading of Nachmanides, who sees two separate revelations here joined by Jacob for the purpose of persuading Rachel and Leah to go with him. See *MG, ad loc.*

33. *The Poetics of Biblical Narrative*, pp. 316-17.

Jacob's telling of the dream will have upon his audience: will Rachel and Leah be persuaded to go with him, or will they prefer the security of their father's house?

The foregoing discussion, while it may have helped to clarify what the narrator hoped to achieve by including the dream report at this point in the narrative, leaves several important questions unaddressed. Why, for instance, if the narrator's interests were primarily rhetorical, did he use a dream report here, rather than some other rhetorical device? It has been noted above that dreams were routinely used in the ancient Near East as justifications for various claims and actions, and perhaps this is explanation enough for the use of the dream here. Yet the matter merits further investigation, and at this point the role of the dream will be examined in the context of the narrative genre in which it appears.

The Dream and Dual Causality

In an article that elaborates upon the work of Y. Kaufmann, Y. Amit discusses the principle of dual causality.[34] Amit is interested primarily in historical texts, but her consideration of von Rad's application of a less-developed form of this theory to Genesis 24 indicates that the frame of reference may be extended to include other narrative types.[35] It will now be applied to the Jacob/Laban narrative, with the aim of shedding more light on the use of the dream in this text.

Briefly stated, 'dual causality' describes the complex interplay of human action and divine intervention employed by writers who were uncomfortable with anthropomorphic or other explicit expressions of divine intervention; who wished to convey a sense of historical realism; who sought to emphasize the role played by human strengths and weaknesses in the fulfilment of God's will; or who were motivated by a combination of all three concerns. In many respects, the dual causality principle is exemplified by the Joseph narrative where for several chapters

34. 'The Dual Causality Principle and its Effects on Biblical Literature', *VT* 37 (1987), pp. 385-400.

35. 'The Dual Causality Principle': 'Von Rad emphasizes that although in most of the individual stories of the Yahwistic compilations the ancient concept of the direct intervention of God is conspicuous, whether by means of sight or hearing, it is already possible to find among them stories which disregard the depiction of tangible and direct divine intervention in the course of historical events, and as an example of a story of this kind he cites the story of the betrothal of Rebekah (Gen. 24)' (p. 387).

the name of God is rarely mentioned, and the course of events is attributed to human nature rather than divine will. Joseph behaves as he
does because he has the advantages (and the disadvantages) of being
handsome, favoured and clever; the brothers' actions are dictated by
jealousy and, later, hunger; Potiphar's wife is motivated by lust and
vanity, and so forth. Eventually, however, it transpires that the entire
cast of characters has been stage-managed by God for the purpose of
bringing Israel down to Egypt (45.5-8). Yet, amazingly enough, this
explicit announcement of divine intervention barely alters the reader's
perception of the human action which precedes it. Joseph, youthful
immodesty aside, continues to be admirable, the brothers still seem
deplorable, and the reader can happily combine an interpretation that
depends upon the supposition of free-will with complete acceptance of
God's controlling hand: the narrator has his cake and eats it.[36]

It is hardly necessary to point out the extent to which the dual causality principle lends itself to a narrative that must demonstrate both that
God chose Jacob, and that Jacob deserved to be chosen. Nevertheless, a
brief comparison with the Abraham narrative may help to underline
this. Abraham's interactions with God are direct and explicit throughout. He usually acts because God tells him to and where he does take
his own initiative, as in 12.10, for instance, there is no later attempt to
define the famine as a manifestation of God's will. On the contrary, the
ensuing narrative suggests that Abraham's trip to Egypt was in opposition to divine will, as is also indicated by God's instructions to Isaac
(26.2) in the third wife-sister text:

וירא אליו יהוה ויאמר אל תרד מצרימה שכן בארץ אשר אמר אליך:
The LORD had appeared to him and said, 'Do not go down to Egypt;
stay in the land which I point out to you.'

Only in ch. 24, when the patriarch despatches his servant in search of a
wife for Isaac, does dual causality come into play. Here divine intervention combines with natural coincidence to enable the servant to identify

36. Not surprisingly, many philosophers are sceptical about dual causality.
H. Frankfurt, however, in *The Importance of What We Care About* (Cambridge:
Cambridge University Press, 1988), pp. 6-8, provides an account of dual causality
which fits well with its biblical application. Frankfurt describes the case of Black
and Jones. Black wants Jones to perform a certain action, but will intervene only if
necessary (i.e. if Jones behaves contrary to Black's desired outcome). He thus gives
the impression that Jones is acting independently when, in fact, he has no alternative but to perform Black's action.

Rebekah as a suitable wife for Isaac, but it is important to bear in mind that this change is accompanied by a shift in focus from the patriarch to his servant. Whereas the dual causality principle features in the Jacob narrative, it plays no significant role at all in the stories about Abraham. We can now return to the question posed above: why was a dream, as opposed to some other rhetorical device, used at this point in the Jacob/ Laban narrative? One plausible answer is that it was used precisely because it fits so well with the dual causality principle. Amit makes the point that the dream, presumably on account of its unusual position between the human and divine spheres,[37] represents an unusually attractive option for the narrator of a dual causality text, permitting the possibility of divine involvement without compromising the prior presentation of human action. The discovery that Jacob had a dream at the time of the mating of the flocks does not force the reader to discard entirely the picture of Jacob the cunning shepherd with his rods at the watering-hole. Rather, the narrator incorporates into this picture an element of divine influence which was not previously considered to be a factor. It may thus be the compatibility of dream revelations with dual causality that persuaded the narrator to terminate Jacob's service to Laban with a dream.

This analysis of the dream of the flocks has been, for the most part, forward-looking. I have claimed that Jacob reported the dream in order to ensure that his wives would follow a certain course of action, and thus the emphasis has necessarily been placed on what will happen after the dream has been reported, rather than what happened before it. Yet it is impossible to overlook the extent to which the dream is also successful in recasting events that have already taken place, revealing them in a slightly different light. The first indication of Jacob's departure from Laban's house comes from the patriarch himself (30.25). Rachel has, at last, given birth to a son, and the time has come for Jacob to focus on the future of his own household. Once he has reported the dream, however, the human circumstances that constituted the background to Jacob's decision pale into insignificance, and the narrator conveys the impression that Jacob left because God told him to. An interesting parallel now presents itself with the circumstances of Abraham's arrival in the land of Canaan. It is initially reported (11.31) that Abraham left Ur as part of his father's household:

---

37. This recalls von Rad's description, *Genesis*, p. 27, of the dream as 'the spiritual plane on which God's revelation meets men'.

ויקח תרח את אברם בנו ואת לוט בן הרן בן בנו ואת שרי כלתו
אשת אברם בנו ויצאו אתם מאור כשדים ללכת ארצה כנען

Terah took his son Abram, his grandson Lot the son of Haran, and his daughter-in-law Sarai, the wife of his son Abram, and they set out together from Ur of the Chaldeans for the land of Canaan.

The fact that everyone is described in terms of his or her relationship to Abraham's father serves to underline Terah's leading role in this journey. 15.7, on the other hand, tells a rather different story:

ויאמר אליו אני יהוה אשר הוצאתיך מאור כשדים לתת לך את הארץ הזאת לרשתה

Then he said to him, 'I am the LORD who brought you out from Ur of the Chaldeans to assign this land to you as a possession.'

Here, as in the dream of the flocks, God assumes responsibility for something that had previously been presented as a human endeavour.

As well as giving the narrator an opportunity to cast a spot-light on God's involvement in Jacob's life, the dream also softens the blow dealt to Israelite theology by certain elements of ch. 30. The precise nature of the black (or white) magic by which means Jacob improves the fertility of his own animals remains somewhat mysterious, but one might imagine that its origins were pagan and thus not entirely acceptable. (With notable exceptions such as Aaron's rod [Exod. 7.8-13] and the bronze serpent [Num. 21.8-9],[38] there are few comparable cases of the use of physical objects to influence the laws of nature.) The dream, however, substantially revises the impression created by ch. 30, implying that divine intervention, not pagan rite, was the source of Jacob's prosperity.

Another question which this analysis has yet to address concerns the dominant images of the two distinct components of the dream of the flocks; the mating sheep and Bethel. Why do these two elements coincide in the dream that finally confirms Jacob's imminent return to his father's house? Since they are, indeed, distinct themes, they will be discussed separately here, and Bethel, being in many ways the more straightforward of the two, will be discussed first.

Bethel

On one level, God's reference to Bethel may be primarily a means of self-identification, similar to the announcement in 28.13, 'I am the

---

38. In the case of the bronze serpent, the Bible registers explicit disapproval in 2 Kgs 18.4.

LORD, the God of your father Abraham and the God of Isaac' (אני יהוה
אלהי אברהם ואביך אלהי יצחק). Yet this does not convey the full extent
of the significance of the allusion to Bethel here. Certainly, it reassures
Jacob that God, the God who appeared to him at Bethel, remains with
him, keeping a watchful eye on events and, when necessary, acting on
his behalf (31.12). Yet it also reminds Jacob that he too has an obligation to perform. Bethel is the place where he anointed the stone and
made a vow, and God is now asking him to take positive steps towards
its fulfilment (31.13):

עתה קום צא מן הארץ הזאת ושוב אל ארץ מולדתך:...
Now, arise and leave this land and return to your native land.

The dream at Bethel leaves behind it a sense of uncertainty and anticipation: will God meet the conditions of Jacob's vow, and what will
Jacob do when he finally returns from his exile? The dream of the
flocks provides a partial answer. As well as guaranteeing his economic
security in Laban's house, Jacob's shepherding activities have earned
him wives to generate offspring and wealth to return to his native land;
God has used the sheep and goats as a means of fulfilling the conditions
of the vow (28.20-22). It now remains for Jacob to keep his part of the
bargain.

It is not difficult to see why God decides to remind Jacob of Bethel at
this point in the story. It is rather more difficult to see why he chooses
animals of the flock as an image of protection and even salvation. The
ensuing discussion will endeavour to show that this imagery is by no
means a matter of chance, but arises from the integral role played by
sheep and goats in the narrative, commencing with the deception of
Isaac in 27.1.

The Speckled Sheep

With the possible exception of the cows seen by Pharaoh (41.1-4, 17-
21), which are mentioned only in the context of the dream report, no
other pentateuchal animals merit so detailed a description as Jacob's
sheep (not even the all-important ram in Gen. 22.13). Before Jacob
leaves his father's house there is little or no indication that he will
become an expert shepherd. On the contrary, he is described (25.27) as
'a mild man who stayed in the camp' (איש תם ישב אהלים), and it seems
likely that his culinary skills (cf. 25.29-34) were acquired at the
expense of outdoor pursuits. Yet in 31.10-13 it is not merely the case

that Jacob the shepherd dreams of flocks; he dreams of the very animals whose breeding patterns he has so carefully manipulated in the preceding narrative. The dream arises directly from his own actions, and its imagery mirrors the mundane details of his daily life. In view of this explicit connection between Jacob's dream and his day-to-day preoccupations, it may seem superfluous to search for additional, unspecified significance in the appearance of the animals there. Yet the extraordinary attention devoted to Jacob's shepherding activities in chs. 30 and 31 demands an analysis that commences well before his employment as Laban's shepherd.

A cursory glance at the Jacob narrative reveals that sheep are a pervasive theme. It is important to note that, prior to the deception which Jacob, aided and abetted by his mother, plays on Isaac, animals appear to have had no significant role in his life. While Esau is described as a hunter and a man of the fields, Jacob, as noted above, is someone who prefers to stay in a tent (25.27). It is only as part of the deception of Isaac that, for the first time, we encounter animals in connection with Jacob: Rebekah prepares a meal of young goat as a substitute for Isaac's favoured game stew (27.9). Despite the fact that Jacob's ability to make soup has been attested in 25.29-34, his mother cooks it for him here. Perhaps his proficiency is limited to lentils, but, more plausibly, this illustrates his rather passive approach to the acquisition of Esau's blessing. Still more to the point, Rebekah clothes Jacob's smooth arms with goat skin so that he can pass as the hairy Esau (27.16), and thus Jacob, the smooth-skinned, tent-dwelling, second-born son, has been transformed into the hairy, field-roaming first-born. Yet we are about to learn that the transformation must be more than skin-deep, and that it must, moreover, be something which Jacob, until now a more-or-less passive participant, effects in his own right.

The text attributes to Isaac and Rebekah, respectively, two distinct motives for sending Jacob to Laban's house. For Rebekah, it is primarily a matter of protecting him from Esau, while Isaac is motivated by his intense desire that Jacob should not marry a Hittite woman but, rather, one of Laban's daughters. The dismissal is followed by another blessing, and this time Isaac's eyes are, at least metaphorically, open wide (28.3-4).

Jacob's departure is followed immediately by his dream at Bethel, in which he asks God to ensure his safe return to the house of his father (28.21), and with this the text has covered the full range of expectations for Jacob's mission in Paddan Aram. He has been forced to flee from Esau's wrath, alone and empty-handed, but he must return with wives and children (the first step in the fulfilment of Isaac's second blessing), and in a state, both material and psychological, conducive for a recon- ciliation with his brother.[39]

It was observed above that certain transformations, far exceeding temporary disguise, must be made before Jacob properly merits the stolen blessing: what was gained dishonestly must now be earned. It should come as no surprise that, in keeping with the biblical commit- ment to measure for measure, the animals that featured in Jacob's deceit are now involved in the proof of his merit.[40] This process of change begins at Bethel, where God demonstrates the validity of Isaac's inadvertent blessing, and where Jacob confirms his commitment to God. Yet it is abundantly clear that the Bethel episode, far from being any sort of culmination of Jacob's relationship with God, is merely a beginning.

The following question now arises: why is it that, following a mo- mentous revelation comprising angels, heaven's gate and the explicit promise of divine blessings, God seems to leave the scene before the next chapter even begins? The answer to this question is inextricably connected with Jacob's shepherding activities and his dream of the flocks. Although the narrative concerning Rachel contains even fewer explicit indications of divine intervention than the story of Rebekah's betrothal (cited in this context by von Rad),[41] it features an extraor- dinarily high density of coincidence. Amit explains the prominence of coincidence in dual causality narrative:

39. While conceding that verbal connections of this sort can be handled over- enthusiastically, it is difficult to resist the pairing of flight (בּרח) with blessing (בּרך) here. Jacob steals a blessing, is forced to flee (from Isaac's house), is blessed by God (at Bethel), flees again (from Laban), and is blessed (again at Bethel). Fokkelman, *Narrative Art in Genesis*, makes a similar point about a possible pair- ing of בּרך (blessing) and בּקר (first-born) (pp. 94-95).

40. For other examples see Exod. 12.29 (the plague of the first-born, cf. 1.16); Est. 7.10 (Haman is impaled on the stake he had raised for Mordecai); Num. 12.10 (Miriam's skin turns white for criticizing Moses' marriage to a black woman, cf. 12.1). This last case depends upon the relevant property of snow being its white- ness not, as is sometimes claimed, its flakiness. Isa. 1.18 may provide evidence for the former interpretation.

41. *Old Testament Theology*, I (trans. D.M.G. Stalker; London: SCM Press, 1989), p. 51.

...through an overwhelming accumulation of circumstances which be-
stow upon the narrative a nuance of the miraculous, that is to say of
supervision from above which causes the events to occur, the narrator
can alert the attention of the reader to a systematic structure which lies
behind the events.[42]

On the one hand, coincidences can be explained and justified in purely
human terms, but on the other they can point to God's governing hand.
A brief analysis of the Jacob/Laban narrative reveals the dominant role
played by coincidence there.

Jacob's first sight upon leaving Bethel is a well, surrounded by
thirsty sheep and covered by a stone. After the Bethel narrative, which
is constructed around the twin columns of the ladder and the standing
stone, and in which Jacob shows himself capable of moving a stone of
possibly astonishing proportions,[43] the reader's expectations are likewise raised. It comes as no surprise that the shepherds know Laban, and
the scene is complete when Rachel, immaculately on cue, arrives with
her father's sheep. That Rachel is explicitly described as a shepherdess
is almost certainly significant here, particularly since, as we later discover, Laban does have sons who could presumably have shepherded
for him.[44] Rachel the shepherdess is the perfect wife for the man whose
mother dressed him up in goat skins; indeed, her very name is propitious.[45] Equally propitious is Jacob's encounter with Rachel next to a
well. Quite apart from the precedent set by Abraham's servant, it seems
likely that wells were regarded as places where God's presence was

42. Amit, 'The Dual-Causality Principle', p. 393.
43. Von Rad, *Genesis*, p. 285, claims that the standing stone may have been
almost seven feet high, in which case Jacob must have possessed colossal strength
to raise it. This view is certainly in keeping with that of the rabbinic commentators,
who saw evidence of Jacob's strength even in the womb. In his commentary on
Hos. 12.4, *MG, ad loc.*, Ibn Ezra suggests that Jacob's ability to grasp Esau's heel
in utero indicates miraculous strength. While this comment was almost certainly
based on the misconception that an unborn child could not move its limbs, it exem-
plifies an interest in tracing Jacob's physical power back to the earliest possible
moment.
44. The unusual nature of Rachel's being called a shepherd(ess) here is noted
by the rabbinic commentators. Nachmanides (*MG, ad loc.*) addresses the matter of
why Leah was not with her, suggesting that Leah's weak eyes made her unsuitable
for the task. The Sforno (*MG, ad loc.*) imagines that she was unusually skilled in
shepherd-craft.
45. See 31.38 for the use of רחל meaning 'young female sheep'.

intensified.[46] At any rate, while God's intervention in the betrothal of Jacob and Rachel is not made explicit, the coincidences that accumulate around Jacob's newly established interest in sheep surely signal a marriage made in heaven.

When Jacob asks for Rachel's hand, Laban agrees to employ him as a shepherd. At one level, then, Jacob is simply working for a wife, but an examination of the episode in its narrative context indicates that his motivation is at least twofold. As well as serving Laban, Jacob is serving God, and his aim, as suggested above, is to reach the point at which he can return to his father's house in good health and in peace. To complicate matters still further, Jacob's tenure with Laban also provides God with the opportunity to fulfil the conditions of the patriarch's vow in 28.20-22.

Once again, the notion of dual causality is helpful in elucidating the text. Since God is largely absent from the narrative, Jacob's success is attributed to hard work and skill in shepherd-craft. From time to time, however, God's involvement is made explicit, and it is interesting to note that, in common with other similar cases, this occurs in connection with a non-Israelite who appears to be in a position of superiority. Thus, the announcement that the LORD was with Joseph (39.2) is followed by Potiphar's recognition of this fact, while Abimelech tells Isaac that he can see that the LORD has been with him (26.28), and, presumably for that reason, seeks to make a pact with the patriarch. Likewise, Laban learns that the LORD has blessed him on Jacob's account (30.27), which explains his eagerness to keep Jacob in his employ long after their original contract has expired. It is difficult to know what conclusions should be drawn from this. On the one hand, these incidents may be intended to illustrate God's promise that non-Israelites will be blessed through the patriarchs (12.3, 26.4, 28.14). Alternatively, they may be seen as naturalistic mechanisms (namely, observation by a third party) for showing that what might appear to be good fortune or the reward for industriousness is, in fact, the result of God's blessing.

46. Concerning the well visited by Abraham's servant in Gen. 24, M. Fishbane, 'The Well of Living Water: A Biblical Motif and its Ancient Transformations', in M. Fishbane and E. Tov (eds), *Sha'arei Talmon: Studies in the Bible, Qumram, and the Ancient Near East Presented to Shemaryahu Talmon* (Winona Lake, IN: Eisenbrauns, 1992), pp. 3-16, observes: 'the events around this well provide diagnostic conditions whereby he divines whether God will fulfill his mission to find a wife for Isaac (vv. 12-27, 42-48)' (p. 4).

I observed above that, commencing with the use of the young goats in Jacob's deception of Isaac, the narrative builds up a series of connections between Jacob and animals of the flock. This motif is further developed in 30.25–31.13, which contains an immensely detailed account of the combination of shepherd-craft, witchcraft and divine intervention by which means Jacob multiplies Laban's flocks. Some exegetes have attributed the length and complexity of this narrative, not to mention its apparent inconsistencies, to the involvement of more than one writer.[47] It may, however, be possible to find a plausible explanation without disturbing the narrative unity.

A possible hallmark of dual causality narrative that Amit does not discuss is a certain amount of confusion. The conflicting information provided by Genesis 37 concerning which brother had scruples about killing Joseph, and precisely who sold him into Egypt, is often attributed to duplication by different sources.[48] E.L. Greenstein, on the other hand, proposes that the confusion may reflect a deliberate attempt to intensify the presence of the divine hand by obscuring human responsibility.[49] In the same way, by making it virtually impossible to determine how Jacob increased his flock, the narrator may be preparing the ground for the announcement that Jacob's good fortune was, in fact, God's doing. Just as God's controlling hand is eventually revealed in the Joseph narrative (45.5-8), so Jacob's dream of the flocks (especially v. 12) reveals that, behind all the confusion, God was pulling the strings. The reader, unable to determine who did what to whom (and when), is open to the suggestion that it was all the result of divine providence.

The attempt to place Jacob's dream of the flocks within its narrative context reveals the extent to which its imagery reflects the central role of sheep and shepherding in Jacob's life. Jacob earns his wives, the acquisition of whom is clearly crucial to Isaac's parting blessing, by

47. Westermann, for instance, in *Genesis 12–36*, p. 480, sees 30.25-43 as the product of one narrative source supplemented by expansions. Unlike von Rad (*Genesis*, p. 305), who divides the narrative between E and J, Westermann is unwilling to specify the origin of the expansions.

48. See, for instance, von Rad, *Genesis*, p. 353.

49. E.L. Greenstein, 'An Equivocal Reading of the Sale of Joseph', in K. Gros Louis (ed.), *Literary Interpretations of Biblical Narratives*, II (Nashville, TN: Abingdon Press, 1982), pp. 114-25: 'By blurring the human factors leading to the enslavement of Joseph, the narrative sharpens our image of the divine factor in bringing it about' (p. 123).

shepherding, and his dealings with the flocks allow him to contemplate a reconciliation with Esau and return to his native land. Far from being a simple vehicle for divine advice regarding shepherd-craft, it is the means by which God conveys the extent of his involvement in Jacob's life, and, inseparably from the acquisition of wives and wealth, God uses the flocks as a means of fulfilling Jacob's vow (28.20-22).

The analysis offered here has endeavoured to account for some of the narrative and linguistic peculiarities of the dream of the flocks, suggesting ways in which they may enhance our understanding of a mysterious episode of the patriarchal traditions. In particular, the dream's rhetorical value has been emphasized, and this suggests that it belongs not, as Ehrlich claimed, to the class of occupation dreams, but rather to that ancient Near Eastern tradition of dreams whose purpose was to validate the claims and confirm the position of their (usually royal) dreamers.

These conclusions fit well with the preceding chapter's interpretation of the dream at Bethel, and the following chapter will attempt to show how Laban's dream confirms the picture which has emerged here of the special role played by dreams in Jacob's life. In the meantime, I will conclude this chapter with a summary of the six themes I have traced through the Genesis dream reports and their application to Jacob's dream of the flocks.

(1) *The dream is received at during a period of anxiety or danger.*
     It occurs at a time of hostile relations between Jacob and Laban (and Laban's sons) following the patriarch's announcement of his decision to leave Paddan Aram.

(2) *The dream concerns descendants, immediate or eventual.*
     Laban is attempting to prevent Rachel and Leah, along with their children, from leaving with Jacob. The dream is reported to convince the wives that they and their children should accompany their husband. Had they failed to comply, Jacob would have returned to his native land effectively childless.

(3) *The dream signals a change in status.*
     It authorizes Jacob to seek his independence by leaving the house of his father-in-law.

(4) *The dream highlights divine involvement in human affairs.*
     Jacob has been serving Laban in Paddan Aram, and seems to have engaged in some form of trickery involving the sheep. The dream confirms that God and not Laban has been his

master, and that his material prosperity was actually the result of divine protection.

(5) *The dream concerns the relationship between Israelites and non-Israelites.*
     It effects an important change, brought about by God's involvement, in the relationship between Jacob and his non-Israelite father-in-law.

(6) *The dream deals with absence from the land.*
     It signals the end of Jacob's exile in Paddan Aram.

Chapter 4

LABAN'S DREAM
(GENESIS 31.24)

Genesis 28.10-22 and 31.10-13 report a pair of dreams, containing God's promise of protection and the subsequent confirmation that he has kept his word, which frame the period of Jacob's service to Laban. These two texts alone offer evidence enough of the special role played by dreams in the life of the patriarch, especially in relation to that part of his life spent in exile in the house of his father-in-law. Yet to Gen. 28.10-22 and 31.10-13 we may add 31.24, the account of a divine dream received by Laban as he pursues Jacob in search of the stolen teraphim. This chapter will attempt to show how Laban's dream, understood in its ancient Near Eastern context, emphasizes the special role of dreams in Jacob's life. It will examine insights into the Israelite attitude towards dreams that may be gleaned from the divine dream of Jacob's Aramean employer and adversary. In particular, some observations will be made about the relationship between dreams and divination, and about the suitability of dreams as a vehicle of revelation for both Israelites and non-Israelites.

Laban's dream is often described as a 'warning' dream.[1] This is a familiar class in the ancient Near East, and is usually included in the broader category of 'message' dreams.[2] Under this latter heading,

1. See, for instance, Ehrlich, *Der Traum im Alten Testament*, p. 131.
2. E.R. Dodds, *The Greeks and the Irrational* (Berkeley: University of California Press, 1984 [1951]) describes the three types of dreams 'in a classification which is transmitted by Artemidorus, Macrobius and other late writers, but whose origin may lie much further back' (p. 107). The categories of 'symbolic' and 'vision' (prophetic) dreams are followed by the *chrematismos* or 'oracle', which occurs when a god or significant person reveals what should or should not be done. Dodds observes that dreams of this sort were common in the ancient world, and feature under different names in other systems: 'Chalcidius... calls such a dream an

Oppenheim describes several dreams whose clear intent is to recommend a course of action, usually involving service to the god responsible for sending the dream, which will divert illness or danger.[3] An interesting example is the dream sent by Ishtar to the father of prince Hattusilis, warning him that the prince is not in good health, and that he should dedicate his son to the service of the goddess. The dream implies that service to Ishtar will cure the prince's ill-health. Ishtar does not appear directly in the dream, however, but sends Hattusilis's brother, Muwatalli, to speak on her behalf.[4] In another 'message' dream report, found in a letter from Mari, the god Dagan appears to a minor provincial functionary, promising that the sheiks of the Benjamin-tribes will be delivered into the hands of Zimri-Lim on condition that the king sends messengers with 'full reports' for the god.[5] The dream is subsequently reported to the king by a member of his court, who apologizes for not having brought the dreamer, or the usual personal token of a lock of his hair and a fringe of his clothing, as witness to the veracity of the dream.

Although not all message dreams are, strictly speaking, warning dreams (those conveying divine approval of plans for a temple, for instance, or recommending cures for infertility), there is a sense in which all divinely sent message dreams contain an implicit warning. Ignoring the advice of the gods is unlikely to bode well in any circumstances, and this explains the urgent quest for interpretation that is often undertaken by dreamers of opaque symbolic dreams. The Talmud draws a pertinent analogy between an uninterpreted dream and an unopened letter.[6] If the unopened letter contains divine instructions that its recipient is thus unable to execute, the consequences are likely to

"admonitio," "when we are directed and admonished by the counsels of angelic goodness" ' (p. 107).

3.   See 'The Interpretation of Dreams', pp. 197-206 (on message dreams).

4.   'The Interpretation of Dreams', pp. 198-99. Oppenheim observes that this dream 'constitutes an example of the appearance of a person still living in a dream to which there are no parallels in the Semitic or ancient Near East' (p. 198).

5.   Oppenheim, 'The Interpretation of Dreams', perceives here political undertones pertaining to a particular sanctuary: 'The receiving of such royal reports on battles was obviously considered the special privilege of a sanctuary and had as such most likely political implications. It seems that we have here an attempt of the priesthood of the sanctuary of Dagan in Terqa to gain or to regain prestige by having the god receive such dream messages from the king of Mari' (p. 195).

6.   *b. Ber.* 55b-57b.

include a double-headed threat of indirect suffering and direct punishment. Thus the urgency with which Pharaoh sought the interpretation of his dreams (Gen. 41.8) was almost certainly prompted, on the one hand, by fear of what would happen if God's warning went unheeded (starvation throughout Egypt), and, on the other, by dread of retribution for ignoring a divine message. It is not difficult to see why the two message dreams described above should also be regarded as warning dreams. Each contains a constructive message which is offered without apparent threat to the dreamer, but the other side of the coin is that, should the messages be ignored, the consequences may be dire: Hattusilis will not recover, and, at best, the battle between Zimri-Lim and the Benjamin-tribes will continue to rage.

In neither of the two reports cited by Oppenheim is the dream received by the person whom it most directly concerns. In the former case, this is not entirely surprising. Although Hattusilis's health was at stake, it was for his father to dedicate him to the service of the goddess. What is surprising, though, is that Ishtar's message was voiced by Hattusilis's brother; she did speak directly to the king. Likewise, Dagan did not appear directly to Zimri-Lim, but sent his message through a minor functionary in a neighbouring province. In view of the established tradition of royal dreaming in the ancient world, one might have expected these kings to receive their own message dreams.[7] Oppenheim, noting especially the official's need to vouch for the trustworthy character of the dreamer, observes that this dream report is atypical, and speculates that it may have been 'based on an actual visionary experience which the person who was so privileged saw fit to report to the officials as a dream'.[8] Ancient Near Eastern politics aside, however, the dreams

7.   Dodds, *The Greeks and the Irrational*, emphasizes the association of divine message dreams (*chrematismos*) with royal dreamers: 'Such dreams played an important part in the life of other ancient peoples, as they do in that of many races today. Most of the dreams recorded in ancient Assyrian, Hittite, and ancient Egyptian literature are "divine dreams" in which a god appears and delivers a plain message to the sleeper, sometimes predicting the future, sometimes demanding cult. As we should expect in monarchical societies, the privileged dreamers are usually kings (an idea which appears also in the *Iliad*); commoners had to be content with the ordinary symbolic dream which they interpreted with the help of dreambooks' (p. 109).

8.   'The Interpretation of Dreams', p. 195. He further speculates that the decision to represent the incident as a dream may reflect a leaning towards Babylon, where dreams were favoured, in some spheres of Mari society.

concerning Hattusilis and Zimri-Lim indicate that the sending and
receiving of message dreams in the ancient world was not entirely
straightforward; the message was not always delivered personally by its
sender, and nor was it necessarily received by the person to whom it
pertained. More specifically, one might infer from these dreams that the
ancient Near East made no proper distinction between a dream dreamt
by a king and a dream dreamt by someone else about him.[9]

Of particular relevance to the discussion of dreaming versus being
dreamt about is Oppenheim's description of a dream and a 'nocturnal
vision' experienced in the same night by an Assyrian priest. Both concern a meeting between Ishtar and Assurbanipal, during which the
goddess promises to protect the king during battle. Oppenheim, following the remarks of Dodds on a similar report from the late Alexandrian
period, links the two events together, and concludes:

> ... what the king experienced and what the priest 'witnessed' in a dream
> seem to have been caused by one and the same act of divine intervention
> ... Stylistically, the reported vision presents itself as a 'message' dream
> of the king, conceived as an objective event and witnessed as such by a
> third person.[10]

Although the dreams in question are symbolic, and the circumstances
different in other ways, it seems possible that a similar idea underlies
the duplication of dreams in the Joseph narrative (cf. Gen. 37.5-11,
40.9-23, 41.1-8). At any rate, it is clear that the ancient Near Eastern
view of through whom and on whose behalf a dream message would be
transmitted is sometimes rather complicated.

It is particularly important to bear in mind this complexity when
analysing Laban's dream in Gen. 31.24. Taken at face value, God's

---

9. J. Sasson, 'Mari Dreams', *JAOS* 103 (1983), pp. 283-93, cites a letter sent
to Addu-duri, a court inhabitant, by Timlû, a social dependent, in which the latter
claims to have a dream on behalf of the former. Sasson concludes from this and
other similar cases that certain individuals may even have been commissioned to
receive dreams on behalf of others (p. 284). *t. Ber.* 55b-57b, likewise makes no real
distinction between a dream received first-hand by x and a dream received by a
third party about x. In this and other respects it may well reflect ancient beliefs
about dreaming. P.S. Alexander, 'Bavli Berakhot 55a-57b: The Talmudic Dreambook in Context', *JJS* 46 (1995), pp. 230-48, maintains that 'the rabbinic
Dreambook fits easily into the pattern of ancient dreambooks' (p. 241), and that it
'simply represents a Jewish version of a system of dream-interpretation widespread
in antiquity' (p. 243).

10. 'The Interpretation of Dreams', p. 201.

warning appears to be directed at Laban, and we may assume that he will not fare well if he ignores it. This is emphasized by the use of the phrase הִשָּׁמֶר לְךָ (take heed), which introduces cautionary statements in the Bible, and usually makes an explicit link between the person being addressed and the content of the warning. Yet the narrator of this story has little interest in Laban or what befalls him, and although failure to heed the dream's message may have been disadvantageous for the dreamer, there is no doubt that Jacob is its intended beneficiary.

Laban's dream contains a type of ambiguity that did not exist in the dreams concerning Hattusilis and Zimri-Lim. In those cases, the interests of the dreamer were identical to, or at least consistent with, the interests of the person to whom the dream pertained. Thus, Hattusilis's health was, in some respects, as important to Hattusilis's father as to the prince himself, and we may assume that the interests of Zimri-Lim's subjects were in line with those of the king.[11] With regard to Laban's dream, an additional complication arises from the fact that, at this point in the narrative, the interests of Laban and Jacob are diametrically opposed. While this does not mean that it cannot be classified as a warning dream, it appears to demand a sub-category in which the dreamer is not a direct beneficiary of the warning dream. This distinction, although subtle, is crucial to a proper analysis of Laban's dream.

A helpful analogy may be found in Judg. 7.13-14, which also reports a dream sent by God to a non-Israelite who does not benefit from it. Here, a Midianite dreamer receives a symbolic dream immediately prior to Gideon's attack on the Midianite camp, and the text reports his recounting of the dream to a friend, followed by the friend's interpretation: Gideon, on God's advice, is conveniently placed to hear both the report and its interpretation and, as God has promised, this instills in him the courage to invade the camp. Although both dreamer and interpreter are Midianites, it is inconceivable that they were the intended beneficiaries of this dream. God did not send the dream to forewarn Midian, so that they could either prepare themselves more effectively for Gideon's imminent attack or else flee from its consequences. On the contrary, God sent the dream for the sole purpose of inspiring Gideon

11. The extent to which the interests of king and people coincided in the ancient world is emphasized repeatedly by Frankfort, *Kingship and the Gods*, but see especially his chapter on government (pp. 251-61).

to attack the camp, and, as far as the Midianites are concerned, defeat is a foregone conclusion.[12]

The Midianite has a dream which, although it pertains to him, he is not expected to act upon, and in this respect it must be distinguished from Laban's dream. Laban's dream does not simply contain information, it contains an instruction that he was presumably supposed to follow. Yet in both cases God sends a dream to a non-Israelite where a dream to an Israelite, or some other form of intervention, would have sufficed. This raises the question of why God did not intervene more directly to inspire Gideon and protect Jacob, which in turn raises questions about the biblical perception of the role played by non-Israelites in Israel's divinely managed history, and about the universalist possibilities of dreams as vehicles of revelation. Not surprisingly, these issues also arise in connection with Abimelech's dream in Gen. 20.1-18, and for this reason it may be helpful to examine some parallels between these two dream reports.

The Dreams of Laban and Abimelech

Genesis contains five dream reports other than Laban's in which God sends a dream to a non-Israelite, but Abimelech's dream in 20.1-18 clearly represents the closest parallel.[13] With regard to textual interpretation, Abimelech's dream report has two important advantages over Laban's. First, it is the focal point of a longer and more detailed narrative (Laban's dream is reported without comment or explanation), and, secondly, it is part of a trio of texts (with Gen. 12.10-20 and 26.1-12)

---

12. McAlpine, *Sleep, Divine and Human*, regards this dream, together with Joseph's dreams and Jacob's dream at Bethel, as evidence for the ironic use of dreams in biblical narrative: 'Of course, vulnerability in general is a concern often addressed in dreams, but at least in the Old Testament the treatment of dreams in situations of vulnerability is often heavily ironic. Joseph dreams of ruling his brothers in the same chapter in which he is sold into slavery (Gen. 37). A Midianite soldier is given a dream portending defeat for the benefit of his eavesdropping opponent (Judg. 7)' (pp. 229-30). It cannot be assumed, however, that the irony perceived by McAlpine here was intentional, and one might well favour a reading that focuses on divine intervention against all odds.

13. The others are received by Pharaoh's butler and baker (40.1-19), and by Pharaoh himself (41.1-8). In these cases, however, the parallels are less interesting: the dreams are symbolic and the dreamers are not in an adversarial relationship with the real beneficiary of their dreams (Joseph).

which offer interesting opportunities for intertextual analysis. It is thus reasonable to hope that Abimelech's dream might help to illuminate the rather obscure report of Laban's.

Like Laban's dream, Abimelech's is a warning dream, but here the issues of precisely who stands to benefit from it, and how, are at once more clear-cut and more complex. On the one hand, Abimelech is a beneficiary of the dream in so far as ignoring its warning would result in his death and the termination of his line. Yet, on the other hand, there can be little doubt that Abraham is the dream's true beneficiary, and that it is on his account that God has intervened. We may wish to claim that Laban, as one who is blessed because of Jacob (cf. 30.27), has a vested interest in his son-in-law's welfare, and thus benefits from a dream advising him against harassing the source of his blessing. Yet this would be a rather contorted reading, and, in any case, Abimelech stands to benefit from both Abraham and Isaac in a similar manner (cf. 26.28).

There are several obvious parallels between the figures of Abimelech and Laban. Both are non-Israelites upon whom a patriarch is temporarily in a position of apparent dependence, and in each case the benefactor turns out to constitute a threat to the continuation of the patriarch's line, Abimelech by taking Sarah as a wife (20.2), and Laban by suggesting that Jacob's wives and children belong to him (cf. 31.43). In each case the matter is resolved only after divine intervention in the form of a dream received by the non-Israelite. It is important to note, however, that the dreams do not contain the solution to the problems, which must be worked out between the patriarch and the non-Israelite. Rather, they pave the way for the peace process that concludes in each episode with a covenant between non-Israelite and patriarch.

An interesting link of a rather different kind concerns the sense in which both Abimelech and Laban span two generations of patriarchs. Abraham and Isaac are involved in similar altercations in Gerar with a king Abimelech, who may or may not be the same man but who certainly fulfils an identical role in the two texts, while Laban first appears as Isaac's potential brother-in-law before being cast in his more memorable role as Jacob's father-in-law. I suggested in the chapter dealing with Abimelech's dream that the wife-sister texts serve to illustrate a development from 12.10-20, where divinely sent plagues are the drastic solution to the difficulties arising between Pharaoh and Abraham, to 26.1-11, where Isaac and Abimelech manage to resolve their problems

without obvious divine intervention or loss of life. Abimelech's dream
in ch. 20, it was argued, provides the blueprint for the relationship
between Israelite and non-Israelite that is eventually realised in ch. 26.
This sense of progression is heightened by the fact that it spans two
generations of patriarchs. Assuming that the wife-sister texts do, indeed, contain the notion of development, and in view of the parallels
between Laban and Abimelech noted above, it seems reasonable to
investigate the possibility that the Laban narrative is similarly motivated by a sense of progression. This requires a brief backward glance
to ch. 24.

Laban's Room for Improvement

Having convinced himself beyond all reasonable doubt that Rebekah is
an appropriate match for Isaac, Abraham's servant proceeds to seek the
approval of Laban and Bethuel. This is an important scene, and Laban's
appearance in it is by no means to be taken for granted. First of all, as
far as familial approval is concerned, Laban was entirely dispensable:
since Rebekah's father was still alive, it was up to him to approve
or disapprove the match. According to Speiser, however, Bethuel was
not alive at this point; his name was either inserted into the narrative
(24.50) by 'some ancient scribe who did not realize that the father had
no place in this narrative', or perhaps appeared as a result of a mis-
reading of the consonants בן בתואל (son of Bethuel).[14] Character-
istically, Speiser also offers a Hurrian parallel to explain the emphasis
on Laban, the surviving older-brother.[15] Yet, awkward as the pairing of
the names of Laban and Bethuel does, indeed, sound, Speiser's theories
fail to account for 25.20, where the pattern is repeated:

14. *Genesis*: '*and Bethuel*. As was pointed out in the NOTE on vs. 28, this
cannot be original. The consonants *wbtw'l* could represent an earlier *bn btw'l* "son
of Bethuel", less probably *wbytw* "and his family." Better still, we may have a mar-
ginal gloss on the part of some ancient scribe who did not realize that the father had
no place in this narrative' (pp. 181-82). Speiser should perhaps have added that the
plural form ויאמרו (and they said) must also have been inserted at some point.
15. *Genesis*: '*in her mother's house*. This phrase can only mean that Bethuel
was no longer alive; hence the immediate reference to Rebekah's brother (29),
whose authority in such circumstances would be an overriding factor in any Hurrian
or Hurrianized society; note the order "her brother and her mother" in 53, 55, and
even "Laban and Bethuel" in 50, where the second personal name is certainly
intrusive for that very reason' (p. 181).

ויהי יצחק בן ארבעים שנה בקחתו את רבקה בת בתואל הוארמי מפדן ארם
אחות לבן הארמי לו לאשה:

Isaac was forty years old when he took to wife Rebekah, daughter of
Bethuel the Aramean of Paddan-aram, sister of Laban the Aramean.

The fact that both father and brother are mentioned here does not prove
that Bethuel was still alive, but it does make it somewhat unlikely that
the appearance of his name in 24.50 was the work of an over-zealous
scribe. At any rate, Bethuel's death is not reported, and Speiser is keen
to infer it primarily in order to make sense of the prominence accorded
to Laban here. A more plausible reading of this narrative might work
from the other direction, assuming that Laban's prominence was determined by the need to give Laban a history against which background
his transformation could occur, and that Bethuel's name was inserted
simply because the narrative was unrealistic without him.[16]

The second, and more important, reason why Laban's approval of the
match was superfluous is because the text has established beyond question that God has confirmed Rebekah's suitability, in which case the
interests of her family are barely worthy of consideration. Twice we
hear the servant's compelling evidence of God's approval of this match,
and, in fact, Laban's response, made in 24.50, in unison with Bethuel,
is uncharacteristically appropriate:

ויען לבן ובתואל ויאמרו מיהוה יצא הדבר לא נוכל דבר אליך רע או טוב:

Then Laban and Bethuel answered, 'The matter was decreed by the
LORD; we cannot speak to you bad or good.'

Since God has made this match, their thoughts, whether positive or negative, are beside the point. Predictably, however, matters are more complicated than they appear.

In a discussion in the preceding chapter on patterns in biblical narrative, it was suggested that dreamers and those to whom dreams are
subsequently reported usually respond appropriately, and that the narrator encourages us to have confidence in their responses. Concerning
Laban, the opposite is true. A brief analysis of his words and actions
reveals that he responds inappropriately in every situation, and that the
truth usually lies at the far extreme from his own version of it.

---

16. Although not making precisely this point, Gunkel, *Genesis* (Gottingen:
Vandenhoeck & Ruprecht, 1966 [1901]), p. 323, emphasizes the parallels between
the two episodes.

In Laban's exaggerated welcome to Abraham's servant (24.29-31), he is only a little less subtle than the miser in a Jonsonian comedy. Our crucial first impression is of Laban hurrying to greet the servant:

ולרבקה אח ושמו לבן וירץ לבן אל האיש החוצה אל העין:

Now Rebekah had a brother whose name was Laban. Laban ran out to the man at the spring (24.29).

In a text that has already developed the theme of hospitality (cf. 24.17-20), the use of 'and [Laban] ran' (וירץ) here rings a loud bell, and we are reminded of Abraham hurrying to greet the angels in 18.2. All the ruder, then, is our awakening when (24.30) we discover what it is that has caught Laban's eye:

ויהי כראת את הנזם ואת הצמדים על ידי אחתו ...

... when he saw the nose-rings and bands on his sister's arms ...

There can be little doubt that his blustering enthusiasm, highlighted (v. 31) by such hail-fellow-well-met phrases as 'come, O blessed of the LORD' (בוא ברוך יהוה) and 'why do you remain outside ...' (למה תעמד בחוץ) is a parody of his sister's kindness to strangers.

Laban's response to Abraham's servant is our forewarning, and it should be no surprise when his seemingly modest refusal in 24.50 to comment upon what God has decreed turns out to be utterly misleading. Laban's words convey a *laissez-faire* attitude that is far from consistent with his almost immediate attempt (v. 55) to influence Rebekah to delay her journey:

ויאמר אחיה ואמה תשב הנער אתנו ימים או עשור אחר תלך:

But her brother and her mother said, 'Let the maiden remain with us some days; then you may go.'

(Once again, Laban is mysteriously unable to speak without the support of one of his parents.) While it is possible that Laban's stalling tactics are reported as evidence of his mercenary nature (he hoped, perhaps, to improve the terms of his sister's dowry), it seems more likely that they illustrate Laban's propensity to go back on his word, in contrast, of course, with his sister's admirable consistency. At any rate, it is clear that Laban's claim regarding the futility of his commenting upon what God has brought about was not spoken from his heart.

In ch. 24, then, Laban plays a prominent role in a narrative that does not demand his presence, and what we learn of him there is both revealing of his character and utterly consistent with the picture that is built up in his subsequent dealings with Jacob. His eventual willingness to give to his son-in-law what rightfully belongs to him, and to make a covenant precluding future false dealings on both sides, is all the more striking against the background of a long history of insincerity. These factors, in combination with the striking similarity between Laban's words to Abraham's servant in 24.50 and God's message to Laban in 31.24, suggest that it is worth analysing the former in the hope that they shed light on the latter.

Fokkelman has written elaborately on the similarity of these two verses, seeing 31.24 as a deliberate echo of 24.50:

> The connection with Gen. 24 has been made explicitly, perhaps, but in any case it is revealing in the words of v. 24 where God warns Laban that he must not 'say a word to Jacob, either good or bad'. When Abraham's servant has shown by his story (24.10-49) how Providence had brought him into contact with Rebekah and when he expressed the wish to leave with her, Laban and his people reacted adequately with: 'This comes from Yahweh! We cannot speak to you "bad or good"'. This was a set phrase expressing the idea, it is not for us to be the judge of this, God has arranged this affair. What Laban saw in Gen. 24 willingly and of his own accord, must now be impressed upon him threateningly by God.[17]

Certainly, the repetition of this uncommon phrase concerning good and evil cannot be dismissed as mere coincidence, yet Fokkelman's account of the narrative's intentions here fails to convince. Given that Laban was almost certainly speaking insincerely in 24.50, it is unlikely that the dream message is a reminder of the time when he had assessed the situation correctly. Neither is it plausible that the repetition is intended to confirm the futility of human interference in divine affairs: Laban's experience with the marriage of Isaac and Rebekah has clearly failed to teach him this general lesson. This leaves the possibility that the narrator was primarily interested in forging a link between these two episodes, and that the importance of making the connection exceeded the weight attached to the sincerity of the words on the first occasion.

Although what follows may sound suspiciously like a circular argument, the very impenetrability of the dream message indicates that its meaning was not of paramount importance. Laban's dream is, as noted above, usually classified as a warning dream, and our attention is drawn to its cautionary element by the use of the stock expression 'take heed'

---

17. *Narrative Art in Genesis*, p. 165.

(הִשָּׁמֶר לְךָ). Elsewhere in the Bible, these words usually preface a clear-cut proscription.[18] In Gen. 24.6, for instance, Abraham warns the servant that he must not take Isaac back to the land of his father's birth, and Deut. 6.12 warns Israel against forgetting the source of her salvation. These are typical of statements usually introduced by 'take heed', which makes it all the more surprising to encounter a similarly prefaced warning—issued, moreover, by God in response to a patriarchal crisis—that fails to establish precisely what is being proscribed.

At first glance it is tempting to assume that the meaning of God's warning here is self-evident: Laban is simply being cautioned against saying anything whatsoever to Jacob. As several commentators have noted, however, this interpretation is worrying, partly because Laban's subsequent behaviour constitutes blatant disobedience in the face of a divine order,[19] but mainly because, in the circumstances, it is not a sensible request to make. Alternatively, God may be warning Laban that he should not even speak to Jacob, much less do him physical harm, which fits well with the use of the phrase מִטּוֹב עַד רָע (from good to bad) to imply the full range of possibilities.

S. Sherwood, in his monograph on the Laban/Jacob narrative, presents several interpretations of 31.24.[20] Most pertinently, perhaps, he cites P. Bovati, who draws comparisons with the legalistic use of this phrase in 2 Sam. 14.17, 1 Kgs 3.9 and Isa. 5.20. On this reading, Laban is prohibited both from passing sentence on Jacob and from implementing it. Yet Sherwood makes little attempt to reconcile the legal connotations which he, following Bovati, perceives here with the fact that it includes an almost word-for-word repetition of 24.50. Of this connection he states only:

> Besides its forensic background, the expression *dbr mtwb 'd r'* echoes 24.50, in which it means that individuals can do nothing to alter what is manifestly God's will. Now Laban learns that God's will is that Jacob not be proceeded against.[21]

18. M. Weiss, 'The Contribution of Literary Theory to Biblical Research Illustrated by the Problem of She'ar-Yashub', in S. Japhet (ed.), *Studies in the Bible* (Scripta Hierosolymitana, 31; Jerusalem: Magnes Press, 1986), pp. 373-86, observes that the word הִשָּׁמֶר (take heed) occurs 16 times in the Bible, and only in Isa. 7.4 is the nature of what is being warned against left unstated (p. 380).

19. See Speiser, *Genesis*, p. 246.

20. *Had God not Been on My Side*, pp. 315-16.

21. Sherwood, *Had God not Been on My Side*, p. 315.

Previously, however, Sherwood has concurred with Speiser's objection to the translation 'dispute with, argue' for דבר here because, although Laban acknowledges God's warning, he ignores it. In view of this, one would have expected Sherwood to raise the same objection here; this is, after all, the second time that Laban has appeared to acknowledge that 'individuals can do nothing to alter what is manifestly God's will', and the second time that he has acted as if this were not the case. Given the unlikelihood of the narrator's reporting, without irony, Laban's acknowledgment of this truth, only to have him act against it, the notion that the link between 24.50 and 31.24 concerns God's will is, to say the least, problematic.

It thus remains difficult to avoid the thought that words that made sense in their original context (24.50) have been repotted in 31.24 with scant regard for the suitability of the conditions. Assuming that the phrase 'from good to bad' (מטוב עד רע) is an idiom of one sort or another, it is quite at home as part of Laban's response to the servant's idiomatically phrased request in 24.49 for the approval of Rebekah's family:

ועתה אם ישכם עשׂים חסד ואמת את אדני הגידו לי ואם לא הגידו לי
ואפנה על ימין או על שׂמאל:

And now, if you mean to treat my master with true kindness, tell me; and if not, tell me also, that I may turn right or left.

The use of חסד ואמת (true kindness) suggests, in this context, a certain cliched formality that does not belong here, while the phrase ואפנה על ימין וא על שׂמאל (that I may turn right or left) is clearly idiomatic. The servant gets what he deserves when Laban responds in kind with another stock expression:

...לא נוכל דבר אליך רע או טוב

… we cannnot speak to you good or bad (24.50).

Laban's words here, like his hearty welcome to the servant (24.31), only underline his insincerity in uttering them. His cliches mean little or nothing, which is precisely what we learn to expect of him (cf., for instance, his lavish but empty 'name your price' in 30.28). Coming from God, on the other hand, particularly in the context of a serious message dream, this idiomatic language sounds rather less appropriate. Furthermore, it should be noted that whereas the prohibition against speech (לא דבר) makes little sense in 31.24, the verb דבר (speak) fits perfectly in 24.50, in response to the servant's request for Laban's verbal commitment, הגידו לי (tell me). Once again, this supports the theory that 31.24 is primarily intended as a reminder of 24.50, and that the evocation of the earlier use was more important than its meaning. Yet this brings us back to the question of the narrator's intentions in making this connection. In an attempt to answer this question, it will be argued below that the evocation of ch. 24 is designed to emphasize Laban's foreignness, and that it is no coincidence that this occurs in the form of a dream.

Laban the Foreigner

Westermann makes the following observation about Laban's dream:

> V. 24 belongs neither in language nor in content to this event. The news that Laban gets is cited literally: ברח יעקב [Jacob has flown]. When Laban takes 'his brethren' in pursuit with him, the narrator is again drawing attention to Laban's superiority, as happens continually throughout the narrative. It is the superiority in power which has occasioned the addition in v. 24, carried on in v. 29. It is a theologizing addition which uses the opportunity to contrast Laban's superiority with God's protecting hand which is Jacob's guarantee (Cf. 1 Sam. 17). Vv. 24 and 29 have no real function in the narrative, which is more tightly knit and clearer without them.[22]

Westermann's exegesis is troubling; he describes the dream as a 'theologizing addition' concerned with contrasting God and Laban, but claims that it has 'no real function in the narrative'. One might, of course, construe this as a claim that the dream has a function that it does not properly fulfil, but, even then, something seems to be missing. The idea of a narrative contrast between Laban and God is, however, important, and, when pursued further, it reveals Laban's dream as being far from superfluous.

As mentioned above, the notion of a contrast between God and a non-Israelite figure of authority also features in the report of Abimelech's dream, and in both cases the narrative is exploring the three-way relationship between the patriarch, a seemingly superior foreign power and God. In both contexts, the foreignness of the apparently superior power is crucial, and it is interesting to compare the formal introductions of the two dreams in this regard. Genesis 20.2 describes Abimelech as king of Gerar, and 20.3 reports that God *came* to him in a dream *by*

22. *Genesis 12–36*, p. 494.

night, while 31.24 announces that God *came* to Laban the Aramean in a dream *by night*. The Midrash claims that this expression is reserved for revelations to non-Israelites,[23] and, indeed, it occurs only in these instances and in Num. 22.9, 20. Since Laban has been mentioned on numerous occasions by this time, the use of the title 'Laban the Aramean' in this context merits consideration. Nachmanides sees this as an allusion to Laban's foreignness and his use of teraphim,[24] and it is difficult to dismiss this as a rabbinic anachronism. On the other hand, the formal appellation may represent an addition to the narrative which, together with a similar reference in 25.20, was inserted at a time when Laban's name and place of birth had become inextricably linked. Genesis 25 contains several suggestions of an exilic redaction,[25] which may indicate an exilic origin for the title 'Laban the Aramean'. This is compatible with the exilic or even post-exilic setting envisaged by recent scholars for the dream of the flocks;[26] it seems likely that both dreams entered the narrative at the same time. It is clear that the story of Jacob's period of service in the house of a foreign master would have resonated in interesting ways for exilic readers of the Genesis narratives. Only one of these issues will be pursued here, however, and this arises from a question that demands an answer regardless of the historical background envisaged for the text. How did the narrator understand the relationships between Laban and God and Laban's other gods?

Genesis 20 leaves no doubt that Abimelech was a God-fearer; Abraham's claim that he expected to find no fear of God in Gerar (v. 11) makes sense only if he was wrong. Yet although we hear nothing of Abimelech's own gods, and although his response to Abraham and his God is not readily distinguishable from that of an Israelite in a similar situation, we know that the king of Gerar must be a pagan. Laban's position is more complicated still. We know that he owns teraphim, and we can be fairly sure that he divines, but, at least at first glance, we have relatively little information about the compatibility of dreams from God with divination or other forms of pagan worship.

---

23. *GR, ad loc.*

24. *MG, ad loc.*

25. The identification of Esau with Edom, for instance, and the use of לאם (people, nation), which appears only here and in Gen. 27.29 in the Pentateuch, but occurs frequently in Deutero-Isaiah.

26. See, for instance, Husser, *Le songe et la parole*, p. 137.

Laban's Other Gods

Much has been written on biblical teraphim, and many scholars have speculated about their nature and their role in the ancient world. Recently they have been associated increasingly with ancestral deities whose functions were mainly domestic,[27] but their use in connection with divination has not been overlooked entirely.[28] Although it seems likely that the teraphim have both a household and a divinatory function in the Jacob/Laban narrative, it is the latter of the two which will be explored in detail here.

27. For a recent treatment see K. van der Toorn, 'The Nature of the Biblical Teraphim in the Light of Cuneiform Evidence', *CBQ* 52 (1990), pp. 203-22. The author concludes that teraphim were probably 'ancestor statuettes' that had acquired a semi-divine status, and were used primarily in a domestic context (p. 215), and compares their presence in Israelite homes to the presence of statues of the saints in Catholic cultures (p. 216). In the context of a less specific discussion of the biblical connection between ancestors and the land, A. Cooper and B. Goldstein, 'The Cult of the Dead and the Theme of Entry into the Land', *BibInt* 1 (1993), pp. 285-303, see the teraphim as Laban's equivalent of Jacob's 'God of your father Abraham, God of Isaac' (אלהי אברהם אביך ואלהי יצחק [Gen. 28.13]). They also attribute to the teraphim the capacity for apotropaic protection, suggesting that דרך נשים may mean 'pregnant' not 'menstruant', and pointing out that 'Rachel dies in childbirth shortly after Jacob has forced his clan to give up their *'elohim* in favour of his' (p. 295). Fishbane, 'Composition and Structure in the Jacob Cycle', offers a literary interpretation of the teraphim that emphasizes their role in conferring blessing: 'During the escape, Rachel counterpoints Laban's deception of Jacob and deceives *her* father by stealing the teraphim. In this theft of the objects of family blessing, Jacob, the trickster, who is also deceitful in this instance against his "brother" Laban (v. 20) has met his match' (pp. 30-31). Greenberg, 'Another Look at Rachel's Theft of the Teraphim', sees them as gods bequeathed to determine who will continue as *paterfamilias*, but claims that possession is not sufficient (p. 242). C. Labuschagne, 'Teraphim: A New Proposal for its Etymology', *VT* 16 (1966), pp. 115-17, sees תרפים (teraphim) as a metathesis of פתרים (petarim), and claims that they were objects used for the interpretation of dreams, and that, being regarded as dangerous, they could not be called by their real name (p. 117).

28. van der Toorn, 'The Nature of Biblical Teraphim', summarizes thus: 'The teraphim are cultic images of—usually—modest proportions, appearing in two capacities. In some texts they are religious items belonging to the household; in other texts they are resorted to for purposes of divination, with nothing suggesting a connection to the domestic realm' (p. 215).

When Jacob tells Laban that he wants to return to his native land with his wives and children and make a home for himself there, Laban responds (30.27) rather strangely:

ויאמר אליו לבן אם נא מצאתי חן בעיניך נחשתי ויברכני יהוה בגללך:

But Laban said to him, 'If you will indulge me, I have learned by divination that the LORD has blessed me on your account'.

Various interpretations of the precise meaning of נחש in this context have been proposed, and Sherwood provides a useful summary.[29] J. Finkelstein, following a suggestion by A. Sperber,[30] rejects the familiar translation of נחשתי as 'I have divined' in favour of 'I have flourished'.[31] Thus 30.27 would read 'And Laban said to him, "I have prospered and the LORD has blessed me on your account" '. Yet this fails to satisfy, partly because it has no obvious biblical parallel,[32] but mainly because comparisons with similar narratives suggest that what belongs here is a verb whose meanings include recognition or discovery, rather than one implying prosperity. In Gen. 26.28, for instance, Abimelech and his officers tell Isaac:

ויאמרו ראו ראינו כי היה יהוה עמך ונאמר תהי נא אלה בינותינו
בינינו ובינך ונכרתה ברית עמך:

And they said, 'We now see plainly that the LORD has been with you, and we thought: Let there be a sworn treaty between our two parties, between you and us. Let us make a pact with you.'

First comes the acknowledgement (we now see plainly) that God has blessed (been with) Isaac, and this is followed by an expression of the desire to derive vicarious benefit from this blessing (let there be a covenant). Genesis 39.3 contains a parallel which is closer still:

וירא אדניו כי יהוה אתו וכל אשר הוא עשה יהוה מצליח בידו:

And his master saw that the LORD was with him and that the LORD lent success to everything he undertook.

Potiphar sees that the LORD is with Joseph, and consequently puts all his affairs into Joseph's hands in order to benefit more fully:

29. *Had God Not Been on my Side*, pp. 213.

30. 'Zu Gen. 30.27b', *OL* 16 (1913), pp. 389-90.

31. 'An Old Babylonian Herding Contract and Genesis 31.38f', in W. Hallo (ed.), *Essays in Memory of E.A. Speiser* (New Haven: American Oriental Society, 1968), pp. 30-36.

32. The use of נחש elsewhere in the Bible will be discussed in more detail below.

ויברך יהוה את בית המצרי בגלל יוסף ויהי ברכת יהוה בכל אשר
יש לו בבית ובשדה:

And the LORD blessed his house for Joseph's sake, so that the blessing
of the LORD was upon everything he owned, in the house and outside
(39.5).[33]

Both texts include an explicit acknowledgment by the non-Israelite
(Abimelech and Potiphar) that God has blessed the Israelite (Isaac and
Joseph), and this is followed by an attempt to capitalize on his good
fortune. If נחשתי is translated 'I have prospered', then this element of
recognition and acknowledgment is missing, and we must assume an
inferential leap by Laban from the objective observation of his own
increased prosperity to the knowledge that God was blessing him because of Jacob. If, on the other hand, it is translated as 'I have divined'
or 'I have learned by divination', then Laban's words to Jacob fit precisely the pattern outlined above: Laban acknowledges that God is
blessing him because of Jacob (נחשתי/I have learned by divination), and
attempts to prolong the blessing (30.28): 'Name the wages due from
me, and I will pay you' (נקבה שכרך עלי ואתנה). F. Delitzsch envisages
a progression from divination as a method of inquiring into the future
by magic to a general 'perceive' or 'remark'.[34] Once again, however,
the absence of a clear biblical parallel is troubling; elsewhere the verb
occurs in contexts where observation by supernatural means is almost
certainly intended. One might, moreover, have expected a change in the
grammatical structure of the sentence to accommodate a semantic shift
of this sort; if נחשתי means simply 'I have seen', the verb would probably be followed by כי (that), rather than by a new clause with the waw
consecutive. H. Torczyner infers from Num. 24.1 that נחש may mean
the opposite of ברך (bless), namely 'curse'. Thus Laban had previously
been under an evil spell that was lifted when God blessed him on
Jacob's account.[35] Sherwood, however, cites the NRSV as evidence that

33. It should be noted that Joseph's master is called 'the Egyptian', despite the
fact that he has previously been introduced as Potiphar, and that the phraseology is
strikingly similar to Laban's words to Jacob in 30.27, 'and the LORD has blessed
me on your account' (ויברכני יהוה בגללך).

34. *A New Commentary on Genesis* (New York: Charles Scribner's Sons,
1889), p. 181.

35. H. Torczyner, 'Zu נחשתי Gen. 30:27', *OL* 20 (1917), pp. 10-12 (11).

נחש does not necessarily mean 'curse' in Num. 24.1.[36] For his own view, he sees נחש as a straightforward allusion to divination, although he claims that Laban's particular mode of practice may appear unusual to an audience familiar with divination.[37]

Assuming that Sherwood is correct to translate נחשתי as 'I have divined' or 'I have learned by divination', it is appropriate to examine the implications of the allusions to divination in this episode, as well as the narrator's intentions in including them. The most obvious explanation for the references to teraphim and divination is that they were meant to cast Laban in a poor light. This fits well with the subtle but persistent textual denigration of Laban discussed above; from the outset our impression is negative, and his involvement with divination and idol-worship is just another nail in the coffin of his reputation. Yet, consistent as it is in some respects, this reading does not quite add up to the sum of its parts. As far as the teraphim are concerned, Laban is not shown in a particularly poor light by his possession of them. On the contrary, it seems unlikely that Rachel would have taken the trouble to steal them if they were seen as truly worthless objects. Similarly, Laban's claim to have learned by divination is reported without aspersion or even comment, which is particularly surprising in view of the hostility directed towards diviners elsewhere in the Bible. Clearly the narrators did not regard this episode as an opportunity for a polemic against foreign abominations.

Yet, despite the absence of polemics, the references to divination and teraphim in the Laban narrative do contribute significantly to the overall impression of Laban's foreignness. Outside Genesis, the verb invariably occurs in a context that is explicitly non-Israelite. Leviticus 19.26 forbids divining and soothsaying along with a number of other pagan practices. Deuteronomy 18.10, 1 Kgs 21.26, 2 Kgs 17.17 and 2 Chron. 33.6 prohibit divination along with the raising of sacred posts, child-sacrifice and other emphatically non-Israelite rituals, while in Num. 24.1 Balaam's refusal to divine is especially significant following upon

36. 'Now Balaam saw that it pleased the LORD to bless Israel, so he did not go, as at other times, to look for omens, but set his face towards the wilderness'.

37. This claim is based on Finkelstein's observation that divination is usually performed for the purpose of predicting the future rather than explaining the past or present, and on the view of N. Waldman, 'A Note on Gen. 30:27b', *JQR* 55 (1964), pp. 164-65, that 'the verb נחש ... is never followed by a clause indicating the content of the act of divination' (p. 165).

the heels of his claim in 23.23 that there is no augury or divination in Israel. Despite the fact that divination was practised in Israel (by Ahab and Manasseh), it was not explicitly condoned, and the Bible invariably identifies it as a foreign custom. In the light of this brief survey, it seems probable that Laban's admission of having practised divination has some bearing on the perception of his foreignness.

The remaining four of the Bible's 13 uses of נחשׁ appear in Genesis 44, and it is worth examining this text for indications of the verb's precise meaning in the Laban narrative. At first glance, it is tempting to take at face value the claim that Joseph practised divination, but a moment's reflection reveals that it is, in fact, an immensely sophisticated literary ploy. The first hint of this comes from the repeated reference to the cup. Clearly, one mention would have sufficed, and the repetition, in combination with the emphatic נחשׁ ינחשׁ (practises divination) suggests that the narrator sought to draw attention to it. Yet what is the purpose of this emphasis? First of all, the divination cup serves to allay the suspicions of Joseph's brothers; his capacity to divine explains Joseph's knowledge of the cup's whereabouts (assuming, of course, that he had a cup in reserve, or knew some other method of divination). Secondly, the divination cup is a valuable component of Joseph's disguise; it did not occur to the brothers that a practitioner of divination might be related to them. This reading is amply supported by Joseph's own words in 44.15:

ויאמר להם יוסף מה המעשׂה הזה אשר עשׂיתם הלוא ידעתם כי נחשׁ
ינחשׁ אישׁ אשׁר כמני:

> Joseph said to them, 'What is this deed you have done? Do you not know that a man like me practises divination?'

Joseph's playful reference to 'a man like me' is perfect here. A man like him, had he been an Egyptian, would have divined, so he has avoided an outright lie, but the irony is that Joseph knows what he knows precisely because he does not divine; he knows because the LORD is with him.

Here again, divination, comprising part of Joseph's disguise as an Egyptian, is clearly identified with foreignness, but again the narrators pass over in silence another opportunity to condemn a practice that is reviled elsewhere in the Bible. There are various possible explanations for this singularly non-judgmental reporting. One might suggest that, since the references to divination in these two texts amount to little more than plot mechanisms, this was not the place for polemics.

More interestingly, however, one might find in these narratives evidence for a certain kind of historical sensitivity on the part of the narrators which resulted in their avoiding anachronisms when reporting the activities of the patriarchs. This is not to say, of course, that the redactors of Genesis were unaffected by the political climate in which they were working. On the contrary, it seems likely that the Jacob/Laban narrative was adapted to reflect exilic and postexilic concerns. Rather, it appears that the insertion of anachronistic attacks on foreign gods into narratives that lacked a consistent presentation of monotheism was not on their agenda. Indeed, it is precisely this sense of historicity that may account for the addition of dream reports to the Genesis text long after they had been downgraded as vehicles of revelation. We must surely infer from the existence of these narratives that the low regard in which dreams were held in their own time did not discourage these narrators from attributing important dream revelations to the patriarchal figures.

Dreams and Divination

It is difficult to imagine that the redactors of Genesis were unaware of many important differences between their own theological outlook and the outlook implied by the patriarchal narratives.[38] This gives rise to an important question in relation to the matter at hand. Did the authors of Genesis envisage a distinction between dreams and various forms of divination? It seems very likely that both dreams and divination are reported in Genesis by writers who would have found them contemptible in a context contemporary to their own, but can we infer from this that they were seen as having been more or less parallel modes of communication between people and God during the patriarchal period?

---

38. Although W. Moberly, *The Old Testament of the Old Testament: Patriarchal Narratives and Mosaic Yahwism* (Minneapolis: Fortress Press, 1992), defines his central project rather differently ('What is the nature of the relationship between patriarchal religion in Genesis 12–50 and Mosaic Yahwism in Exodus onward?' [p. 105]), he sees as important corollaries such questions as whether the pentateuchal narrators were aware of theological differences in their material, and whether they were capable of 'imaginative consistency' (pp. 84-85). See also G. Wenham, 'The Religion of the Patriarchs', in A.R. Millard and D.J. Wiseman (eds.), *Essays on the Patriarchal Narratives* (Leicester: Inter-Varsity Press, 1980), pp. 157-88.

F. Cryer, in his study of divination in ancient Israel, claims that we can.[39] In his view, dreaming was simply one of many forms of divination in ancient Israel, and the Bible, in contrast to later Jewish exegetes, makes no real distinction between dreams and liver examination or the study of patterns in bird flight. In making these claims, Cryer acknowledges his opposition to many scholars (and to Y. Kaufmann in particular)[40] who emphasize the foreign associations of most types of divination, and especially of divination signified by נחש.[41] What follows will attempt to show that Cryer is wrong on this matter. It should, perhaps, be mentioned at the outset that, in a book on divination in ancient Israel, Cryer mentions Gen. 30.27 and 44.5, 15 only once in passing, despite the fact that they provide five of the Bible's 13 occurrences of the verb נחש. Moreover, there is room to differ with his analysis of the Joseph episode.[42]

The capacity of modern scholars to draw distinctions between dreams and divination does not, of course, have any bearing upon whether or

39. *Divination in Ancient Israel and its Near Eastern Environment: A Socio-Historical Investigation* (JSOTSup, 142; Sheffield: Sheffield Academic Press, 1994).

40. See also A. Guillaume, *Prophecy and Divination among the Hebrews and Other Semites* (London: Hodder and Stoughton, 1938), who observes in the Bible a favourable comparison of dreams and prophecy, and discusses several narratives that confirm trust in dreams (pp. 214-16), but classifies all types of divination used in Israel, other than Urim and Thummim, as a form of lying (pp. 204-205).

41. *Divination in Ancient Israel*: 'As we saw above, Kaufmann is too realistic to invent a pseudo-category for divination so as to differentiate it from magic. Thus, if he wants to insist on the exclusiveness of the specifically Israelite practices (and his work is nothing if not a fine exercise in theological apologetic), he has no alternative but to distinguish sharply between (purportedly foreign) nahash-divination and (avowedly Israelite) ephod and Urim-and-Thummim divination. As we shall see presently, this distinction is both overly artificial and also fails adequately to account for the passages in which Israelites make use of nahash divination' (pp. 233-34). Cryer seems not to acknowledge that when Israelites do make use of nahash-divination, as in 1 Kgs 21.26; 2 Kgs 17.17; 2 Chron. 33.6, it is made clear that they are offending the LORD with their *foreign* abominations.

42. *Divination in Ancient Israel*: 'Accordingly, we should note that Joseph, the paragon of the late collection in Genesis, claims (falsely in this case) to have discovered the "theft" of his divining-cup by divination: "Do you not know that such a man as I can indeed divine?" (Gen. 44:15); and, since, his cup is in his brother's bags, he obviously does not mean them to think that lecanomancy was the means in question available to him in this instance' (p. 285).

not such distinctions were made in ancient Israel. Indeed, it is hard to know what ancient Israelites did believe, since we can be quite sure that the Bible does not contain an accurate reflection of the true state of affairs. We have many texts to illustrate the diverse means by which other ancient Near Eastern cultures contacted their gods, sought approval for human actions, predicted the future and so forth, and the Bible contains only glimpses of practices that are assumed to have been widepread throughout the ancient Near East, ancient Israel included.[43] What is almost beyond doubt, however, is that, with the few exceptions (lots, the ephod and Urim) noted by Kaufmann,[44] biblical references to divination by Israelites are either disguised or openly condemned while this is far from being the case with dream reports. This alone suggests that they were not held in equal esteem in ancient Israel.[45]

In the patriarchal narratives, God's word was accessible to Israelites by a few methods, limited mainly to direct speech, visions and dreams, with the latter accounting for a number of important cases. In later books, dreams are associated with divination, which may be why Cryer classifies them among divination's sub-classes. Plato, in the *Timaeus*, describes the extensive role played by the human intellect in divination, and discredits most divination rituals because they have no place for divine inspiration. According to him, reliable contact with the gods can be achieved only when the human mind is fettered by sleep or madness.[46] One might suggest that the biblical writers shared this point of

---

43. This discrepancy between reality and its biblical representation is a central concern of Robinson, 'Dreams in the Old Testament'.

44. Y. Kaufman, *The Religion of Israel: From its Beginning to the Time of the Babylonian Exile* (trans. and abridged M. Greenberg; Chicago: Schocken Books, 1972 [1960]): 'Dreams, prophets, teraphim and lots are common to Israel and the nations; the ephod and Urim are peculiarly Israelite' (p. 89).

45. V. Hurowitz, 'Eli's Adjuration of Samuel (1 Samuel 3:17-18) in the Light of a "Diviner's Protocol" from Mari (*AEM 1/1, 1*)', *VT* 44 (1994), pp. 483-97, argues: 'The dichotomy between Israelite and Mesopotamian modes of contact with the divine is not as sharp as has often been assumed and as might be implied by biblical prohibitions of divination, prohibitions which explicitly juxtapose divination and prophecy as two contrasting and mutually exclusive alternatives (Deut. 18:9-22)' (p. 495). Indeed, Hurowitz sees in 1 Sam. 3.17-18 an echo of a Mari diviner's oath, used 'to assure full prophetic disclosure of the divine word' (p. 486). The observation that the Bible does not explicitly condone, or even openly discuss, divination rituals practised by Israelites is, however, consistent with Hurowitz's reading of this text.

46. *Plato: Collected Dialogues* (eds. E. Hamilton and H. Cairns; Princeton:

view and, indeed, were motivated by similar concerns about the authenticity of methods of divination that depended so heavily upon human reason. The preference for dreams may have been based on the feeling that they were more reliable because, unlike divination, they were involuntary.[47]

Yet the biblical writers, even if they did favour dreams over divination, did not necessarily see the latter as ineffective. Divination worked even for the God of Israel; Laban divines effectively in 30.27, and Jonah contains a vivid example of successful divination.[48] Thus it appears that certain forms of divination were acceptable in certain circumstances; the sailors need information from God that is provided via lots, and Laban must discover that he is being blessed on account of Jacob, which is effected, at least in the first instance, by divination. In both cases, however, the divination is practised by non-Israelites for the purpose of discovering something that concerns an Israelite, and this suggests that the identity of the practitioner and the nature of his intentions must be considered relevant to the issue.

There is one respect in which Plato's distinction between the role of the human intellect in deciphering God's will by means of messages received in sleep (dreams) as opposed to divination may constitute an over-simplification. This is in the area of interpretation. While it may be the case that the mind is fettered by sleep when the dream occurs, the intellect is not likewise fettered during the waking state in which the dream is interpreted. Since Laban's dream, although somewhat obscure, does not require interpretation, this issue will not be pursued here. It should be noted, however, that the attempts of scholars to distinguish between dreamers of symbolic dreams and dreamers of

Princeton University Press, 1971 [1961]): 'And herein is a proof that God has given the art of divination not to the wisdom, but to the foolishness of man. No man, when in his wits, attains prophetic truth and inspiration, but when he receives the inspired word, either his intelligence is enthralled in sleep, or he is demented by some distemper or possession' (*Timaeus* 71e, p. 1194).

47. Speaking of prophetic visions, Hurowitz, 'Eli's Adjuration of Samuel', argues that, despite the basic contrast between the psychic nature of prophecy and the mechanical nature of divination, 'the two had much in common, both on a conceptual, theological level and on a practical, operative plane' (pp. 494-95). It is possible that dreams were regarded as a form of divination, but were considered acceptable in some circumstances because of their similarity to prophecy.

48. By means of lots, the foreign sailors discover that God is angry with Jonah (Jon. 1.7).

straightforward message dreams are often misleading. Gnuse's claim that symbolic dreams are reserved for non-Israelites,[49] does not take account of Gen. 37.9-10, while it is difficult to reconcile the dreams of Gudea of Lagash and Pharaoh (Gen. 41.1-7) with the class-based distinction envisaged by Cryer:

> ... it is a standard *topos* of ancient Near Eastern dream reports that kings receive clear and unambiguous 'message' dreams while the *hoi polloi* receive dreams which require to be interpreted (ie. symbolic dreams)...[50]

In view of all this it is, perhaps, somewhat surprising to note that in the ancient Near Eastern cultures surrounding Israel, dreams were often held in lower esteem than other forms of divination. Oppenheim attributes this to the belief that they were less easily verified:

> A deep seated distrust of dreams and their messages speaks out of the perpetual desire for confirmation. The objectivity of a 'sign' activated by the god himself is clearly preferred to the subjectivity of the dream experience.[51]

A related objection to dreams concerns their ephemeral quality, and Gnuse suggests that Job 20.8, 'he shall fly away as a dream', may have been inspired by similar criticisms from Egyptian wisdom.[52]

Yet objections of this sort seem to have had surprisingly little influence over the chroniclers of dreams in the ancient world, since dream reports and dream books have been recovered even from societies, such as Assyria,[53] which held dreams in low regard. A possible explanation for this is that although forms of divination such as liver examination and lots may have seemed less ephemeral than dreams in the short run, they were less likely than dreams to survive for posterity. The reporting and recording of dreams is a relatively simple matter, and this, in combination with their literary appeal, made dream reports an attractive tool in the hands of kings and politicians. By contrast, a detailed account of a liver inspection or the casting of lots could hardly

49. *The Dream Theophany of Samuel*: 'symbolic dreams only come to foreigners. Dream interpretation was a magic art never accepted in Israel' (p. 59).

50. *Divination in Ancient Israel*, p. 265.

51. 'The Interpretation of Dreams', pp. 204-205.

52. *The Dream Theophany of Samuel*, p. 34.

53. Gnuse, *The Dream Theophany of Samuel*: 'Oneiromancy was often held in low esteem in Mesopotamia, especially Assyria. Even when dreams were viewed with respect there was some distrust' (p. 33).

command a guarantee of literary immortality and thus, in the long term, divination was more ephemeral than dreams, whose reports, at least, endured in a readable form.[54]

This consideration of the ancient view of the divinatory aspect of dreams, both inside and outside Israel, raises some important points in relation to Laban's dream. First of all, the narrative is not concerned with distinctions between acceptable and unacceptable or effective and ineffective methods of discerning God's will. (It is, however, concerned with Laban's foreignness, and the reference to divination almost certainly reflects this.) Secondly, the Bible regards dreams as vehicles of revelation that did not distinguish between Israelites and non-Israelites. Thirdly, despite concerns about the verifiability of dreams, dream reports were recorded throughout the ancient Near East, which suggests that their veracity was not of the utmost importance.

Dreams and Transformation

The section of this chapter entitled 'Laban's Room for Improvement' explored the possibility that the text attempts to show a transformation in the character of Laban, commencing with his obsequious and self-serving involvement in the betrothal of Isaac and Rebekah (24.29-60), and concluding with his covenant with Jacob (31.44-48). Laban's dream represents the crucial turning-point in this scheme, as is underlined by God's echo of the words that Laban himself uttered insincerely to Isaac in his youth (24.50). Thus, although neither Laban's dream nor his subsequent report of it to Jacob does much to alter the narrative structure, it has, like Abimelech's dream in Genesis 20, effected a significant change of status for both Laban and Jacob, clearing the path for a covenant between them. This is partly because Laban is changed by the dream experience; he may have been able to learn something of God's will by means of divination, but his subsequent actions make it plain

---

54. This contrast is discussed by R. Caillois, 'Logical and Philosophical Problems of the Dream', in G.E. von Grunebaum and R. Caillois (eds.), *The Dream and Human Society* (Berkeley: University of California Press, 1966), pp. 23-51: 'In fact—even though suspect by nature, fleeting, fantastic, and absolutely unverifiable—it [the dream] tends to become institutionalised whenever it contributes to the basis of practical policy, its use regulated, and its area of competency carefully outlined' (p. 31). With regard to a dream of Nabonidus, Caillois observes: 'The most indestructible stone was used to record the most fleeting of visions' (p. 38).

that divination did not teach him reverence. The dream, on the other hand, marks a mile-stone in the development of his character, or at least in our perception of it. It changes him, not immediately but irrevocably, from a seemingly superior figure who persisted in thinking that he could outwit Jacob and benefit from his divine blessing, to a man who acknowledges God's blessing of Jacob and asks to make a covenant with him as, at best, an equal. As with Abimelech, this transformation does not occur miraculously or without further ado, but there can be little doubt that it commences at precisely the point when God comes to Laban the Aramean in a dream by night. More importantly, perhaps, and once again like Abimelech's, Laban's dream also confirms that God is protecting the patriarch. Laban himself is forced to acknowledge this, and his subsequent report of the dream to Jacob (31.29) is one of the means by which the patriarch can witness God's intervention on his behalf.

Most importantly, however, Laban's dream reflects a change in Jacob's status. Had God's dream revelation to Laban been justified on the basis that dreams were an inferior form of revelation, worth little more than divination, and thus appropriate for non-Israelites, then the two dreams received by Jacob himself in the same episode would have been compromised in some way. Yet in the context of an ancient Near Eastern view of dreams in which the person dreamed about may be more significant than the dreamer and messages were not always delivered directly, it is plain that Laban's dream raised Jacob's status as well as his own, working with the dream at Bethel and the dream of the flocks to confirm the patriarch's standing with God.

I will conclude with a summary of themes common to all the dreams of the patriarchal narratives and a brief account of how they are manifested in Laban's dream.

(1) *The dream is received during a period of anxiety or danger.*
     It occurs while Laban is pursuing Jacob, who is thus in danger. Laban could presumably endanger himself by failing to heed God's warning.

(2) *The dream concerns descendants, immediate or eventual.*
     Laban is trying to prevent Jacob from leaving with his wives and children.

(3) *The dream signals a change in status.*
     Laban was previously aware that he had been blessed by God through Jacob, but the dream reveals the full extent of God's

superior power. A covenant between Jacob and Laban is now possible.

(4) *The dream highlights divine involvement in human affairs.*
It confirms God's involvement in what had previously been presented as an ordinary human struggle between Laban and Jacob.

(5) *The dream concerns the relationship between Israelites and non-Israelites.*
It is received by the non-Israelite Laban (whose foreignness is again underlined), revealing the extent of God's protection of Jacob.

(6) *The dream deals with absence from the land.*
It cautions Laban against preventing Jacob's return to his native land.

Chapter 5

THE COVENANT OF THE PIECES
(GENESIS 15.1-21)

Although Genesis 15 describes what is termed and traditionally understood as a vision, the obvious dream-like characteristics of Abraham's
experience have convinced many scholars that it is, in fact, a dream
report.[1] Yet few exegetes, if indeed any, have seen the identification of
the vehicle of revelation as a central issue in the interpretation of this
text. I will argue here that the events associated with what is usually
described as the Covenant of the Pieces must have occurred within the
context of a dream, and that an acknowledgment of this is an essential
precursor to understanding the text. As to why the narrator does not
simply call a spade a spade, I will suggest that, for a variety of reasons
that will emerge during the course of the chapter, it was preferable, and
even necessary, to maintain a level of ambiguity concerning the precise
form of the revelation.

Some Recent Scholarship and its Application to
the Possible Dream Format of Genesis 15

Genesis 15 has inspired a vast canon of scholarly exegesis, of which
space does not permit an adequate summary here.[2] There are, however,

1. See A. Jirku, 'Ein Fall von Inkubation im Alten Testament (Ex. 38:8)', *ZAW*
33 (1913), pp. 151-53 (p. 153); Resch, *Der Traum im Heilsplan Gottes*, p. 63;
Gnuse, *The Dream Theophany of Samuel*, p. 64. J. Lindblom, 'Theophanies in Holy
Places in Hebrew Religion', *HUCA* 32 (1961), pp. 91-106, connects the use of
תרדמה (deep sleep) with dreaming (p. 94), but sees a separate tradition reflected in
vv. 7-11 and 17-18 which does not concern a dream (p. 95).
2. Westermann, *Genesis 12–36*, pp. 209-31, provides a typically thorough
resume of recent scholarship. J. Ha, *Genesis 15: A Theological Compendium of
Pentateuchal History* (BZAW, 181; Berlin: W. de Gruyter, 1989), pp. 33-36, offers
a useful survey of studies that treat Gen. 15 as a literary unity. For a more recent

several works that merit particular attention in this context, and it may be helpful to begin with some brief observations about them and their relationship to each other. R.E. Clements argues for a link between the patriarch and the king and their respective covenants in Genesis 15 and 2 Samuel 7:[3]

> At this point we can consider the importance of the fact that this type of covenant [promissory] is precisely that which we have found to be reflected in Genesis 15 as the original nucleus of the Abrahamic covenant. In view of our argument for the antiquity of this covenant, and in agreement with the close links which bound David to Hebron where the Abrahamic covenant was located, we may reasonably assume that the form of the Davidic covenant was influenced by the recollection in Jerusalem of the ancient covenant with Abraham. This is the position advocated by G.E. Mendenhall, and with it we substantially agree.[4]

M. Weinfeld offers evidence from ancient Near Eastern sources that substantially undermines Clements's position. Weinfeld suggests that Mendenhall's case, upon which Clements's view was partly constructed, was weakened by the subsequent discovery of a group of treaties between Esarhaddon and his vassals dating from 672 BCE. These documents demonstrate, at least to Weinfeld's satisfaction, that the covenant formula remained essentially unaltered from the Hittite period to the neo-Assyrian era.[5] Thus it cannot be assumed that the Hittite ritual, regarded by Clements as evidence for an early date for the formulation of Genesis 15, was a direct influence upon the Abrahamic covenant, and nor is it possible to assume that 2 Samuel 7 was based on the memory of it. It should be noted, though, that not all scholars are convinced by the Assyrian parallels; J.H. Walton expresses concern about the assumption of an Assyrian model for late biblical covenants

study see H. Hagelia, *Numbering the Stars: A Phraseological Analysis of Genesis 15* (ConBOT, 39; Stockholm: Almqvist & Wiksell, 1994).

3.   *Abraham and David: Genesis 15 and its Meaning for Israelite Tradition* (Studies in Biblical Theology; Second Series, 5; London: SCM Press, 1967).

4.   *Abraham and David*, p. 54. It should be noted here that Clements revised his view of an ancient covenant tradition in *Prophecy and Tradition* (Oxford: Basil Blackwell, 1975); see especially pp. 14-17. He does not, however, offer a reassessment of Gen. 15 in this context.

5.   *Deuteronomy and the Deuteronomic School* (Oxford: Clarendon Press, 1983 [1972]). See p. 60 for this discussion.

because they lack the historical preface which is, however, found in the Hittite covenant formula.[6]

Exercising due caution, Clements admits that both Davidic and, less directly, Abrahamic covenants may have been influenced by other ancient Near Eastern concepts of kingship.[7] (Even if one is unable to accept the route by which Clements traces this influence, the royal associations fit well with the occurrence of a dream report in the context of God's choice of Abraham.) Clements also allows that the account of the covenant in Genesis 15, which he attributes to the Yahwist, may have been 'moulded in an attempt to emphasize similarities between the two'.[8] Several striking parallels (cf. especially 2 Sam. 7.12 with Gen. 15.4, 15, and 2 Sam. 7.4, 17 with Gen. 15.1) indicate that Clements is correct to doubt that the two accounts were composed independently. Weinfeld attributes these similarities to common 'literary and historical antecedents',[9] but the instances noted above seem rather too specific to be thus explained. The following discussion will be based on the premise that the textual relationship between Genesis 15 and 2 Samuel 7 is not, as Clements suggested, primarily a case of the former influencing the latter. Rather, Genesis 15 contains deliberate echoes of 2 Samuel 7.[10]

6. J.H. Walton, *Ancient Israelite Literature in its Cultural Context: A Survey of Parallels Between Biblical and Ancient Near Eastern Texts* (Regency Reference Library; Grand Rapids, MI: Zondervan, 1989), pp. 106-107.

7. In *Abraham and David* he speculates that 'it is antecedently probable that the royal covenant of 2 Sam. 7 was influenced in its origin by other Near Eastern concepts of kingship, especially that which was current in the Canaanite city states. It is a false contrast to set Israel's idea of the divine election of its kings too sharply against the elaborate court style of the ancient Near East, since the idea of the divine election of kings was current in the ancient world, and the dynastic covenant of 2 Sam. 7 shows us the distinctive form which this belief in royal election took in Israel' (p. 55).

8. Clements, *Abraham and David*, p. 55.

9. *Deuteronomy and the Deuteronomic School*, p. 80. More recently, Weinfeld has provided a detailed account of these common antecedents in *The Promise of the Land: The Inheritance of the Land of Canaan by the Israelites* (Berkeley: University of California Press, 1993), see especially pp. 222-64 on the covenantal aspect of the promise of land.

10. Although Clements attributes Gen. 15 to the Yahwist, he does not rule out modification for the purpose of emphasizing a perceived link between Abraham and David: 'We must recognise consequently that the account in Genesis 15 of the Abrahamic covenant has been influenced in its formulation by features drawn from

Additional evidence that the form of Abraham's covenant in Genesis 15 was influenced by David's in 2 Samuel 7, and not the other way round, may be drawn from the reflections of other covenants that are observable in Genesis 15. As J. Ha has demonstrated, the narrator of the Covenant of the Pieces was certainly familiar with the Sinai covenant,[11] and he also seems to have known the preamble to Joshua's covenant (cf. Gen. 15.16, 19 with Josh. 24.8-11). Clearly, the question of the relationship between these various traditions is fraught with uncertainty, and it may be unwise to stake too much on supposedly historical claims about any of them. Yet it seems to be the case that the echoes of 2 Samuel that Clements correctly perceives in Genesis 15 are but one element of a complex web of inner-biblical allusions, the result, I will argue here, of a politically motivated attempt to create a direct link between Abraham and the Israelites in exile.

Van Seters[12] criticizes Clements for the absence of a form-critical approach in *Abraham and David* and objects strongly to the identification of Abraham with a particular king:

> Frequently we are told that this statement [Gen. 12:1-3] reflects the Davidic or Solomonic period and functioned as a legitimation of the empire. But is this really the case? What this statement has in mind is a purely ethnic form of identity with no necessity for a monarchy whatever. Abraham is not the beginning of a royal line, but of all the families in Israel. Now in the Davidic-Solomonic period there does not seem to be any such sense of unity, even between Judah and Israel, let alone all the other disparate elements. The king was the sole basis of unity, and

the Davidic covenant of Jerusalem. This does not preclude, however, that we should also recognise that the latter covenant was indebted for its origin to certain features belonging to the tradition of the Abrahamic covenant of Mamre. The fact that this influence was important has led to a conscious assimilation of the form of the two covenants to each other in their respective written accounts. This further strengthens our main contention that there was a close connection, both in historical significance and religious interpretation, between the Abrahamic and the Davidic covenants' (p. 55).

11. *Genesis 15*, pp. 135-48.
12. *Abraham in History and Tradition*, p. 252 n. 9. Van Seters himself advocates a form-critical analysis to identify the smaller or larger unities in the text and the environment from which the text comes, and a source-critical analysis which 'may bring to the surface a compositional design and movement that might otherwise be lost through various attempts at source division and thus constitute a strong argument for the text's unity' (p. 252).

there is not a hint anywhere of the monarchy being traced back to Abraham. So the significance of the statement must be otherwise.[13]

To this one might add that it is not merely the case that the historical narratives dealing directly with the Davidic-Solomonic period fail to make any explicit connection between the figures of David and Abraham.[14] Several Psalms refer to one or other of the covenant traditions, but none links them. Thus Psalm 89 mentions the Davidic covenant, but not the covenant with Abraham, while Psalm 105 mentions only the covenant with Abraham.[15] N. Lemche, who places Psalm 105 in the postexilic period, characterizes the Psalm as part of a trilogy (with 104 and 106) which encapsulates Israel's history from creation to exile,[16] and if the link between Abraham and David had made a significant impact on the national consciousness, one might expect to find it reflected here.[17]

Yet although Van Seters rejects the notion of an explicit connection between Abraham and David, he is convinced that a royal ideology underlies the Abraham narrative. He perceives the shift in Genesis 15 from the barrenness of the matriarch to the patriarch's lack of an heir as a shift 'from the story type dealing with ancestry to the ancestor as king'.[18] He also envisages a royal *Sitz im Leben* for the salvation oracle in v. 1, equating its offer of reward to the spoils of war, and notes

13. Van Seters, *Abraham in History and Tradition*, p. 271.

14. There are, of course, certain words and phrases which occur in connection with both Abraham and David. Thus, it might be argued that the reference to the sand on the seashore in 1 Kgs 4.20 is intended to recall Gen. 22.17. Yet this image occurs in a promise to Jacob (32.13) in a form which is even closer to 1 Kgs 4.20, and is also used in contexts which have no connection with Abraham, David, or their descendants (see, for instance, Gen. 41.49, where it describes the produce amassed by Joseph). It is, therefore, difficult to see it as representing an explicit link between patriarch and king.

15. Certainly, Ps. 105.10 includes the term עולם ברית (eternal covenant), which also occurs with reference to David (see 2 Sam. 23.5). Yet this is a term that appears in contexts which have no connection with either the Abrahamic or the Davidic covenant (see, for instance, Gen. 9.16; Exod. 31.16; Lev. 24.8), and it thus seems unlikely that Ps. 105.10 is an intentional allusion to the covenant with David.

16. *Early Israel: Anthropological and Historical Studies on Israelite Society Before the Monarchy* (VTSup, 53; Leiden: E.J. Brill, 1985), pp. 350-51.

17. In fact, 105.42-44 suggests a link between Gen. 15 and the Exodus, which must be treated quite separately.

18. *Prologue to History* (Louisville, KY: Westminster/John Knox Press, 1992), p. 49.

parallels with the dynastic promise to David (2 Sam. 7.12, 16). As he
makes clear in a subsequent discussion of Genesis 12, Van Seters sees
these similarities as the result of the narrator's attempt to democratize
the royal ideology by applying it to the forefather of the people; any
link with David that they may suggest is purely incidental.[19]

Finally, for present purposes, Van Seters diverges from Clements in
tracing the theme of blessing and curse to the influence of the Assyrian
and Babylonian empires of the eighth to sixth centuries BCE, rather than
to the imperial monarchy of the Davidic-Solomonic period.[20] For his
own account, Van Seters places Genesis 15 in the late exilic period,[21]
identifying its theological provenance with that of Deutero-Isaiah.[22] Its
function is as a message of hope to the exiles, particularly, perhaps, in
its predating of the conditional promise at Sinai, now broken almost
beyond repair, with an unconditional promise to the descendants of
Abraham.[23]

19. Van Seters, *Abraham in History and Tradition*, p. 256; Hagelia, *Numbering
the Stars*, reconciles apparent Davidic and presumed exilic themes as follows: 'This
[the correspondence between the borders mentioned in Gen. 15 and those of the
Davidic-Solomonic era] does not have to mean that Gen. 15:18 historically reflect
the time of David and Solomon. We have seen many ties between the content of
Genesis 15 and the time around the exile, a time when many were exiled at River
Euphrates and others were refugees in Egypt. The particular promise of land in
Gen. 15:18 may reflect a dream from contemporaries: one time the areas where the
descendants of Abraham are now exiled or refugees will be theirs, and there will be
a re-establishing of the great kingdom of David and Solomon. At least it should be
admitted to see in the promise of Gen. 15:18 a remembrance of this great kingdom
and that great time' (p. 171).

20. *Abraham in History and Tradition*, pp. 274-75.

21. *Prologue to History*: 'The land was given to Egypt after the exodus from
Egypt and through the conquest of ancient inhabitants. The wilderness became a
preparation for life in the Promised Land ... Loss of the land in the exile confirmed
the prophetic judgement based on the land's conditionality. Any subsequent right to
the land was jeopardised ... An alternative tradition of national origin, based upon
the eponymous ancestors, allowed for a prior unconditional claim to the land that
could be interpreted as the promise to the forefathers *before* the generations in
Egypt—the patriarchs—and so permitted a new possibility of continued association
and claim upon the land ... I attribute this daring combination of antiquarian traditions to the Yahwist in the exilic period. It is this combination that is fully confirmed by the Priestly writer as well (see esp. Ex. 6:2ff)' (p. 242).

22. He elaborates on the relationships between the patriarchal narratives and
Deutero-Isaiah in *Prologue to History*, pp. 241-42, 256.

23. *Abraham in History and Tradition* (p. 269): 'Of course ... there is nothing

If Van Seters and others are right to see in the patriarchal narratives
an editorial attempt to address the plight of the exiles,[24] then we might
expect to find some hint of this in prophetic literature from the period.
The exilic prophets contain surprisingly few explicit references to Abraham but those which do exist are clearly concerned with establishing a
claim on the land for those in exile (Ezek. 33.24; Isa. 41.8-9, 51.1-2).[25]
The task of analysing prophetic references to Abraham is not straightforward, though, and it is difficult to determine how much significance
should be attached to each case. A good example of this difficulty is
discussed by F. Holmgren.[26]'Holmgren suggests that the unusual choice
in Neh. 10.1 of the word אמנה for 'covenant' or 'binding declaration' is
a deliberate echo of Neh. 9.8. The merit of his exegesis cannot be
assessed here, but it certainly illustrates the problem of determining the
full extent of prophetic allusions to the patriarch.[27]

contradictory about a Jew who held to this promise and yet who wanted to know on
what basis he could lay claim to the land, especially since the old covenant basis
was broken. The explanation of this new basis is set forth in vv. 7-21 and includes a
reorientation of YHWH's confessional identity, a new land-promise covenant, and
an accounting for the delay in the fulfillment. In this way the whole chapter became
a very close-knit unit, fully intelligible to the Jew of the exile, telling him exactly
where he stood and what his future was if he would exercise faith in this word of
salvation from the God of Abraham'.

24. See also R.N. Whybray, *The Making of the Pentateuch* (JSOTSup, 53;
Sheffield: JSOT Press, 1987), who emphasizes the need for historical reassessment
in the exilic period (pp. 229-30), and agrees with Van Seters's reading of exilic
resonances in the mention of Ur in Gen. 15.7. J.A. Emerton, 'The Origin of the
Promises to the Patriarchs in the Older Sources of the Book of Genesis', *VT* 32
(1982), pp. 14-32, is sceptical of Van Seters's claim that the reference to Ur reflects
Nabonidus's favouring of Ur and Harran, but thinks that v. 7 'may represent a
modification of a formula that originally spoke of bringing Israel out of Egypt' (p.
30). Emerton concludes that the promises in vv. 4-5, 18 are probably original to the
text, but that the text itself is late (p. 23).

25. For a discussion of these references to Abraham and their connection to the
land, see S. Japhet, 'People and Land in the Restoration Period', in G. Strecker
(ed.), *Das Land Israel in biblischer Zeit* (Göttingen: Vandenhoeck & Ruprecht,
1983), pp. 103-25, especially pp. 106-109.

26. 'Faithful Abraham and the *'amâna* Covenant in Nehemiah 9:6–10:1', *ZAW*
104 (1992), pp. 249-54.

27. It is worth noting here that Neh. 9.8 contains rare example of a reference
to God's promise of land to Abraham which almost certainly alludes to Gen. 15.

Van Seters's overall view, although without his emphasis on Deutero-Isaiah, is shared substantially by Ha, who makes the following observations:

> The author's scriptural familiarity favours a late datation for his work. His concern for the land and, to some extent, his concern for a great posterity point to the exilic period as the probable time in which he composed his work ... Given this date for the composition, the author's intention would evidently be to strengthen the faith of the exiles and provide them with a hope of a return to the land ... The Pentateuch was offered as the foundation of this faith and hope because it recorded an almost similar experience made by Israel's forefathers in a foreign land and their liberation by YHWH their God on the ground of his unilateral oath to their patriarchs ... This unilateral oath was valid for all generations of Abraham's descendants. YHWH's destruction of the Egyptians and the Assyrians had taken place. It should now serve to guarantee the destruction of the Babylonians, the present oppressors of Abraham's descendants, thereby securing the latter's liberation and return to the promised land.[28]

Where Van Seters emphasizes Deutero-Isaiah, Ha identifies two other prophetic texts as having exerted a significant influence on Genesis 15: Jer. 34.18-20 and Isa. 7.1-17. The question of dependency on Jeremiah will be discussed below in relation to the covenant ritual. The possible connection between Genesis 15 and Isaiah 7 is a more complex matter, however, and the general thrust of the Genesis text must be characterized quite differently according to whether or not it is accepted.

Faith in Signs or Faith in God's Word?

Ha sees the Covenant of the Pieces as centrally concerned with the notion of 'faith supported by signs',[29] and, in this respect, he regards it

J. Weingreen, 'הוֹצֵאתִיךְ in Genesis 15:7', in P. Ackroyd (ed.), *Words and Meanings: Essays Presented To David Winton Thomas* (Cambridge: Cambridge University Press, 1968), pp. 209-15, sees in the use of הוֹצֵאתִיךְ (brought you out) in both Genesis and Nehemiah an allusion 'to Abraham's fortitude in his faith and his deliverance by divine grace' (p. 215).

28. *Genesis 15*, p. 216.

29. Ha deals at some length with this aspect of the Exodus and Sinai traditions in the Pentateuch: 'Like the 'exodus narrative' (Ex. 1–14), the Sinai tradition also furnishes evidence of the theologoumenon of history taking on the character of a sign to support faith. YHWH's announcement to Moses of his first theophany on Sinai characterises the theophany as a sign to elicit faith in Moses (19.9). The sign

as the positive antithesis of Isaiah 7. In Isaiah, God offers a sign to an unwilling recipient, and in Genesis 15 a worthy recipient asks for and receives a sign from God.[30] While Ha is right to note textual similarities between Isaiah 7 and Genesis 15,[31] it is difficult to accept his view that 'faith supported by signs' is a central concern of the Covenant of the Pieces. Without exception, the signs mentioned by Ha are, in one sense or another, widely accessible. The plagues in Egypt and the miraculous crossing of the Red Sea are visible to Israelites and Egyptians alike, the audio-visual effects at Sinai are witnessed by all the Israelites present there, and the tabernacle, if one includes it in this list, is available to the entire community. The birth of the son predicted in Isaiah 7 must also have entailed some form of physical presence, since its effectiveness as a sign is ultimately dependent on its tangibility. In Genesis 15, by contrast, only Abraham experiences whatever signs are offered; the intensely communal aspect of the Exodus-Sinai signs, emphasized repeatedly in Deuteronomy and prophetic texts, is entirely absent here.

Certainly, there are several plausible candidates for signs in this text: the row of dissected animals, the birds of prey, the great darkness, and of course, the smoking oven and fiery torch. Yet the statement of faith in v. 6 is preceded by a description that cannot reasonably be interpreted as a sign:

ויוצא אתו החוצה ויאמר הבט נא השמימה וספר הכוכבים אם תוכל
לספר אתם ויאמר לו כה יהיה זרעך:

He took him outside and said, 'Look toward heaven and count the stars, if you are able to count them.' And he added, 'So shall your offspring be.'

character of the theophany is marked by the audibility and visibility; thick cloud, thunder, lightning, trumpet blast (v. 16) and fire and smoke (v. 18)' (p. 159). He identifies God's destruction of the Egyptians as a sign intended to elicit the faith of Moses and the Israelites, and the tabernacle as a sign of God's presence among the people.

30. Ha, *Genesis 15*, writes: 'Basically, therefore, a close literary and theological affinity exists between Gen. 15:1-6 and Is. 7:3-9, especially v. 9b. The only significant difference lies in their human protagonists: Abraham, a man of great faith, and Ahaz, his opposite. But then, in view of the above-traced affinity, it is reasonable to postulate that the two protagonists are intended to form an antithetic parallelism, that is, as type and anti-type' (p. 87).

31. Ha notes that both Gen. 15.1 and Isa. 7.4 include the formulaic reassurance 'fear not' (אל תירא), both speak of belief or faith (cf. Gen. 15.6 and Isa. 7.9 and both texts contain the promise of a son.

The stars of the heavens, although they might well bear witness to God's creation as part of a different theological outlook (such as that of Deutero-Isaiah and some wisdom literature) are clearly not signs in the same sense as the plagues in Egypt or the thunder and lightning at Sinai. The fact that the statement of faith in Genesis 15 is not linked to a sign, combined with the absence here of the term אות (sign) (cf. the covenants described in Gen. 9.12, 17, 17.11), makes Ha's emphasis on signs seem overstated.

If, moreover, one assumes with Ha an exilic background for Genesis 15, it is difficult to see what the appeal of a faith based on signs might have been, either for the narrator or for his intended audience. The signs and wonders that had been revealed to the wilderness generation were by now conspicuous only by their absence, and miraculous defeats of Israel's enemies, exemplified by the crossing of the Red Sea, had been replaced by subjugation. Certainly, it is not surprising that requests for new signs should occur in this historical context,[32] but the exiles were unlikely to have derived much comfort from the mere recounting of signs experienced by previous generations. It was surely time to look for an alternative to sign-supported faith, which is precisely what Genesis 15 provides with its emphasis on God's unconditional promise of the land to the descendants of Abraham.

If we return to the relationship between Gen. 15.6 and Isaiah 7, we find that Westermann understands it rather differently:

> Earlier, before Isaiah, the hiph. of אמן [believe] occurred mainly with the negative. It was the normal, natural thing for one to believe in God's word; there was no need to state it. What was unusual was not to believe in God's word; this merited mention; hence in the earlier period the word was used rather often with a negative. Isaiah experienced the disbelief of the king, God's anointed, who did not believe the word of God which came to him (Is. 7). The consequence was an awareness of the meaning of faith, and the necessity of explaining the culmination of this problem in Isaiah. This is also the theological background of 15:6.[33]

Where Ha emphasizes faith in God's signs, Westermann focuses on trust in God's word. This is surely a more plausible reading than Ha's of the significance of Gen. 15.6.

The most obvious consequence of preferring Westermann's view over Ha's is a renewed emphasis on the vision. Abraham's fears that

32. Ps. 74.9-11 includes a good example.
33. *Genesis 12–36*, p. 222.

God's promise may not be fulfilled are quelled by means of an auditory message confirmed by the image of multitudinous stars. The subsequent announcement of his trust in v. 6 is less likely to be a general statement of faith than a specific response to what he has just experienced; the patriarch finds God's vision reliable.[34] This emphasis on the vision demands a detailed analysis of the precise nature of Abraham's experience, and, in particular, an assessment of how its narrator intended it to be understood.

The Covenant of the Pieces: Vision or Dream?

Taken at face value, Gen. 15.1 would seem to indicate that the experience attributed to Abraham in this chapter is a vision. Yet while it is literally correct to translate the word מחזה as 'vision', and while the notion of vision is of considerable significance, one might suggest that מחזה should be understood as 'dream' rather than 'vision' if a coherent reading of the text is to be uncovered.

Semantic evidence from several sources indicates that, at the least, מחזה refers to a vision with distinctly dream-like characteristics—a form of revelation which is, in fact, barely distinguishable from a dream, particularly if it is received at night. The Bible has several words for vision, and מחזה appears only three times elsewhere: in Num. 24.4 and 24.16 it denotes the visions of Balaam,[35] and in Ezek. 13.7 it is used in connection with false prophecy and lying divination.

Two of Balaam's pronouncements are introduced in more or less identical manner. The first, beginning with Num. 24.3-4, reads as follows:

... נאם בלעם בנו בער ונאם הגבר שתם העין

נאם שמע אמרי אל

אשר מחזה שדי יחזה נפל וגלוי עינים

34. Ha considers but rejects this possibility in a discussion of Hab. 2.4: 'No doubt both texts do bring out YHWH's trustworthiness. Nevertheless, in Hab. 2:4b the real emphasis is on the reliability of the vision and YHWH's trustworthiness on which it is grounded is drawn only as an implicit conclusion. In Gen. 15:6, *byhwh* explicitly affirms this quality of YHWH's. Moreover, in Gen. 15:6 Abraham's faith is highlighted while in Hab. 2:4 it is very faintly implied and, even then, it is not so much faith in YHWH as confidence in his vision' (p. 87).

35. Gnuse, *The Dream Theophany of Samuel*, assumes that Balaam is dreaming in Num. 22.8-13 and 19-21, referring to 'these two night dreams of Balaam...' (p. 71).

Word of Balaam son of Beor, Word of man whose eye is true, Word of
him who hears God's speech, Who beholds visions of the Almighty,
Prostrate but with eyes unveiled.

The second, in 24.15-16, differs from this only in that 'Who obtains
knowledge from the Most High (וידע דעת עליון) is inserted after 'God's
speech' (אמרי אל). Pedersen claimed that the only difference between a
dream and a vision is that 'the vision is received while awake',[36] and
the terms are often used interchangeably, especially in Daniel.
Regrettably, the verses from Numbers include no explicit reference to
the time of day, but there are several reasons to believe that Balaam
received his visions at night. In Num. 22.8 Balaam tells Balak's
messengers, 'Spend the night here, and I shall reply to you as the
LORD may instruct me' (לינו פה הלילה והשבתי אתכם דבר כאשר
ידבר יהוה אלי).[37] This episode is more or less repeated in v. 19, and
v. 20 reports, 'That night God came to Balaam' (ויבא אלהים אל בלעם
לילה). This suggests that Balaam's visions came during the night. It is
worth noting that the gods also come by night in the non-biblical text
about Balaam from *Deir 'Alla*.[38]

Translators have disagreed on the appropriate rendering of נפל in
Num. 24.4, some favouring 'falling down'[39] and others preferring 'prostrate'.[40] Balaam's entirely matter-of-fact attitude casts doubt over the
former; there is nothing to indicate that his visions would have made
him fall down in reverence.[41] On the other hand, if the visions do,

36. J. Pedersen, *Israel I–II: Its Life and Culture*, (London: Oxford University
Press, 1959), p. 140.
37. Robinson, 'Dreams in the Old Testament', cites A. Caquot's comparison of
the occurrences of לין in Isa. 65.4 and Ps. 91.1. Caquot suggests that the use of the
verb here may imply passing the night for the purpose of obtaining something, such
as a divine revelation. This is clearly of interest with regard to Num. 22.8.
38. See K. Smelik, *Writings From Ancient Israel* (trans. G.I. Davies; Edinburgh: T. & T. Clark, 1991), p. 83.
39. See, for example, NRSV:
       'Who sees visions of the Almighty,
       Who falls down, but with eyes uncovered' (Num. 24.4, 16).
40. NJPS: 'Who beholds visions from the Almighty,
       Prostrate but with eyes unveiled' (Num. 24.4).
41. NJPS treads the tight-rope with 'prostrate, but with eyes unveiled'. 'Prostrate' can imply that he was lying flat on his back, but also suggests an act of
prayer.

indeed, occur at night, then we might expect Balaam to be lying prostrate when he received them. Finally, there is the question of the precise
meaning of וגלוי עינים (but with eyes unveiled). BDB cites Num. 24.4,
16 as containing the two biblical usages of גלה to mean 'open' in a
literal sense, as opposed to the less literal *JPS* translations cited here.[42]
Against this, it should be noted that the verb appears shortly afterwards
(in the episode of Balaam's ass) in a context where it cannot possibly
carry the literal meaning of 'open'.[43] Yet the notion that a dream in
some sense awakened the dreamer is commonplace in the ancient Near
East. Indeed, the Egyptian word for dream, *rswt*, is related to the verb
'to be awakened' and was written with the symbol of an open eye.[44]
Thus וגלוי עינים, literally 'and with open eyes', may be understood here
as an idiom with the fuller sense of 'and capable of receiving a revelation'.[45] Taken together, these observations surely entitle us to understand Balaam's visions as dreams. Indeed, it is possible that the term
was used precisely because it represented a middle ground between
dream and prophetic vision; a more straightforward form of the latter
may have presented difficulties when used in connection with a non-
Israelite.

On account of the abstract nature of Ezek. 13.7 it is less easy to
defend a reading of מחזה that implies a specifically dream-like vision:

הלוא מחזה שוא חזיתם ומקסם כזב אמרתם
It was false visions you prophesied and lying divination you uttered.

The text gives no clue to the time of day, nor to the state in which the
'prophets' received their false visions. Yet false prophets often are
discussed in connection with dreams,[46] and Ezekiel's failure to mention
dreams in this tirade against false prophecy (13.1-7) may mean simply
that he used מחזה in a sense that included both vision and dream. At
any rate, and perhaps this is the most that can be claimed, there is

---

42. See, for instance, NJPS.
43. When the angel of the Lord first appears on the road in front of Balaam and
his ass, he is visible to the animal but not to the man. Only when Balaam has beaten
his mount for its wayward behaviour does the Lord enable Balaam to see what has
been visible to his ass all along: 'Then the Lord uncovered [גלה] Balaam's eyes and
he saw the angel of the Lord standing before him' (Num. 22.31).
44. See Oppenheim, 'The Interpretation of Dreams', p. 190.
45. I am grateful to Dr G.I. Davies for suggesting this interpretation.
46. See, for instance, Deut. 13.2 and Jer. 29.8.

nothing in this verse to preclude the possibility that the term refers to a nocturnal vision-dream.[47]

Abraham's vision in Genesis 15, unlike Jacob's in 46.2, is not explicitly called a vision of the night.[48] Yet the allusion to the stars directly following its announcement suggests that it almost certainly is a nocturnal vision. While Abraham may have been transported by his vision from daylight to dark, it seems more likely that, as Ehrlich thought, the stars were there in reality, offering themselves as a ready comparison to Abraham's descendants.[49] This is not necessarily to say that Abraham was sleep-walking when he saw the stars, but rather that the narrative blurs the distinction between external reality and the world of the vision. Just as we cannot be sure, nor do we need to be sure, whether the sheep mentioned in Jacob's dream of the flocks (31.10-13) are real or imagined, nor do we need to determine in which realm Abraham's stars exist; sheep and stars are both literally present and part of the dream imagery. Finally on this point, one might observe that the very mention of stars, particularly without any specification that they featured solely in the vision, evokes an immediate impression of darkness. Had the narrator wished to convey the impression that Abraham's vision occurred in daylight, an image other than stars would surely have been preferable.[50]

In a discussion of the relationship of Genesis 15 to Numbers and Ezekiel, Ha observes that the prophetic potential of מחזה is not realized in Abraham's vision:

> As we have seen, the formula of the advent of the divine word in Gen. 15:1 is clearly prophetic. As such, it is the equivalent of *ne'um yhwh* found in prophetic oracles. If *mahazeh* is used with it, there is every reason to take Gen. 15:1 as intending to bring out the double dimension of a prophetic oracle: audition and vision. What was communicated to Abraham was precisely what YHWH was uttering and seeing... Yet Abraham is not presented as exercising a prophetic role. He had no audience

47. מחזה has unmistakable negative connotations both in Numbers, where it is used in connection with the ambiguous non-Israelite prophet, and in Ezekiel, where it is linked to false prophecy. One might infer from this that it was regarded as a particularly weak form of prophetic vision which was thus almost interchangeable with a dream.

48. In 46.2 the term מראת הלילה is used.

49. See *Der Traum im Alten Testament*, p. 36.

50. Images such as the sands of the seashore (Gen. 22.17) or the dust of the earth (Gen. 28.14) would have been more appropriate for a daytime setting.

with which to communicate his message. Moreover, the message was more a promise, or to be precise, an oath than a prophecy. Therefore, the prophetic traits, especially in the formula of the advent of God's word and *mahazeh*, strictly speaking do not belong to Gen. 15.[51]

Yet a slightly different reading of the significance of the term may help to resolve the inconsistency noted by Ha here. Thus, it is possible that the narrator selected it because, on the one hand, it denotes a dream-like experience that would not have appeared anachronistic or out of place in the patriarchal narratives and, on the other, because its prophetic associations indicate that its import extended far beyond the figure of Abraham the dreamer.[52] Yet although Genesis 15 is, in many respects, concerned primarily with a time long after the death of Abraham, it is by no means the case that the narrator's interest in this event was entirely future-orientated. Indeed, the effectiveness of the chapter's prophetic element is largely dependent upon its convincing insertion into the Abraham story as a pivotal event in the patriarch's life.

Immediately following the announcement of the vision (15.1), God addresses Abraham:

אל תירא אברם אנכי מגן לך שכרך הרבה מאד

Fear not, Abram, I am a shield to you; your reward shall be very great.

The reassuring 'fear not' frequently accompanies divine revelation, although the context in which it occurs here suggests that the reassurance was intended to exceed the duration of the vision: Abraham need never fear because God will continue to act as a protecting shield for him. Abraham, however, is not satisfied with this vague promise of reward, and takes the opportunity to remind God of a specific problem—his childlessness. God responds by showing him the stars, assuring Abraham that his descendants will be as numerous. Fears of this kind were often the basis of dream reports in the ancient world. In a discussion of dream incubation in a study of dreams in Ugaritic literature and the Bible, A. Jeffers shows that dreams are frequently sought

---

51. *Genesis 15*, p. 68.

52. It is also possible that the narrator chose מחזה because the negative contexts in which it appears in Num. 24.4, 16 (with reference to the ambiguous figure of the non-Israelite prophet Balaam) and Ezek. 13.7 (in connection with false visions and lying divination) suggested a proximity to the dream as a second-rate vehicle of revelation.

in situations of extreme necessity, and particularly in connection with childlessness.[53] In examples from Ugaritic literature,[54] Keret requests a dream after his seven sons die, leaving him with no heir to the throne, and Danel undergoes a complex incubation ritual, involving a sacrificial offering and the purification of his dwelling, because he has no son. The ritual results in a dream in which El assures Danel that his sterility will be cured and he will be given a perfect son. These parallels suggest that readers from this period may well have associated requests for an heir with dream reports, regardless of whether a dream is specifically mentioned.

Verse 7 makes the transition from one of Abraham's concerns, his lack of an heir, to another, his lack of land (both of which had been promised to him in ch. 12):

ויאמר אליו אני יהוה אשר הוצאתיך מאור כשדים לתת לך את הארץ
הזאת לרשתה:

Then he said to him, 'I am the LORD who brought you out of Ur of the Chaldeans to assign this land to you as a possession.'

The fact that the dream-vision provides the patriarch with an opportunity to seek reassurance on these subjects, combined, perhaps, with the description of his cutting of the animals in v. 10, has prompted some scholars to ask whether 15.12-17 might represent an incubated dream report.[55] As Ehrlich has made clear, though, this theory depends upon the assumption that the events occurred in a holy place,[56] and although Wellhausen and others have surmised that Hebron was the location of the Covenant of the Pieces,[57] this must remain a matter for speculation. An additional problem for the theory that Genesis 15 reports an incubated dream arises from the lack of an explicit reference to sacrifice,

---

53. 'Divination by Dreams', pp. 167-83.

54. See J.C.L. Gibson (ed.), *Canaanite Myths and Legends* (Edinburgh: T. & T. Clark, 1978), for translations of, and commentaries, on other ancient Near Eastern dream texts.

55. Jirku, 'Ein Fall von Inkubation', pp. 151-53.

56. *Der Traum im Alten Testament*: 'Der Aufbau der zweiten Erzählung ist folgender: 1. Selbstoffenbarung JHWH's; 2. Opferhandlung; 3. ein Traumgesicht; 4. die Erklärung dieses Traumgesichtes und dessen Verwirklichung durch die *berit*' (p. 39).

57. J. Wellhausen, *Der Text der Bücher Samuelis* (Göttingen: Vandenhoeck & Ruprecht, 1871), pp. 21-22.

another essential element of the incubation ritual. Proponents of this theory must thus take the cutting of the animals as the functional equivalent of sacrifice, which may or may not be the case. At any rate, the issue of whether or not 15.12-17 is an incubated dream is raised here not because it seems especially likely, but because it demonstrates that at least some elements of ch. 15 have struck exegetes as distinctively dream-like. Even readers who remain unconvinced by the incubation theory, however, have noted the extent to which the smoking oven and the flaming torch resemble the imagery of symbolic dreams.[58]

Most commentators on biblical dreams have attempted to provide some form of classification based on the content and the presumed purpose of the dream narrative.[59] Gnuse considers two main categories, 'the simple message dream and the symbolic or ambiguous dream', adding that the second category may be further divided to distinguish between 'symbolic' dreams, which contain one or two symbolic statements or images, and 'mantic' dreams, which are more complex and usually require skilled interpretation.[60] It is immediately obvious that a dream reading of Genesis 15 involves considerable overlap between Gnuse's two main categories, since it contains both simple messages from God and symbolic images. This is, however, precisely the case for Genesis 28, which also contains an auditory message and the symbolic images of the ladder and angels.

Yet although ch. 15 fits imperfectly into either one of these broad categories, it contains many of the individual elements that are frequently found in dream narratives. Gnuse outlines components of the so-called Elohist's dream narratives as follows:

1. Theophany
2. Recipient
3. Dream reference
4. Time
5. Auditory address formula
6. Message
   A. Introductory formula or particle *hinneh*
   B. Divine self-identification

---

58. Ehrlich, *Der Traum im Alten Testament*, pp. 40-41, cites many allusions to light and fire in symbolic dreams of the ancient Near East.

59. See, for instance, W. Richter, 'Traum und Traumdeutung im Alten Testament: Ihre Form und Verwendung', *BZ* 7 (1963), pp. 202-20.

60. *The Dream Theophany of Samuel*, p. 16.

       C.   Assurance and promise/warnings/commands
       D.   Dialogue
  7.   Formal termination.[61]

He proceeds to use this structure as a basis for analysing the dreams of Gen. 20.3, 28.13, 31.10, 31.24, 46.2; Num. 22.9, 22.20 and 1 Kgs 3.5. Of these, Abimelech's dream in Genesis 20 corresponds most closely to the prototype, but none of these dreams includes all of Gnuse's components.

A similarly structured analysis of Genesis 15 yields the following:

  1.   והנה דבר יהוה, היה דבר יהוה (the word of the LORD, vv. 1, 4)
  2.   אל אברם (to Abram, v. 1)
  3.   במחזה (in a vision, v. 1)
  4.   –
  5.   לאמר (saying, vv. 1,4)
  6.

       A.   אל תירא אברם (fear not Abram, v. 1)
       B.   אנכי מגן לך (I am a shield for you, v. 1), אני יהוה אשר הוצאתיך
           (I am the LORD who brought you out, v. 7)
       C.   Assurances and promises (vv. 1, 4-5, 7, 13-16, 18-21)
       D.   Lengthy response (vv. 2, 3, 8)
  7.   –

While some biblical dreams contain either no speech (Gen. 37.5-11) or only divine speech (Gen. 31.10-13), dialogue of the kind that occurs between God and Abraham here is not unparalleled (Gen. 20.3-18; 1 Kgs 3.5-15), and Oppenheim states that it is attested, though rare, in other ancient Near Eastern sources.[62] Moreover, we should not be surprised to find Abraham dreaming in character: 'what can you give me, seeing that I shall die childless?' (v. 2) and 'how shall I know that I am to possess it?' (v. 8) typify the patriarch's interactions with God. At any rate, the dialogue between Abraham and God here presents no obstacle to the identification of Genesis 15 as a dream text. In addition, ch. 15 contains three occurrences of הנה, which commentators have often associated with dream narratives,[63] and concludes with what might be

61. *The Dream Theophany of Samuel*, pp. 75, 76.

62. He mentions the dreams of the priest of Ishtar and Thutmose IV, 'The Interpretation of Dreams', p. 191, and also a dream report in which Nabonidus argues with Marduk (p. 203).

63. This observation is made several times by Ehrlich in *Der Traum im Alten Testament*, and he draws attention to the הנה (behold) which precedes the appearance of the oven and the torch (p. 38). Gnuse, *The Dream Theophany of Samuel*,

regarded as the dream's 'fulfilment': God makes a covenant with Abraham on that day.

Thus far, I have explored several justifications for interpreting Genesis 15 as a dream text. Those who share von Rad's view that 15.1-11 describes a waking vision[64], however, will be quick to point out the difficulties posed by v. 12 for the theory that ch. 15 is one long dream. If Abraham only falls asleep in v. 12, how can he have been dreaming throughout the preceding 11 verses? Moreover, if the sun is only now about to set, why were the stars in the sky in v. 5?

One possible explanation for these inconsistencies concerns the meaning of the term תרדמה, usually translated as 'deep sleep'. We cannot assume that Abraham was falling asleep from a waking state in v. 12, since the term may refer to a certain quality of sleep that was achieved, without waking, during the night.[65] *Genesis Rabbah* describes it as the torpor of prophecy,[66] and McAlpine's study of the varieties of biblical sleep suggests that this particular form of deep sleep is almost invariably associated with divinely-given sleep.[67] The reference to night visions in Job 4.13 also supports this reading since it implies that the

likewise emphasizes the use of הנה: 'The dream structure of the Elohist parallels ancient Near Eastern dreams. A setting is given in which the dream reference, recipient, place, time and conditions under which the dream is received are given. The theophany occurs with the address of the recipient, self-identification of the deity, and the message. The actual message is introduced with the particle *hinneh*, it is short and direct, there are either promises or commands, and the message may be interrupted by pious dialogue from the human recipient' (p. 64).

64. In *Genesis*, p. 183, von Rad likens Abraham's vision to Job's (4.12-16) which was, he claims, received at night, 'in intensified wakefulness with attendant physical circumstances' (p. 183).

65. Lindblom, 'Theophanies in Holy Places in Hebrew Religion', connects תרדמה (deep sleep) with significant dreams: 'Using the term תרדמה the narrator wanted to say that in a heavy sleep Abraham was dreaming and in his dream he heard God speaking to him. The Hebrew term means an abnormally deep sleep or lethargy (Gen. 2:21, 1 Sam. 26:12, cf. Judg. 4:21, Jonah 1:5, Prov. 10:5, Ps. 76:7, Dan. 8:18, 10:9); it can also refer to a mental state of apathy (Prov. 19:15) or obduracy (Isa. 29:10, cf. 6:10). Sometimes the תרדמה is connected with significant dreams (Job 4:13, 33:15). This is the case in our passage' (p. 94).

66. *GR, ad loc.*

67. *Sleep, Divine and Human*: 'Study of the occurrences of *rdm* suggested that it was generally limited to divinely influenced sleep (the exceptions being in Proverbs). This rather than the quality of the sleep (deep, etc.) appeared to be the operative distinction' (p. 76).

visions and the deep sleep come together in the middle of the night
when the sleeper is already asleep:

בשעפים מחזינות לילה בנפל תרדמה על אנשים

In thought-filled visions of the night, when deep sleep falls on men.

The deep sleep of 15.12 may thus be the vision-inducing sleep that fell
upon Abraham in the middle of the night in preparation for the appearance of the smoking oven and the flaming torch in v. 17. On the basis
of the assumption that Abraham is asleep when the vision is announced
in v. 1, one might ask whether that sleep is not also in some sense
divinely-given. It is impossible to answer this with any certainty, but
there is a qualitative difference between the nature and function of
Abraham's two visionary experiences in this chapter (namely, the stars
and the oven and torch), and this is consistent with the notion that two
different types or levels of sleep were intended.

Ha, while understanding Abraham's deep sleep as a form of prophetic sleep, consistent with the prophecy given to him in the verses
immediately following, sees in Genesis 15 a double vision: 'one extending from v. 1 to v. 5 and the second from v. 12 to v. 17'.[68] These two
visions are, in Ha's opinion, interrupted by the day:

> But if we bear in mind the Hebrew way of reckoning the day from sunset
> to sunset, then there is no difficulty in seeing the event reported in v. 12
> as marking the end of the day that began with the sundown just before
> the event in v. 5. This interpretation finds support in Abraham's slaugh-
> tering of the animals described in vv. 9-10. It is hardly conceivable that
> this was done in the darkness of night. It must have been carried out in
> broad daylight.[69]

Yet the matter may be more complicated than he allows. Comparable
texts suggest that we should expect to find an explicit description of
Abraham's awakening and his execution of God's instructions (cf. Gen.
22.3, 28.18). The absence of such a statement means an intervening
period of daylight cannot be assumed. Moreover, since the animals certainly appear in the context of the vision in v. 17, they must surely have
been gathered, killed and dissected in the context of a vision (vv. 10-
11).

The dream reading also helps to resolve another problem arising
from the account of the animals in Genesis 15: God told Abraham to

68. *Genesis 15*, pp. 50-51.
69. Ha, *Genesis 15*, p. 51.

bring the animals, but not what to do with them, so how did he know that he should cut the animals, but not the birds, in half and set the pieces opposite each other? The argument that he was performing a familiar act and thus needed no instructions is not entirely plausible, as comparison with similar texts will show. In Judg. 6.25-26, Gideon is left in no doubt about how he should perform this fairly routine sacrifice of (at the most) two bulls.

How much more precise, then, would one expect God's instructions to be when a veritable menagerie is involved, and when the act in question, at least in its biblical context, is far from routine? Moreover, in striking contrast with other texts where animals are required (Gen. 22.13, for instance, explains carefully that the ram was at hand because it had been caught in the thicket by its horns), there is no explanation here for the surprising availability of the three three-year-old animals and the birds. If we assume, however, that the animals are creatures of Abraham's divine dream, then neither their availability nor the patriarch's knowledge of what to do with them need present a problem.

The occurrence of the animals in the context of a dream also allows for an element of symbolic interpretation that would be out of place if they are considered flesh-and-blood creatures.[70] This applies likewise to the birds that swoop down on the carcasses and are driven away by Abraham. Although they may be understood as real birds of prey attracted by the flesh of the carcasses, many commentators, and not just rabbinic ones, have focused on their symbolic potential.[71] Von Rad, for instance, suggests that the birds may be bad omens, as in Virgil's *Aeneid* 3.235, or evil powers intent on thwarting the covenant,[72] and V. Hamilton speculates that the animals may represent Israel and the birds hostile outsiders.[73] Gnuse suggests that the birds may originally have been connected with a Mesopotamian divinatory practice in which the flight of birds was observed, although he concludes that 'for the

70. *PRE, ad loc*, states that the animals represent the four kingdoms, their dominion and their downfall.

71. Contrary to Zimmerli's assertion, cited by Westermann, *Genesis 12–36*, p. 226, that the swooping birds have no parallel in the Hebrew Bible, one can find an obvious comparison in the baker's dream (Gen. 40.16-19) where, in strikingly similar dream-imagery, the birds which come down to eat from his basket are equated with the birds which will eat his flesh when Pharaoh has hanged him.

72. *Genesis*, p. 187.

73. See *The Book of Genesis: Chapters 1–17* (NICOT; Grand Rapids, MI: Eerdmans, 1990), p. 432.

narrator of this account, however, it has become a half-forgotten practice which Abraham performs for the purposes of the literary account'.[74]
An argument for the symbolic significance of the birds is strengthened
by a comparison with prophetic texts such as Isa. 18.6, 46.11, Jer. 12.9
and Ezek. 39.4, where birds of prey (also עיט) represent the hostile
nations gathering against Israel. At any rate, it is clear that the reading
of Genesis 15 as a dream text not only helps to fill awkward gaps in the
narrative of Genesis 15 (where did Abraham find the animals, and how
did he know what to do with them?), but it also enables the reader to
overlay natural or ritual acts with symbolic significance. We can now
move from the 'bestial' to the temporal difficulties of Genesis 15.

It may be possible to draw evidence about the narrator's intentions
for the role of the dream-vision in this chapter from a comparison of vv.
12 and 17. Verse 12 reports what we are entitled to understand as the
beginning of the sunset or the period immediately preceding it. It is not
yet clear whether the sun is setting in reality or in the dream-vision.
What is clear, though, is that the great darkness that falls upon Abraham has a strong metaphorical component, in keeping with the tenor of
the prophecy he is about to receive in v. 13. Verse 17 reports what must
be the conclusion of the sunset which began in v. 12. By this time
Abraham is already asleep, so the precise stage of nightfall in the real
world is irrelevant. In terms of the dream-vision, on the other hand, the
darkness is an all-important backdrop to the appearance of the oven and
the torch, whose images would have been infinitely less potent in daylight. If the sun that has set in v. 17 is thus part of Abraham's dream-
vision, then it may be assumed that the sunset in v. 12 is likewise of his
own making.

Westermann offers a rather different reading of these events. Clearly
he must acknowledge that Abraham falls asleep at the beginning of
v. 12. Yet his wish to deny the visionary quality of the patriarch's subsequent experiences leads him to conclude that the second half of v. 12
is redundant:

> As he is aware of nothing in the deep sleep (cf. 2:21), the following
> sentence is not necessary, whether one deletes one of the nouns or not: 'a
> great terror came upon him' or 'the terror of a great darkness came upon
> him'. The two words occur together again in Job 4:12-15 in the descrip-
> tion of a vision out of which an oracle is addressed to an individual: deep
> sleep and terror (there פחד). The two passages have something further in

74. *The Dream Theophany of Samuel*, p. 64.

common: the oracle as it is communicated in this divine manifestation has, as in Job, an interpretative meaning; it is to reinforce, to legitimate the explanation. The conclusion from its proximity to Job 4 is that the insertion vv. 12(11)-16 is very late.[75]

Westermann's reference to Gen. 2.21 in this context implies that he attributes to the deep sleep anaesthetic properties incompatible with sensations of fear and dread. This is mysterious, partly because such sensations do occur in deep sleep, even under anaesthetic, but mainly because Westermann himself supplies a biblical example (Job 4.13-14, cited above) of this very phenomenon. A possible clue to the meaning of Westermann's exegesis here may be found in his comment on 15.17:

> The carrying out of the rite follows in v. 17. If vv. 12-16 are a subsequent insertion, then the deep sleep and great terror are also part of it; the action in vv. 9-10, 17-18 does not contain any visionary traits; it is nothing but an enactment of an oath by God which Abraham experiences in full consciousness (so already A. Dillmann); peculiar to it is merely that it takes place in complete darkness (v. 17a). This is a necessary precondition for the action because no person may see God (Exod. 33.20). Only signs, fire and smoke, which represent God, may be seen in the darkness.[76]

His commitment to the idea that certain elements of Genesis 15 did not occur in the context of a vision-dream report may have led him to an interpretation that fails to convince on many levels. The assumption that the text in its entirety reports a dream is surely less problematic than the unparalleled enactment of an oath in complete darkness, undertaken after Abraham's unannounced awakening from a deep sleep, which Westermann envisages here.

An explanation of the significance of v. 12b, dismissed by Westermann as unnecessary, may be found in standard ancient Near Eastern representations of divine presence in dreams. Oppenheim remarks on the widespread use of imagery that suggests that the god in question comes to 'awaken' the dreamer, standing, in fact, out of sight at his head.[77] Even in dream narratives from cultures that had no taboo against physical descriptions of divine beings, dream messengers tend not to appear as a physical presence. The continuation of the verses from Job quoted above may seem to present a counter-example (Job

75. *Genesis 12–36*, p. 226.
76. *Genesis 12–36*, p. 228.
77. 'The Interpretation of Dreams', p. 190.

4.15-16). Yet the form described here is shadowy and indistinct,[78] and the report focuses on the dreamer's response to its presence, rather than on the precise nature of the apparition itself. These observations, combined with the fact that darkness and fear are often associated with divine revelations,[79] suggest that the 'great dark dread' (אימה חשכה גדלה) which descended upon Abraham may have been a standard dream-manifestation of the divine presence.[80]

Thus far in this discussion it has been suggested that the treatment of Genesis 15 as a dream report resolves apparent textual inconsistencies, such as those concerning the time of day at which the various events occurred, and fills perplexing gaps, such as how Abraham knew what to do with the animals God commanded him to take. It also encourages a reading in which physical objects or acts—the setting sun or the cutting of the animals—acquire an additional layer of symbolic significance. Yet the question remains: why did the narrator fail to state explicitly that the events of Genesis 15 occurred within a dream? This question almost certainly has a complicated array of answers, but it may be appropriate to begin with a discussion of the prophetic intentions of Genesis 15.

Abraham's Dream, Israel's Vision

Westermann claims that 15.4 does not constitute a standard annunciation message:

78. NJPS translates לא אכיר מראהו 'its appearance was strange to me', but a comparison with Ruth 3.14 suggests that NRSV's 'I could not discern its appearance' may be more accurate.

79. Cf., for instance, Deut. 5.20.

80. Additional support for this reading may be derived from the juxtaposition of vv. 12 and 13:

ויהי השמש לבוא ותרדמה נפלה על אברם והנה אימה חשכה גדלה
נפלת עליו: ויאמר לאברם ידע תדע כי גר יהיה זרעך בארץ
לא להם ...

> As the sun was about to set, a deep sleep fell upon Abram, and a great
> dark dread descended upon him. And he said to Abram, 'Know well that
> your offspring shall be strangers in a land not theirs ...'

Since none of the four preceding verses has mentioned God's name, one might have expected v. 13 to specify that God was speaking to Abraham. The absence of an explicit reference here may indicate that the narrator regarded the great darkness in v. 12 as a divine manifestation.

> In Genesis 15:4, the promise has undergone major changes. In fact, the statement in 15:4 that the offspring of Abraham's own body will be his heir is not really a promise of a son except by implication. The statement is obviously patterned after Abraham's lament in 15:3; Abraham laments that one of his house slaves will be his heir. The actual lament of child-lessness appears in verse 3: 'I continue childless!' The natural response would be the direct promise of a son. The placing of the whole emphasis on the heir in God's response to the lament appears to indicate a stage in which the handing on of property, inheritance, was the truly important consideration.[81]

His observations are to the point. Genesis 15.4 is not really concerned with the promise of a particular son, which is usually made more explic-itly (Gen. 18.10), to a woman (Judg. 13.3) or at least with reference to her (Gen. 18.10), and with some indication of when the birth will occur (Gen. 18.10). The combination of these elements makes it relatively straightforward to identify exactly which son is being promised, whereas Gen. 15.4-5 is strikingly vague on this matter.[82]

Pronouncements concerning offspring, born and unborn, are wide-spread (see Gen. 17.16-21, 21.18, 27.29-40; Judg. 13.5). Yet although they invariably involve predictions about the future, they do not consti-tute prophecy in its developed form. Genesis 15, by contrast, offers no predictions specific to Isaac, but only general pronouncements; Abra-ham will have an heir who is the product of his own loins, and his de-scendants will be numerous. The emphasis is not on a specific son, but rather on the people of Israel as a whole.

Although Westermann acknowledges that inheritance is of greater importance than the heir in Gen. 15.4-5, he nevertheless overstates the significance of the son. This is particularly evident in the contrast he makes between Gen. 15.4-5 and Isa. 51.1-2. In Gen. 15.5 he sees prom-ises of both a son and descendants, but in Isa. 51.2 he sees only the latter:

---

81. C. Westermann, *The Promises to the Fathers* (trans. D. Green; Philadelphia: Fortress Press, 1980). See p. 135.

82. Some might suggest that the ambiguity at this stage is attributable to a plot development in which the apparent heir is not the heir apparent. Thus, Ishmael is introduced in Gen. 16 only to be ruled out in ch. 21. Against this, however, it should be noted that the narrator is not coy about revealing from the outset that Jacob and not Esau will be the chosen son. Rebekah is told that her older son will serve her younger while they are still in the womb (25.23), and the suspense comes in watching the drama unfold.

This verse shows how even a factitious narrative can achieve the poetic power of a real narrative. Even though what God shows Abraham does not touch directly the point which gave rise to the lamentation, namely, that his wife cannot have children, it is nevertheless the vitalization of the promise of many descendants pronounced in unforgettable language at a time when the people was under threat. The promise to Abraham in this adapted form continues to live in an adapted situation. In Gen. 15:1-6 the promises of a son and of descendants are still clearly juxtaposed; in Deutero-Isaiah there is only the promise of descendants: 'Look to Abraham your father and to Sarah who bore you; for when he was but one I called him, and I blessed him and made him many' (Is. 51:2).[83]

Yet while he may be literally correct in seeing the promise of a son in the Genesis text, his emphasis is misleading, and a closer look at Gen. 15.5 and Isa. 51.2 suggests that they are simply two sides of the same coin. In Gen. 15.5 God tells Abraham to 'look to' his descendants. In Isaiah, using the same verb (נבט), God tells the descendants to look to Abraham. In Genesis 15 God shows Abraham that one will become many, while in Isaiah 51 he shows the many that they came from one. Both texts are primarily concerned with establishing a direct link between Abraham and his descendants.[84]

It is not difficult to see why Westermann wishes to include the son in the Genesis equation; Abraham is, after all, promised that his own son will be the heir to his house. Yet there are several reasons for minimizing the significance attached to the son. First, as mentioned above, the narrative itself is vague about the matter, failing to provide specific details about who the son will be and when he will be born; even the identity of his mother remains a mystery. Secondly, the promise of a son was an essential precursor to the promise of numerous descendants. Even if the narrator was not interested in making a formal birth announcement, it would have been disturbingly illogical to promise descendants without addressing the matter of Abraham's childlessness. In this respect, the allusion to an actual son may be little more than a peg on which to hang the promise of descendants. Thirdly, and perhaps

83. *Genesis 12–36*, p. 221.

84. Ezek. 33.24 pursues a similar theme in its message to those who had left Judah in 587 BCE. Van Seters, 'Confessional Reformulation in the Exilic Period', *VT* 22 (1972), pp. 448-59, notes the difficulty of assessing the significance of the one-to-many argument in this first reference to Abraham in the prophets, and makes the important observation that the theme of the promise to the patriarch and his descendants is not used (p. 449).

most importantly, the promise that Abraham would have an heir from his own loins emphasizes the direct connection between the patriarch and his descendants.

The earlier discussion of Clements's *Abraham and David* was sceptical about the links he perceives between the patriarch and the Davidic monarchy. Yet it is one thing to doubt that the author of either the Abrahamic or the Davidic covenant was interested in connecting the two figures, and quite another to hold that a general royal prototype was used as a basis for the depiction of Abraham. As noted above, biblical parallels suggest that Abraham's royal associations were drawn in part from the Israelite tradition: thus Gen. 15.4, 5 is reminiscent of the royal promise of descendants in 2 Sam. 7.12. Yet, as Van Seters observes, the royal theme was as likely to be drawn from Assyrian and Babylonian models:

> The theme about blessing those who bless Israel and cursing the one who curses Israel also has its origins in the concept of an imperial monarchy. This is true of the related theme of Abraham's offspring possessing 'the gate of their enemies' (22:17, 26:4). Such an imperial monarchy does not have in mind the Davidic-Solomonic period, which never had any such effective dimensions. It is, instead, an imitation of the great Assyrian and Babylonian empires of the eighth to sixth centuries.[85]

Genesis 15 may thus reflect what Van Seters describes as the 'democratization of royal forms'.[86] Abraham is presented as a proto-royal figure, not in order to validate the Davidic-Solomonic monarchy, but simply as a mechanism for ensuring that divine promises made to him applied also to his descendants. The ancient Near Eastern model of a covenant in which dynasties were included under the auspices of the king, much as citizens also benefited from the esteem in which their king was held by the gods, proved ripe for adaptation. Israel's claim on the land was guaranteed by its inclusion in a covenant made with the proto-royal figure of the patriarch, and the people were likewise beneficiaries of God's love for Abraham on account of his righteousness.[87]

A glance at the narratives that describe the Sinai covenant confirms the importance of establishing precisely who was bound by its terms.

---

85. *Abraham in History and Tradition*, pp. 274-75.

86. *Abraham in History and Tradition*, p. 275.

87. Even Isaac's claim on the land is credited to Abraham, and Gen. 26.3-5 refers explicitly to the latter's obedience and his willingness to keep God's commandments, statutes and laws (Gen. 26.5).

Exodus 19.9-11 contains various indications that the people are regarded as an active party in the covenant. God insists that the Israelites must
hear with their own ears the agreement he will make with Moses, and
although the reason given is to foster trust in their leader, it may also be
taken as a sign of their acceptance of the terms of the covenant that he
is making on their behalf, and, of course, their willingness to keep their
side of it. This is further underlined when they are instructed to keep
themselves pure during this period, which implies that they, as well as
Moses, will be in God's presence during the making of the covenant.
Finally, God promises to come down to the people on Mount Sinai
when the covenant has been made, and this makes it quite clear that
they are bound by its terms.

Deuteronomy 29.9-11 is still more specific on this matter. The inclusion of the stranger in the camp and everyone from the wood-cutter to
the water-drawer establishes that no Israelite present at Sinai could
claim exemption from the covenant, and, in the verses that follow (vv.
13-14), the obligation is extended to all those who were not present,
appearing to encompass those as yet unborn, as well as those who were
simply elsewhere at the time.

If it is, indeed, the case that Abraham's covenant with God was intended to establish an Israelite claim on the land that preceded the Sinai
covenant, then we might expect to find in Genesis 15 a strong indication that the covenant was not just with Abraham, but also with his
descendants. In some respects, the need was less pressing than at Sinai,
where it was important to show that the people had obligations under
the terms of the covenant. Yet in other respects, the need was more
pressing still. The narrator, presumably expressing the point of view of
the people, had to demonstrate beyond all doubt that God's unconditional promise of land in the form of a covenant with Abraham extended also to them, regardless of their behaviour in the meantime.

This is achieved in two ways. First, as discussed above, the insistence
that the Israelites were direct descendants of Abraham makes it possible
to see the Abrahamic covenant in terms of a dynastic promise. Leaving
nothing to chance, though, the narrator creates an interesting alternative
to the Deuteronomic emphasis on the presence of the Israelites when
the covenant was being made, and here the image of God's taking Abraham outside to see the stars (15.5) turns out to have central importance.
The explicit identification of stars with descendants means that they
may be seen not as a symbol of God's promise to Abraham, much as

the rainbow was in Genesis 9, but as actual witnesses to the covenant ceremony. This reading is supported by texts such as Deut. 4.25-26, 30.19, 32.1 and Isa. 1.2, in which heaven and earth are invoked in the role of witnesses to a divine agreement. It also fits well with observations by Mendenhall[88] and others concerning the appeal to heaven and earth and other parts of the cosmos to serve as witnesses in ancient Near Eastern treaties.[89] In these cases elements of the cosmos do not, of course, represent the people in the symbolic sense envisaged here for Genesis 15, but nor are they signs of the covenant (cf. the rainbow in Gen. 9). It seems thus plausible that the narrator of Genesis 15 merged the practice of invoking heaven as a treaty witness with the use of stars as a metaphor for the people in order to suggest that the Israelites, although not there in person when God made a covenant with Abraham, were represented as witnesses by the stars.

The Form of the Covenant

The description of the covenant ritual itself (15.9-10) has generated a great deal of discussion and as much disagreement:

וַיֹּאמֶר אֵלָיו קְחָה לִי עֶגְלָה מְשֻׁלֶּשֶׁת וְעֵז מְשֻׁלֶּשֶׁת וְאַיִל מְשֻׁלָּשׁ וְתֹר וְגוֹזָל:
וַיִּקַּח לוֹ אֶת כָּל אֵלֶּה וַיְבַתֵּר אֹתָם בַּתָּוֶךְ וַיִּתֵּן אִישׁ בִּתְרוֹ לִקְרַאת רֵעֵהוּ
וְאֶת הַצִּפֹּר לֹא בָתָר:

He answered, 'Bring me a three-year-old heifer, a three-year-old she-goat, a three-year-old ram, a turtledove, and a young bird.' He brought him all these and cut them in two, placing each half opposite the other; but he did not cut up the bird.

The great variation in scholarly interpretations is not without justification. M. Weinfeld identifies the sacrificial element of Genesis 15 with other ancient Near Eastern traditions:

Treaties of the third and second millennium were ratified by sacrifices. Thus, in the treaty between Naram Sin and the Elamites (2300–2250 B.C.) we find sacrifices offered and statues erected at the Elamite sanctuary.

88. G. Mendenhall, *Law and Covenant in Israel and the Ancient Near East* (Pittsburgh: The Biblical Colloquium, 1955).

89. D. Hillers, *Covenant: The History of a Biblical Idea* (Baltimore: The Johns Hopkins University Press, 1989 [1969]), claims that the appeal to heaven and earth 'is a standard feature of second-millenium Hittite treaties, is attested at Ugarit, recurs in a different form in one of the Aramaic Sefire treaties (eighth century B.C.), and stands in Hannibal's treaty with Philip V of Macedon which, although it is preserved only in Greek, is a translation of a Punic original' (p. 128).

The stele of the vultures also tells us about sacrificing a bull and two
doves. In the Mari documents we even meet with two different traditions
of covenantal sacrifices: the provincial tribes seem to prefer a goat and a
puppy for the ritual ceremony of the covenant, whereas the king of Mari
seems to insist on killing an ass. In the Alalah documents the covenant
involves cutting the neck of a lamb, and in one instance there is an explicit reference to 'cutting the neck of a *sacrificial* lamb'. A later
Alalahian covenantal text mentions an offering and a brazier in connection with the oath that the parties had taken. Similar features characterise
the ancient Israelite covenants.[90]

According to Ha, however, Abraham's actions are based on the similar
covenant ritual described in Jer. 34.18-19. He notes that both concern
liberation from slavery, and that both contain the root בתר (piece),
which appears elsewhere only in Song 2.17.[91] The account in Jeremiah
together with a Mari text in which a donkey is cut up for the same
purpose,[92] suggest that it was usual to use a single animal for the covenant ritual. As many commentators have noted, however, the additional
animals mentioned in Genesis 15 are all fit for sacrifice, and they may
have been included to evoke sacrificial associations. These associations
are further underlined by the information that the birds are not
divided,[93] as well as by the precise wording of God's instructions. The
numbering of the animals is similar to that found in lists of offerings
such as those prescribed for the week culminating with Shemini Atzeret
in Num. 29.20:

וביום השלישי פרים עשתי עשר אילם שנים כבשים בני שנה ארבעה
עשר תמימם:

Third day: Eleven bulls, two rams, fourteen yearling lambs, without
blemish.

The expressions 'take for me' (קחה לי) and 'he took for him' (ויקח לו)
are likewise resonant of the language of sacrifice, as is clear from a
comparison with texts that are unambiguously concerned with this

90. *Deuteronomy and the Deuteronomic School*, p. 103.
91. *Genesis 15*, pp. 74-75. Ha also claims that, in both cases, the superior party
passes through the pieces. This is not actually true in Jer. 34, since the covenant is
between God and the officers, officials, priests and so forth. Yet since the terms of
the covenant concern these people and their slaves, there is sense in which they are
the superior party.
92. Westermann, *Genesis 12–36*, p. 225.
93. Cf. Lev. 1.17. Rashi, *MG*, *ad loc.*, claims that the birds were not divided
because they symbolize Israel (cf. Song 2.14).

subject, such as Exod. 25.2. The offerings are not simply brought, but are brought *for God*, and this idea of dedication is surely present in Genesis 15.[94]

L. Perlitt describes vv. 7-21 as being 'rather crammed with motifs',[95] and this, one might argue, captures precisely the narrator's intentions. While avoiding the blatantly anachronistic approach to patriarchal sacrifice which occurs in the book of *Jubilees*, for instance, the narrator has achieved a description of an ancient covenant ritual in terms that evoke the distinctive piety of sacrifice. Indeed, vv. 9 and 10 not only provide a means of introducing the theme of sacrifice, but also serve to purge the ritual of pagan overtones which it almost certainly had. The partial transformation of the cutting up of the animals into a sacrifice performed by Abraham has the additional advantage of blurring a problem that arises in connection with the appropriation of a conditional covenant ceremony intended for two parties. In its original form, the ritual of dividing the animals was probably intended to evoke a concrete image of the fate that would befall the party who transgressed the terms of the covenant.[96] (Indeed, it may be an indication of the extent to which this aspect of the ritual was identified with transgression that, just as the verb כרת (cut) applies both specifically to the animals and generally to the covenant, so the verb עבר (cross) denotes both the passing between the pieces and the transgression of the covenant.) Since the Abrahamic covenant was intended to be unconditional, it was necessary to dilute the original conditional element of the ritual, and this is achieved, in part, by the introduction of the element of sacrifice. It is also achieved by the extraordinary account of God, in the form of a smoking oven and a flaming torch, passing between the pieces. Not only is God making a covenant with Abraham in which no conditions are imposed upon the patriarch, but he is using a ritual form which suggests that failure to keep its terms will entail God's taking upon himself the fate of the animals.[97]

94. This is compatible with the view of S.E. Loewenstamm, 'Zur Traditionsgeschichte des Bundes zwischen den Stucken', *VT* 18 (1968), pp. 500-506, who sees Gen. 15 as a late attempt to combine sacrifice with symbolic representation.

95. Cited by Westermann, *Genesis 12–36*, p. 225.

96. See M. Weinfeld, 'The Covenant of Grant in the Old Testament and in the Ancient Near East', *JAOS* 90 (1970), pp. 184-203 (198).

97. Hagelia, *Numbering the Stars*, supports with many biblical citations his claim that 'the choice of metaphors תנור עשן [smoking oven] and לפיד אש [fiery torch]

Turning from the ritual to more general issues of presentation, it is helpful to compare Genesis 15 with Joshua 24, particularly in relation to the preamble that precedes the cutting of the covenant in both cases. In Genesis this takes the form of a prophetic statement (vv. 13-15), while in Joshua 24 it is more of a historical overview (vv. 2-13), but both texts refer to Egypt and Israel's subsequent sojourn in the wilderness (Gen. 15.13-14, 16 and Josh. 24.5-7), both describe Canaan as the land of the Amorites (Gen. 15.16 and Josh. 24.8), and both contain similar lists, culminating with the Jebusites, of the peoples who occupied the land promised to Israel (Gen. 15.19-21 and Josh. 24.11). There are, however, some important differences, most notably in the area of conditionality. Joshua's covenant (24.27), like the Sinai covenant, is strongly conditional and depends absolutely upon the faithfulness of the Israelites. Genesis 15, on the other hand, contains no mention of conditions, and the expulsion of the existing inhabitants from the land is linked not to the righteousness of the Israelites, but to the iniquity of the Amorites. Joshua 24 contains no suggestion that the Amorites are iniquitous. On the contrary, their eviction from the land is presented rather naturalistically as the result of a typical skirmish between invader and existing occupant (24.8). Genesis 15, however, is clearly written against a theological background, such as that described in Deut. 9.5, in which the Amorites are removed as a punishment for their sins.

The similarities and differences between Genesis 15 and Joshua 24 are most unlikely to be accidental, but probably result instead from a careful adaptation by the Genesis redactor, in which process certain aspects of existing material are highlighted at the expense of other aspects no longer seen as compatible. The deuteronomic idea that the expulsion of the land's previous inhabitants was a punishment for their own wrong-doing is emphasized, while the concurrent emphasis on

was obviously not by chance. In fact, the main metaphors for divine presence are that of fire and smoke, corresponding to the two metaphors in Gen. 15.17' (pp. 144-45). No exegete, however, seems to have commented on a possible similarity between the imagery of this verse and the concluding lines of the Hittite 'Soldier's Oath', cited by J. Pritchard, *Ancient Near Eastern Texts Relating to the Old Testament* (Princeton: Princeton University Press, 1969 [1950]): 'They light [a fire]*brand* and trample it underfoot so that it scatters here and there and he says: "Just as this one flies apart(?)—whoever breaks these oaths, even so let this man's house be robbed(?) of men, cattle (and) sheep!" ... You will place before them an oven. Also a plow, a cart (and) a chariot you will place before the congregation ...' (p. 354).

conditionality is overlooked altogether.[98] This creative reconstruction of a chronologically earlier land-related covenant fits well with the notion that Abraham's righteousness is a basis for the promise of the land,[99] and would surely have appealed to an exilic audience anxious to minimize their own responsibility for historical events.

Prophecy and Typology

The down-playing in Genesis 15 of the conditional nature of the land covenant tradition is not the only means by which the Covenant of the Pieces may have been used to offer reassurance to the exiles in Babylon. As noted above, Van Seters posits a link between Genesis 15 and Deutero-Isaiah, but an aspect of Deutero-Isaiah's theology that he does not mention in this context is the prophet's particular emphasis upon God's ability to predict the future. This is exemplified by 41.26-27, which contrasts idols who cannot predict anything with God who has foretold everything. Deutero-Isaiah is primarily interested in God's ability to predict and, indeed, to control the future, as opposed to the impotence of foreign idols. Yet this form of thinking is more than a tribute to God's power, and leads inevitably to the assertion that everything was

98. N.C. Habel, *The Land is Mine: Six Biblical Land Ideologies* (Minneapolis: Fortress Press, 1995), contrasts the theme of peaceful relations in the Abraham narrative with the militant overtones of Joshua: 'This classic list [Gen. 15:19-21] might conjure up memories of the conquest tradition, but no explicit indications are given here that these people are to be expelled or destroyed. On the contrary, the narratives that surround this land covenant suggest that Abraham provided a model of how to live at peace with the host peoples of the land and share ownership of the land. In this ideology, possessing the land does not demand annihilation or expulsion of these peoples. The militant Joshua story is not the logical conclusion of the patriarchal narratives, but an alternative tradition and ideology about possessing the land. The land ideologies of the book of Joshua and the Abraham narratives are apparently in political tension' (p. 125).

99. B. Halpern-Amaru, *Rewriting the Bible: Land and Covenant in Postbiblical Jewish Literature* (Valley Forge, PA: Trinity Press International, 1994) suggests that it may be wrong to assume that the patriarch is promised land as a reward for merit: 'However, in both these cases fidelity is defined in terms of the patriarch's surety that God would keep promises that had initially been made without reference to the merits of the recipient. Here, in the biblical narrative Abraham's merit does not elicit the covenant so much as offer justification for it after the fact' (p. 12). As noted above, however, even Isaac's claim on the land is attributed to Abraham's righteousness (cf. 26.5).

planned by him; nothing has occurred by accident. There can be little doubt that this message would have been received enthusiastically by the exiled community for whom it was intended. The confirmation that the Babylonian Exile was not an unforeseen setback, but an event engineered by God to curb the excesses of the people, would have reassured the exiles on two points. First, regardless of outward appearance, they remained in God's control, and secondly, he would bring them back to the land he had promised to their ancestors.

G.H. Jones, following B.W. Anderson, comments as follows on Deutero-Isaiah's historical perspective on the Exodus:

> Deutero-Isaiah's eschatological pattern, which he had inherited from prophetic tradition, was based on the assumption that the end-time will correspond to the beginning (*Endzeit gleich Urzeit*). The exciting events of the day, namely the rise of Cyrus, the fall of Babylon and the release of the exiles, were described as a new exodus, corresponding to the Exodus under Moses. The prophet interpreted current events in the light of events from Israel's sacred history.[100]

This raises another mechanism, closely related to the theological outlook of Deutero-Isaiah, by which Genesis 15 could serve as a message of hope for the exiles. If Jones is correct in his general claim that Deutero-Isaiah creates what he describes as a 'typological' connection between Abraham and Cyrus, then the link between Abraham and the Exodus that is evident in Genesis 15 may indicate a three-way interaction between patriarchal history, the Exodus, and the Exile. This is clearly the view taken by M. Fishbane:

> Indeed, one might further add that the typological use of Abraham in connection with the 'new exodus' may have its roots in an earlier association made between Abraham and the original exodus.[101]

Fishbane goes on to note parallels between Abraham's sojourn in Egypt and Israel's slavery there, and between the plagues brought by God following Pharaoh's advances to Sarah and the plagues which preceded the Exodus, concluding that 'Abraham came to serve as the prototype of Israel for later generations'.[102]

---

100. 'Abraham and Cyrus: Type and Anti-type?', *VT* 22 (1972), pp. 304-19. See pp. 304-305 for this citation.

101. *Biblical Interpretation in Ancient Israel* (Oxford: Clarendon Press, 1991 [1985]), p. 375.

102. *Biblical Interpretation in Ancient Israel*, p. 276.

The first clear case in Genesis 15 of an attempt to suggest a connection between Abraham and the Exodus appears in v. 7. Van Seters sees this as a reformulation of the confessional 'I am the LORD your God who brought you out (הוֹצֵאתִיךָ)[103] of the land of Egypt' (Exod. 20.2; Deut. 5.6; cf. Lev. 25.38):

> This statement is the divine declaration of Israel's election through the exodus. Now the form and content in Gen. 15:7 is the same, except that 'Ur of the Chaldeans' is substituted for 'land of Egypt', but there can be little doubt that the reference to the exodus is the more original. Therefore Gen. 15:7 must be understood as representing a deliberate shift from the election of the exodus to the election through Abraham.[104]

This is surprisingly close to J. Calvin's observation that Abraham's safe passage from Ur of the Chaldeans to Judea served the Jews exiled in Chaldea as 'a pledge or mirror of their deliverance to come'.[105]

---

103. The use of הוֹצֵאתִיךָ (brought you out) here implies divine involvement in the strongest possible terms. It is difficult to generalize on this point, but it seems to be the case that יצא (bring out) occurs mainly where the statement that God brought the Israelites out of Egypt has a credo-like quality (cf. Deut. 5.6), while עלה (bring up) is used (far less frequently) in cases which are not declarations of belief. A particularly clear example is Exod. 32.4, which uses 'bring up' not 'bring out' with reference to the golden calf: 'This is your god, O Israel, who brought you [up] out of the land of Egypt' (אלה אלהיך ישראל אשר העלוך מארץ מצרים).

104. 'Confessional Reformulation in the Exilic Period', p. 455. Van Seters, *Abraham in History and Tradition*, sees the reference to 'Ur of the Chaldeans' in Genesis 15.7 as a strong indication of the text's late exilic background: 'It is best to start with the second part, and v. 7 in particular, because it contains a fairly precise date for the whole unit. There we have a reference to 'Ur of the Chaldeans' and this can only have meaning in the neo-Babylonian period, during the period of Chaldean dominance and the reign of Nabonidus in particular. So the period from which the Abraham tradition is being viewed is the late exilic period, and it is to the exilic community that the words of this chapter are being addressed' (p. 264). Westermann, however, in *Genesis 12–36*, questions Van Seters's confidence in this claim: 'J. Van Seters has concluded from the name Ur of the Chaldees that 15:7 can have originated only in the exile, because such a designation makes sense only in the late Babylonian period ... One must concede the possibility; but as the language of the text as a whole favors rather the seventh century, according to L. Perlitt's study, one cannot be so certain in assigning it to a later period merely on the basis of the one name. However, it can certainly not have originated in the tenth century' (p. 224).

105. Cited from Calvin's *A Commentary upon the Prophecies of Isaiah* (1609) by G. H. Jones in 'Abraham and Cyrus: Type and Anti-type?', p. 306.

Certainly, the idea that miraculous acts of liberation bear repetition is the basis of an important prophetic use of the Exodus theme (see Isa. 43.9, 18; 46.9). A prophet working in exile would inevitably have been drawn to the link between Abraham and the Exodus, offering as it does a perfect vehicle for a message of hope in the shape of historical precedent.[106]

Another comforting aspect of the association of Abraham and Moses is its emphasis on God's direct and active intervention in the life of the patriarch. This is evident in a comparison of Gen. 15.7 with 11.31. The occurrence in both texts of Ur of the Chaldeans makes it unlikely that the author of 15.7 was unaware of 11.31, and yet the two accounts represent different versions of the same story; according to ch. 11 it was Terach and not God who brought Abraham out of Ur. Yet it is important to consider that, when used with reference to Egypt (see Exod. 20.2; Lev. 25.38; and Deut. 5.6), this formulaic phrase is not used primarily to evoke specific details of God's extraction of Israel from the house of bondage. Rather, it is a statement of ultimate responsibility, a form of self-identification, almost a divine attribute. The issue of who brought who out of Ur was thus submerged in a general statement concerning God's relationship with Abraham. In any case, the patriarch himself clearly holds God responsible for bringing him out of Ur. There can be no doubt that Abraham's statement to his servant in 24.7, made during his quest for a wife for Isaac and carrying an explicit reiteration of God's promise of the land to Abraham's descendants, seeks to associate God's initial call of Abraham with the claim of his offspring on the land.

---

106. In a discussion of the typlogies of Genesis, M. Brettler, *The Creation of History in Ancient Israel* (London: Routledge, 1995), emphasizes the power to reassure of cyclical depictions of history: 'By creating an exodus-liberation pattern in Genesis that then gets repeated in Exodus (and still later again in Deutero-Isaiah), the community, even when in a state of subjugation, will feel that the cycle is about to turn, that liberation is again around the corner' (p. 54). There is, however, an important distinction to be made between this view, in which the exodus is seen as a prototype for the return from exile, and the opinion of P.R. Ackroyd, *Exile and Restoration: A Study of Hebrew Thought of the Sixth Century BC* (London: SCM Press, 1968), who, following Zimmerli, sees the return from exile as a fulfilment of the exodus: 'It is a recurrent theme [of Deutero-Isaiah] that the events by which the exiles are to be restored are the reality of what is proclaimed in the Exodus events' (p. 130).

Van Seters attaches great significance to 15.7:

> In Gen. 15:7, however, the reference to Egypt has been changed to Ur of
> the Chaldeans, and with it there is a fundamental shift of the whole elec-
> tion-tradition. YHWH is now the God of Abraham and his offspring.
> Just when this shift took place can be quite clearly traced in the biblical
> texts. Jeremiah and Ezekiel, the last prophets of the monarchy and the
> early exilic period, still held to the theme of divine election through the
> exodus event and the promise of land to Israel *at that time* (Ezek. 20:5-
> 6). Ezekiel, it is true, does mention Abraham once (33:24), and he is the
> first prophet to do so. But the claim to land based on the Abraham tra-
> dition is treated in rather disparaging terms ... But with Deutero-Isaiah
> the situation has entirely changed. Isa. 41:8f contains a clear reference to
> election through the forefathers ... Here God's election and call of
> Abraham from a distant land is viewed as Israel's election also. And the
> relevance of this for the exiles is that God can again bring them from
> these same distant regions to the promised land.[107]

The occurrence in Genesis 15 of the usually Deuteronomic formulation
לתת לך את הארץ הזאת לרשתה (to assign this land to you as a possession) applies to Abraham the connection between bringing out and inheritance which is more often associated with the exodus from Egypt,[108]
and the repetition of the root ירש (inherit, possess, vv. 3, 4, 7, 8) may
seek to underline the link between Israel's claim on the land and the
promise to Abraham.[109]

The centrality of the promise of the land in Genesis 15 is marked. As
discussed above, vv. 7-21 deal almost exclusively with the land, and,
where descendants are mentioned, it is primarily in the context of their
relationship with the land. Verses 13-16 address the question of when
Israel will be able to return to it. The placement of this prophecy of
postponement between Abraham's preparations for the covenant ceremony and its occurrence confirms that the delay was known to God

107. *Abraham in History and Tradition*, pp. 264-65.
108. Ha, *Genesis 15*, considers, but ultimately rejects, the possibility that this
phrase may have been borrowed from Gen. 28.4.
109. Westermann, *Genesis 12–36*, assumes this interest in 15.7: 'The third sentence of v. 7 says that the purpose of God in bringing Abraham from Ur was to give
him "this land" as his possession. There is here the same close link between the
bringing out and the promise of the land as in the parallel in Lev. 25:38, which in
turn goes back to the promise in Ex. 3:7f. This confirms that the bringing of Israel
out of Egypt and the grant of the land is the background of the formula used here'
(p. 224).

from the outset, and should not raise doubts about the eventual fulfilment of his promise. The confusion over the 400 years and the four generations has occupied a good deal of attention.[110] Although it is not possible to debate the matter further in this context, it seems appropriate to observe that the ambiguity created by the discrepancy between the two periods mentioned in vv. 13 and 16 helps to shift the focus away from the particular historical situation (the years of slavery in Egypt) to a less specific representation of exile. This is compatible with Kreutzer's view that these two periods of time should be understood typologically rather than historically.[111] The notion of a typological reading is further supported by the absence of an explicit reference to Egypt, and while it is impossible to assert beyond doubt that an allusion

---

110. Van Seters, *Abraham in History and Tradition*, explains the apparent discrepancy between the four-hundred years and the fourth generation by interpreting the latter as 'a prediction about the actual end of the exile'. He likewise understands the allusion to the guilt of the Amorites as a statement concerning the delayed return from exile' (p. 267). M. Anbar, 'Genesis 15: A Conflation of Two Deuteronomic Narratives', *JBL* 101 (1982), pp. 39-55, sees in Gen. 15.16 'a combination of two traditions concerning this span of time' (pp. 47-48). He observes that the phrase 'return here' ישובו הנה occurs only here and with reference to the returning exiles in Jer. 31.8. J. Emerton, 'The Origin of the Promises to the Patriarchs', thinks that Gen. 15.13-14 'may have had the Babylonian exile in mind'. S. Kreutzer, '430 Jahre, 400 Jahre oder 4 Generationen—Zu den Zeitangaben über den Ägypten-aufenthalt der "Israeliten"', *ZAW* 98 (1986), pp. 199-210, perceives exilic resonances, but associates them with the Assyrian exile.

111. '430 Jahre, 400 Jahre oder 4 Generationen', p. 209. Similarly, Kreutzer offers a metaphorical interpretation for the allusion to the Amorites in v. 16, claiming that it may be a code-name for a people, such as the Assyrians or Babylonians, who represented a later threat to Israel (p. 206). A variant on this theme is offered by S. Geller, 'The Sack of Shechem: The Use of Typology in Biblical Covenant Religion', *Prooftexts* 10 (1990), pp. 3-15: 'More immediate is the function of the "Canaanites". Through this concrete, almost accidental image covenant religion opened a slot, as it were, in its view of the world, a new "natural" category: the "unnatural", the cosmic foe of divinely created order. Covenant religion identified this inimical principle with a group no longer extant. Later generations were not so careful. The Canaanite "slot" came to be filled already in the fifth century by an oddly hybrid congeries termed, significantly, the "peoples of the land(s)". Ezra lists the groups with whose women returning Jews have intermarried as "Canaanites, Hittites, Perizzites, Jebusites, Ammonites, Moabites, Egyptians and Amorites" (Ezra 9:1)... They serve here only to state the prototype ... "Peoples of the land(s)" has come only to mean all those who threaten Israel's ethnic solidarity' (p. 13).

to Babylon was intended in Gen. 15.13-16, it seems reasonable to see this as a text that points beyond its ostensible subject.

The Placement of Genesis 15 in the Patriarchal Narrative

Since the discussion in this chapter is based on the premise that Genesis 15 was inserted into a more or less complete form of the patriarchal narrative, it would be inappropriate to conclude without comment on its placement. It goes without saying that the redactor was limited by the pre-established order of events; ch. 15, with its promise of an heir, could not, for instance, have appeared after the birth of Isaac.

Ha provides an extensive discussion of the placement of this chapter, and, with the exception of his commitment to a late date for the controversial Genesis 14, it contains little to disagree with.[112] It is not possible to enter into the Genesis 14 debate here, but, regardless of whether ch. 14 or ch. 15 was the earlier of the two, their proximity raises questions about the methodology of the biblical redactor that are particularly relevant to the subject at hand.

Ha speculates that the author of Genesis 14 'might have been struck by the military overtone of Gen. 15 and thought his work might provide a fitting setting to it'.[113] Indeed, it appears that biblical covenants almost invariably follow some form of unrest, whether global, as in God's covenant with Noah after the flood (Gen. 9.8-17), or merely between two individuals, as with Jacob and Laban (Gen. 31.44). That a covenant should be preceded by a disagreement between the two parties concerned is hardly surprising. What is more interesting is that covenants are sometimes preceded by the successful conclusion of a conflict that is not obviously connected with the covenant itself. Thus, the Sinai covenant in Exodus 19 is preceded by the defeat of Amalek in 17.8-15, interrupted only by a description of Jethro's solution to the problem of internal wrangling in the wilderness.[114] Joshua's covenant (Josh. 24.25-

---

112. Ha, *Genesis 15*, follows Van Seters' claim that ch. 14 belongs to neither the D nor the P sources. He takes its assumption that Abraham is already in possession of the land as a sign that it is later than ch. 15 (pp. 202-203).

113. *Genesis 15*, p. 204.

114. Admittedly, viewed in the sweep of Israelite history, the battle with Amalek has the appearance of a minor skirmish. Yet the episode has a symbolic importance which the text makes quite plain through its depiction of Moses's remote control of the battle, and through its statement in Exod. 17.14-16 that God, and not merely Israel, is engaged in an unending war against Amalek.

28) is likewise reported after peace has been achieved between Israel and her enemies (Josh. 23.1), and the description of David's covenant in 2 Samuel 7 begins with the announcement (v. 1) that God had given him respite from his enemies.[115] What thus appears to be an established link between resolved conflict and covenant makes the placement of the account of Abraham's successful intervention in the battle between the kings next to the description of God's first covenant with Israel seem unlikely to be coincidental.

A number of verbal parallels between chs. 14 and 15 suggest that one or the other (or both) was adapted to emphasize the points of contact suggested above. Exegetes have commented on possible links between Abraham's refusal to become rich at the king of Sodom's expense (14.21-23) and God's promise of great reward (15.1), between מגן (delivered) in 14.20 and the noun מגן (shield) in 15.1, and on the occurrence of שכר (reward) in 14.21 and 15.14.[116] The use of verbal similarities to carry forward a text is, of course, precisely the mechanism that governed the flow of later midrashic literature, and although it would be difficult to establish that this hermeneutic device was already at work in the Bible, textual evidence points strongly in that direction.[117]

In the context of a discussion of another familiar midrashic device, the juxtaposition of two texts to express a new idea, A. Shinan and Y. Zakovitch discuss the appearance of the Covenant of the Pieces immediately before Abraham's expulsion of Hagar in Genesis 16:

> It can be shown that chap. 16 serves to justify the slavery in Egypt which is foretold in chap. 15—'Then the LORD said to Abram, "Know ... that your descendants will be sojourners in a land that is not theirs, and will be slaves there, and they will be oppressed there (וענו אתם) for four hundred years ..." ' (vv. 13-14). The reason for the delay in giving the promised land to Abraham's descendants is expressed in v. 16: 'for the iniquity of the Amorites is not yet complete'. This does not explain,

---

115. Kapelrud, 'Temple Building', pp. 56-62, identifies peace in this case as a necessary condition for the building of a temple (see 1 Kgs 5.1-19), but since David does not build a temple despite being granted rest from his enemies, it is possible that 2 Sam. 7.1 actually refers to the peace required prior to the making of a covenant.

116. See Sarna, *Understanding Genesis*, pp. 121-22.

117. A. Caquot, 'L'alliance avec Abram (Genèse 15)', *Semitica* 12 (1962), pp. 51-66, actually sees Gen. 15 as a form of midrash (prefiguring the Davidic dynasty) (p. 66). In this discussion, however, it is claimed merely that its author seems to use techniques now identified with post-biblical Jewish midrashists.

however, why the Israelites, who did not commit any sin, need suffer in the meantime. Chap. 16 provides an answer. The Egyptian Hagar is oppressed in Abraham's house—'Then Sarai oppressed her (ותענה) ...' (vv. 6-9)—in a way parallel to the affliction of the Israelites in Egypt (Gen. 15:13 and Exod. 1:11, see also Deut. 26:6).[118]

Other parallels are offered: the Egyptians oppress the Israelites lest they multiply (Exod. 1.10), and Sarah oppresses a pregnant Hagar; both Israel and Hagar flee to the desert, the angel's reference to Hagar's affliction (v. 11) is mirrored in God's words to the Israelites (Exod. 3.7, also 2.24, 6.5); and in both stories a slave-girl's son (Ishmael and Moses) is adopted by a woman in the master's house (Sarah and Pharaoh's daughter). Although not all scholars would be convinced by the case made by Shinan and Zakovitch for what they describe as another example of 'the well-known principle of "measure for measure" ', the parallels they observe must certainly be weighed in with other evidence for the possible midrashic intentions in tbe placement of Genesis 15.

Another glimpse of the redactor's hand may be found in the formulaic opening phrase of Genesis 15, אחר הדברים האלה (after these things). Westermann cites R. Kilian's view that this is 'an editorial connecting link which looks backwards', and adds that it is not a sign of immediate continuation, but 'always spans back an interval to what had preceded'.[119] He claims that its three occurrences in texts concerning Abraham (15.1, 22.1, 22.20) presuppose a coherent narrative, so that it must have been introduced at a time when the Abraham cycle was no longer regarded as a series of independent units: it is a redactional device, 'linking ch. 15 with what precedes'.[120]

Yet the dream format itself may function as an editorial tool in this context. The fact that the dream operates in a separate sphere of the character's existence, namely the realm of the unconscious, minimizes the need for connective links with the surrounding narrative. The prophetic component inherent in dreams means that future events can be accounted for without the risk of disturbing anachronism, and, as is illustrated by the variation between the two accounts of how Abraham left Ur of the Chaldeans, dreams lend themselves well to the subtle

118. 'Midrash on Scripture and Midrash within Scripture', in S. Japhet (ed.), *Studies in Bible* (Scripta Hierosolymitana, 31; Jerusalem: Magnes Press, 1986), pp. 257-77 (270).

119. *Genesis 12–36*, p. 217.

120. Westermann, *Genesis 12–36*, p. 217.

revision of impressions created by pre-existing narratives.[121] Most importantly, perhaps, the dream provides the narrator with a format that combines a prophetic application to future generations with intense attention to the individual dreamer; the emphasis on his descendants in no way diminishes the significance of the experience for Abraham.[122]

Sarna describes the Bible's assimilation and adaptation of ancient Near Eastern material for its own purposes.[123] What he has in mind is, of course, the biblical reworking of creation and flood narratives, by which means reassuringly familiar stories and beliefs were reinterpreted by the biblical narrator. Yet there is a sense in which Genesis 15 is the product of a remarkably similar process. Its narrator has created a compendium, not so much of history, but of aspects of Israelite and non-Israelite culture that had the power to reassure by their familiarity. The slight but significant changes which he effects casts these established traditions and beliefs in a new light, but they lose little or none of their original appeal or authority. A brief overview of the text provides a graphic illustration of this process.

Verse 1, with its formulaic introduction, its reference to a vision and its familiar 'fear not', imbues all that follows with prophetic significance; this is not just the account of an event, but a message for its readers. Verses 2-5 rework the theme of the childless head of a dynasty on whose behalf divine intervention is required; the promise of a son is almost entirely submerged in the promise of the nation. Verse 6 elaborates the concept of unsupported faith, which had become increasingly important in the exilic period. Verse 7 simultaneously backdates the Exodus to Abraham, linking the promise of the land to his being brought out of Ur, and creates a link with the exiles, who are awaiting the time when God will bring them out of Babylon. Verses 9-11 endow an ancient covenant ritual with sacrificial resonances which evoke cultic piety. Verses 13-16 merge exodus and exile in a prophetic recapitulation of relations between Israel and Egypt. Verses 17 and 18 recall Sinai, and 19 and 20 address the occupation and eventual reoccupation

121. This feature is evident in other Genesis dream reports. Thus, Jacob's dream of the flocks (31.10-13) revises the impression that magic as opposed to divine protection was responsible for the patriarch's success in sheep breeding.

122. Whybray, *The Making of the Pentateuch*, observes that dreams and oracles, providing warnings that are later fulfilled, are used as a connective device by Herodotus (p. 228).

123. *Understanding Genesis.* See especially pp. 1-27.

of the land. Thus Genesis 15 reassures by the very familiarity of the
elements it incorporates. Yet it also contrives to claim authority for
ideas that were far from familiar, such as the notion of an unconditional
promise of the land to Abraham, by clothing them in traditional garb
which, though altered, was easily recognizable.

Does Genesis 15 Contain a Useful Type of Ambiguity?

A variety of explanations have been offered for the absence in Genesis
15 of an explicit reference to dreaming. On the one hand, the dream
report had many distinct advantages. As observed above, it could be
inserted almost seamlessly into an existing narrative; it can convey
prophetic significance without obvious anachronism in pre-prophetic
circumstances; and, while appearing to focus on the dreamer, it can
address other issues, particularly those which, in reality, have not yet
arisen, in a way that is not possible in straightforward narrative. Against
all this, however, was the ambivalence with which dreams were regarded as the concept of prophecy was developed. The extraordinary
attempt to precede the Sinai covenant with a more favourable alternative would almost certainly have been jeopardized by explicit
identification with a dubious form of revelation. By implying but not
stating that Abraham was dreaming in Genesis 15, the narrator is able
to tread a tightrope between the advantages and disadvantages inherent
in the dream format.

Yet there may be advantages of an entirely different nature that arise
from the narrator's failure to specify the real nature of Abraham's
revelation. It should be clear by now that, as this discussion of Genesis
15 has progressed, the intended reader has emerged at the very heart of
the text. The claim that the use of the dream format is primarily for the
benefit of the intended reader may seem banal, but, in fact, it promotes
a level of engagement with the text which would have been difficult to
achieve by any other means.

In a discussion of gap filling and midrashic indeterminacy, D. Boyarin
characterizes gaps as 'those silences in the text which call for
interpretation if the reader is to "make sense" of what happened, to fill
out the plot and the characters in a meaningful way.' He goes on to
explain that he is:

> extending the application of the word 'gap' to mean *any* element in the
> textual system of the Bible which demands interpretation for a coherent
> construction of the story, that is, both gaps in the narrow sense, as well

> as contradictions and repetitions, which indicate to the reader that she
> must fill in something that is not given in the text in order to read it. The
> reason for broadening the extension of the term is that all of these textual
> phenomena, when read synchronically, turn out to function similarly;
> that is, they are resolved by assuming that something has been left out of
> the text which can be restored by a more or less motivated activity of the
> reader.[124]

Boyarin's interest here is the role of midrash in filling the Bible's textual gaps, but his discussion of texts which, according to a rabbinic saying, cry out 'interpret me' is helpful in determining an appropriate
approach to Genesis 15. Thus, its numerous gaps may be explained not
as the result of inferior redaction, but as a deliberate device employed
by the redactor to engage the reader. Yet there is an obvious sense in
which the text itself contains signs directing the reader as to precisely
how the gaps should be filled. Although there may seem to be something inherently paradoxical about the claim that a text that cries out for
interpretation provides clear directions about how its gaps should be
filled instead of simply filling them, it is easy to reconstruct circumstances in which a biblical redactor might wish to preserve textual gaps
and inconsistencies while simultaneously providing the reader with a
means of filling or resolving them. The motivation may be a straightforward desire to maintain more than one tradition, even if this must
occur at the expense of narrative coherence, and gaps and inconsistencies may also be used to invite, or even force, the reader to make
critical judgments which the redactor may prefer not to voice aloud. In
the case of Genesis 15, however, the inconsistencies reflect the tensions
between the text's real and stated concerns. The redactor's decision to
arm the reader with an implicit solution while refusing to express it
explicitly is, in part, a device enabling him to minimize the contra-
dictions inherent in the narrative. Moreover, in creating a text that
demands interpretation, and which is, in fact, incoherent without it, the
redactor has forced the exilic readers posited here to participate in a text
of which they, as well as Abraham, are the subjects.

  Genesis 15 is a narrative that is most centrally concerned with delay.
Abraham is promised numerous descendants at a time when even one
child seems unlikely, and he is promised land while still a nomad,
unable, as 12.10 shows swiftly and indisputably, to depend on the land

---

124. *Intertextuality and the Meaning of Midrash* (Bloomington: Indiana University Press, 1990), p. 41.

to sustain him. The Covenant of the Pieces reassures him that these promises will be fulfilled, but, more importantly, it implies that the delay is not an inconvenience to be endured, but rather an essential element of God's plan for patriarch and people. That the covenant is preceded by a reference to the delay that will occur before the Israelites can occupy the land promised here to Abraham reassures the patriarch that God will not necessarily fulfil promises immediately. The fact that he has neither son nor land is not a cause for great concern, and certainly does not justify the doubts he expresses here. On the other side of the coin, God's dealings with Abraham established a pattern of promise and fulfilment punctuated by delay. It is not difficult to see the optimism and acceptance that could have been generated in the exilic reader by this message, and, although its suitability for this purpose does not prove that it was thus intended, I have attempted here to show that the text may well have been constructed with this end in view. In this respect, the placement of Genesis 15 in the Abraham narrative is a matter of critical importance. The covenant occurs at the point when God's promises to the patriarch seem least likely to bear fruit, and its capacity to quell the uncertainty of the exiles is based in no small measure upon its power to reassure the patriarch that delay need not entail doubt.

As with each of the preceding chapters, I will conclude with an outline of themes shared by all the patriarchal dreams of Genesis and a brief account of how they are manifested in the Covenant of the Pieces.

(1) *The dream is received during a period of anxiety or danger.*
Abraham is anxious because God has yet to fulfil his promises of land and offspring.

(2) *The dream concerns descendants, immediate or eventual.*
Abraham voices his concern that he will be succeeded not by a child of his own, but by his servant Eliezer, and God promises descendants numerous as the stars of the heavens. The troubled future of Abraham's descendants is contrasted with his own peaceful death.

(3) *The dream signals a change in status.*
It prepares Abraham for a covenant in which God's promises are confirmed.

(4) *The dream highlights divine involvement in human affairs.*
It reveals that God brought Abraham out of Ur as part of his plan. What appeared to be a natural delay in Abraham's

acquisition of offspring and land is now presented as an integral element in the divine scheme of things.

(5)   *The dream concerns the relationship between Israelites and non-Israelites.*
God confirms that Abraham's house will not be inherited by the non-Israelite Eliezer, and prophesies Israel's future bondage to (and eventual redemption from) a foreign master.

(6)   *The dream deals with absence from the land.*
It predicts a delayed inheritance of the promised land.

Chapter 6

CONCLUSION

My decision to limit the scope of this study to the patriarchal dreams of Genesis arose at first from a desire to fill a perceived gap in the literature. Previous writers on biblical dreams, having cast their nets wide to include dream reports from Israelite and, often, other ancient Near Eastern sources from throughout the biblical period, and sometimes beyond, have, for the most part, been unable to provide a detailed analysis of any individual text. That scholars should be drawn to the wide-net approach is not surprising. Although the Bible itself contains varying assessments of dreams and their theological value, certain aspects of dreams and dream interpretation remained consistent throughout the ancient Near East and for a remarkable duration. One might note, for instance, striking parallels between the Talmudic dream book and the Assyrian work that acted as the catalyst for Oppenheim's study of ancient Near Eastern dreams.[1] Yet the failure to examine individual texts in detail represents a serious limitation. The dreams of the Bible, whether or not they were based on real dream experiences, have survived in their present form as literary texts, and it is as such that they must be examined and assessed. A brief structural survey is inadequate for this purpose.

My decision to limit the scope of this study was also motivated by a second factor, quite separate from the belief that the significance of literary creations is most effectively revealed through close textual analysis which, in turn, is best conducted on a small number of texts. Without wishing to insist that the patriarchal dreams originated from the same hand, or even in the same historical circumstances, there is a *prima facie* case for claiming that, at least at the level of final redaction,

---

1. For another similar work see 'The Egyptian Dream Book' (British Museum Papyrus 10683), cited by N. Lewis, *The Interpretation of Dreams and Portents* (Toronto: Hakkert and Co., 1976), pp. 7-15.

they have a common narrative purpose. This belief, if correct, justifies a treatment in which the dreams of Genesis are analysed as a distinct corpus, inter-connected by links which they do not share with other biblical dreams.[2] It does not, however, preclude the possibility that the same narrative purpose is evident elsewhere in Genesis, and, in a separate study, it would be interesting to explore the relationship between the dream reports and other texts with a similar concentration of themes.[3]

At the end of each of the preceding chapters I have outlined six themes common to the five patriarchal dreams. My analysis has shown that each dream is (1) received at a time of anxiety or danger; (2) concerns descendants; (3) signals a change in status; (4) highlights divine involvement in human affairs; (5) deals with the relationship between Israelites and non-Israelites; and (6) concerns absence from the land. A variety of conclusions may be drawn from these themes. That at least four of them are shared by standard dream reports from throughout the ancient Near East confirms the value of examining biblical dreams through the lens of surrounding cultures, and the correspondences observed here suggest that royal figures were used as models for the biblical representation of the patriarchs. As discussed in connection with Genesis 15, however, there is no reason to presume links with a specific monarchy from either within or outside Israel.

The *political* use of the dreams of kings in the ancient Near East has been well documented, and, in view of these additional connections, it would be unwise to understate this aspect of the patriarchal dreams.[4] There are two distinct, though compatible, senses in which the dreams may serve a political purpose. On the one hand, they may operate in their immediate narrative context to further the interests of the patriarchs, and this function has been perceived in all the texts examined here: Abimelech's dream demonstrates Abraham's superiority over the

---

2.   Structural and stylistic matters pertaining to the presentation of the dream reports have been well-treated by scholars such as Ehrlich and Gnuse.

3.   I am grateful to Professor J. Rogerson for suggesting 21.1-21, 22.1-19 and 32.23-33 as examples of Genesis narratives which could profitably be explored in this context.

4.   P.E. Dutton, *The Politics of Dreaming in the Carolingian Empire* (Lincoln: University of Nebraska Press, 1994), uses ancient models to elucidate his treatment of political dreams in ninth-century Europe, and his conclusions point to a use of dreams which changed remarkably little over many centuries.

foreign king; Jacob's dream at Bethel reveals God's preference for Jacob over Esau; Jacob's dream of the flocks sanctions his trickery and emphasizes his advantage over Laban; Laban's dream shows that he is powerless against Jacob; and the Covenant of the Pieces underlines Abraham's position as the father of a nation.

On the other hand, the patriarchal dreams may have political implications that extend beyond their immediate narrative sphere. The two themes outlined above which have no obvious ancient Near Eastern resonances, namely the relationship between Israelites and non-Israelites and absence from the land, point to a political value for future descendants as well as for the patriarchs themselves. Thus Abimelech's dream works within the wife-sister narratives to develop a blueprint for the peaceful coexistence of Israelites and non-Israelites, in opposition, perhaps, to the model of violent conquest offered elsewhere; Jacob's two dreams indicate that absence from the land, although a stage in the divine plan, is neither permanent nor a desirable end in itself; Laban's dream shows that God will deal directly with non-Israelites to protect Israel; and the Covenant of the Pieces demonstrates again that the delayed inheritance of the land is intentional.

In addition to their political value in revealing God's position with regard to Israel's short-term and long-term history, the patriarchal dreams also operate in a third way, which is, once again, both distinct from and compatible with the other two. I have emphasized the role of dreams not simply as a mechanism for confirming status, but also as a means of revising or supplementing an impression conveyed by the preceding narrative. Not surprisingly, this revision or supplementation almost invariably takes the form of accenting, and even introducing, divine involvement in human affairs. The role of dreams in recasting in a more favourable light what are represented as historical events, emphasizing, in particular, divine sanction of human acts and decisions (especially misguided ones), suggests an interesting comparison with the use of inscriptions in the ancient world. A. Laato has argued persuasively that inscriptions recording the results of a battle are not necessarily reliable historical accounts. Rather, they may represent the creative revisions of kings who feared that military defeat in battle would be seen as a sign that they were no longer favoured by the gods.[5]

---

5. 'Assyrian Propaganda and the Falsification of History in the Royal Inscriptions of Sennacherib', *VT* 45 (1995), pp. 198-226.

Dream reports were, in many ways, well-suited to perform a similar function.

Several theological and literary points have been made to account for the particular suitability of dreams for effecting historical revisions. Dreams were, as von Rad observed, the biblical meeting place of divine and human spheres, and they thus represented an attractive tool for narrators faced with the challenge of introducing notions of divine responsibility or even approval into a text which previously dealt only in human action. In this capacity as a meeting-place for human action and divine will, dreams were ideally suited to what Y. Amit has described as 'dual causality' narrative, enabling a narrator to preserve a sense of ambiguity between the two spheres.

Dreams have, in addition, a number of 'editorial' advantages that make them ideal for creating revisions of the type envisaged here: they can be inserted seamlessly into an existing text with minimal disruption of the narrative flow; they can function as connective devices of the sort observed by Whybray and others in the historical accounts of Herodotus; they can fill unexplained gaps in human knowledge or account for an otherwise inexplicably reversed decision; and, in some ways most importantly, they can enhance the portrayal of an individual character by revealing something of his inner-life while simultaneously achieving the less overt goals outlined above.

There can be little doubt that redactors of existing patriarchal material strove for authenticity, and, in this respect too, dream reports were particularly useful. On the one hand, the desire that the patriarchal narratives should address in some way future generations called for the introduction of a prophetic element that was unlikely to have been present in the most ancient texts. On the other hand, the insertion of straightforwardly prophetic forms would have seemed anachronistic and out of place in the context of the patriarchal relationship with God. Together with birth announcements and promises made in connection with blessings (whether divinely or humanly conferred), dream reports balance immediate personal relevance with the suggestion of a future application as yet unrevealed, and in this respect they seem to have been the narratively conceived, if not actually chronological, predecessors of prophecy.

The effectiveness of dreams in revising the past, particularly in the direction of heightened divine involvement in human affairs, their flexibility as editorial (especially connective) devices, and their forward-looking, even prophetic, quality combine to make them ideal tools in another kind of textual operation, namely the creation of narrative typologies. There are obvious respects in which typology may function as a supplement to prophecy, adding a reassuring sense of precedent to outright prediction. A redactor wishing to emphasize similarities between the patriarchal experience and later episodes in Israelite history might well look to dream reports as a means of achieving this goal. Dreams were, furthermore, eminently compatible with the typological ideal, well-formulated by Fishbane, of emphasizing the 'homological likeness' of two events while preserving their 'historically unique character'.[6] The question remains, however, as to whether it is possible to determine the historical context in which textual revisions intended to create or emphasize typologies are most likely to have been made.

The research described in this study has pointed repeatedly to the Babylonian Exile as the time when historical circumstances and theological outlook might most plausibly have combined to encourage redactional activity of the sort envisaged here. This was a time when classical prophecy was falling short of meeting the needs of its recipients, as Deutero-Isaiah seems tacitly to acknowledge when he supplements comforting predictions with the reassuring notion that what had happened before would happen again (cf. Isa. 46.3-4; 51.1-2, 9-11; 54.9-10). The prophet's frequent use of images of the creation and the Exodus to confirm his continuing involvement in Israel's history is surely auspicious for a similar use of patriarchal material.

The increasingly universalist outlook of the exilic state of mind (as reflected in Deutero-Isaiah) also resonates in the patriarchal dreams. This study has emphasized the flexibility of dreams as vehicles of revelation which were equally appropriate for Israelites and non-Israelites, and has also demonstrated a strong interest, evident in all five texts, in the relationship between the two. The emphasis on peaceful coexistence and Israel's role as a source of blessings for the nations which pervades the dream texts is clearly in keeping with the attitude towards non-Israelites exemplified by Deutero-Isaiah.

Not surprisingly, however, the connection between the patriarchal dreams and the time of the Babylonian Exile that commands closest attention concerns the attitude to the land itself. The brief thematic survey presented above reveals that all five dream reports deal in one way or another with absence from the land or, to use a less neutral term,

6. *Biblical Interpretation in Ancient Israel*, p. 350.

exile. This theme is, of course, most evident in the three dreams of the
Jacob cycle, which may indicate a special typological relationship between Jacob and Israel in exile. In any case, taken as a group, the
patriarchal dreams present a picture in which absence from the land
entails potential danger, or, at the very least, subservience to a seemingly superior foreign power, and in which additional divine protection
is required. Far from recommending violent conquest or even complete
separation, however, the dream texts idealize peaceful coexistence,
with God's intervention taking the form of revelation and not force.
This picture fits well with a historical context in which re-entry into the
land was dependent upon the generosity of a foreign power against
whom physical force was not even a remote option. The Israelite
humility appropriate to this situation is, however, tempered by the
dreams' insistence that God is superior to any foreign power, and that,
all appearances to the contrary, the duration of Israelite absence from
the land is actually in his hands.

There is, of course, another dimension to the exile that is only tangentially connected with absence from the land, and this concerns the
destruction and anticipated rebuilding of the temple. Since the theme of
temple building occurs only in Jacob's dream at Bethel, it would be
wrong to dwell on it in concluding comments that focus on interests
shared by all five patriarchal dream reports. Yet it seems clear both that
the twin themes of the relationship between Israelites and non-Israelites
and absence from the land find their most intense expression in the
three dreams of the Jacob cycle, and that, of those three dreams, the
dream at Bethel is pivotal. For these reasons, it is appropriate to observe that, although not a pervasive theme, the emotive issue of rebuilding the temple is addressed in the typological model which has been
envisaged here.

One final question remains: how effectively would the patriarchal
narratives have conveyed the typological interests ascribed to them here
without the patriarchal dreams? On the one hand, the dream reports are
tightly interwoven with the fabric of the narrative, and there is ample
evidence elsewhere of the pervasive themes of anxiety or danger, threatened descendants, the relationship with non-Israelites, and absence from
the land. Nor is it the case that only the dream texts deal with altered
status or divine involvement in human affairs. Yet the dream reports,
though not unique in the themes they treat, are surely the best examples
of texts that combine all these themes to create a sense of perpetual

divine stage-management, especially in times of danger or duress. In terms of the typological effectiveness of the patriarchal narratives, this theological dimension is extremely important, if not indispensable. The presentation of a set of striking coincidences between the lives of Israel's ancestors and her own historical experience would be interesting, but little more. It is only the involvement of divine will that transforms chance parallels into messages of hope and reassurance concerning God's continuing love for Israel.

Throughout the ancient world dreams were sought and interpreted in response to illness, fear and uncertainty, both personal and political. It is strangely moving to consider that the biblical narrators too may have sought comfort in dreams, not, in this case, by means of the direct divine response they envisaged for their ancestors, but through hope inspired by patriarchal precedent. For the Jews of the exilic period it must have seemed increasingly unlikely that God's promises to Abraham, Isaac and Jacob, and extended to their offspring, would ever be fulfilled; the hope of multitudinous descendants inhabiting the promised land and bringing blessings to the nations was hardly a realistic one during a period of exile and subservience to a foreign power. Through the patriarchal dreams of Genesis, God reassures the patriarchs that the delayed fulfilment of these promises is only temporary, and provides an inspirational glimpse of what is to come. Through the same dreams the biblical narrators, seeing their own fears and concerns mirrored in the lives of their ancestors, comforted themselves with the hope that what had come before would come again.

BIBLIOGRAPHY

Ackroyd, P.R., *Exile and Restoration: A Study of Hebrew Thought of the Sixth Century BC* (London: SCM Press, 1968).

Alexander, P.S., 'Bavli Berakhot 55a-57b: The Talmudic Dreambook in Context', *JJS* 46 (1995), pp. 230-48.

Alexander, T.D., 'Are the Wife/Sister Incidents of Genesis Literary Compositional Variants?', *VT* 42 (1992), pp. 145-53.

Alt, A., 'Die Wallfahrt von Sichem nach Bethel', in *idem, Kleine Schriften zur Geschichte des Volkes Israel* (3 vols.; Munich: C.H. Beck, 1953), I, pp. 79-88.

Alter, R., *The Art of Biblical Narrative* (London: George Allen & Unwin, 1981).

Amit, Y., 'The Dual Causality Principle and its Effects on Biblical Literature', *VT* 37 (1987), pp. 385-400.

—'The Multi-Purpose "Leading Word" and the Problems of its Usage', *Prooftexts* 9 (1989), pp. 99-114.

Anbar, M., 'Genesis 15: A Conflation of Two Deuteronomic Narratives', *JBL* 101 (1982), pp. 39-55.

Berlin, A., 'Literary Exegesis of Biblical Narrative: Between Poetics and Hermeneutics', in J. Rosenblatt and J. Sitterson (eds.), *'Not in Heaven': Coherence and Complexity in Biblical Narrative* (Bloomington: Indiana University Press, 1991), pp. 120-28.

Boyarin, D., *Intertextuality and the Meaning of Midrash* (Bloomington: Indiana University Press, 1990).

Brettler, M., *The Creation of History in Ancient Israel* (London: Routledge, 1995).

Buber, M., '*Leitwort* Style in Pentateuch Narrative', in M. Buber and F. Rosenzweig, *Scripture and Translation* (trans. L. Rosenwald; Bloomington: Indiana University Press, 1994), pp. 114-28.

Caillois, R., 'Logical and Philosophical Problems of the Dream', G.E. von Grunebaum and R. Caillois (eds.), *The Dream and Human Societies* (Berkeley: University of California Press, 1966), pp. 23-51.

Caquot, A., 'Le Psaume XCI', *Semitica* 8 (1958), pp. 21-37.

—'L'alliance avec Abram (Genèse 15)', *Semitica* 12 (1962), pp. 51-66.

Carlson, R.A., 'Temple et Somnium (Temple and Dream)', *Svensk Exegetisk Arsbok 54* (1989), pp. 50-56.

Cartledge, T.W., *Vows in the Hebrew Bible and the Ancient Near East* (JSOTSup, 147; Sheffield: JSOT Press, 1992).

Cassuto, U., *Commentary of the Book of Genesis* (trans. I. Adams; Jerusalem: Magnes Press, 1974 [1964]).

Charles, R.H. (ed.), *The Apocrypha and Pseudepigrapha of the Old Testament in English* (Oxford: Clarendon Press, 1913).

Clements, R.E., *Abraham and David: Genesis 15 and its Meaning for Israelite Tradition* (Studies in Biblical Theology, Second Series 5; London: SCM Press, 1967).

—*Prophecy and Tradition* (Oxford: Basil Blackwell, 1975).

Clines, D.J.A., *The Theme of the Pentateuch* (JSOTSup, 10; Sheffield: 1978).

—*What Does Eve do to Help? And Other Readerly Questions to the Old Testament* (JSOTSup, 94; Sheffield: 1990).

Cooper, A., and B. Goldstein, 'The Cult of the Dead and the Theme of Entry into the Land', *BibInt* 1 (1993), pp. 285-303.

Cooper, H., 'Connecting Heaven and Earth: Biblical and Psychological Perspectives on Jacob's Dream', lecture delivered at Leo Baeck College, 8 June 1994.

Cryer, F.H., *Divination in Ancient Israel and its Near Eastern Environment: A Socio-Historical Investigation* (JSOTSup, 142; Sheffield: Sheffield Academic Press, 1994).

Delitzsch, F., *A New Commentary on Genesis* (New York: Charles Scribner's Sons, 1889).

Dicou, B., *Edom, Israel's Brother and Antagonist: The Role of Edom in Biblical Prophecy and Story* (JSOTSup, 169; Sheffield: Sheffield Academic Press, 1994).

Dodds, E.R., *The Greeks and the Irrational* (Berkeley: University of California Press, 1984 [1951]).

Donner, H., 'Zu Genesis 28:22', *ZAW* 74 (1968), pp. 35-38.

Dutton, P.E., *The Politics of Dreaming in the Carolingian Empire* (Lincoln: University of Nebraska Press, 1994).

Emerton J.A., 'The Origin of the Promises to the Patriarchs in the Older Sources of the Book of Genesis', *VT* 32 (1982), pp. 14-32.

Ehrlich, E.L., *Der Traum im Alten Testament* (Berlin: Alfred Töpelmann, 1953).

Exum, J.C. 'Who's Afraid of the Endangered Ancestress?', in J.C. Exum and D.J.A. Clines (eds), *The New Literary Criticism and the Hebrew Bible* (JSOTSup, 143; Sheffield: Sheffield Academic Press, 1993), pp. 91-124.

Finkelstein, J., 'An Old Babylonian Herding Contract and Genesis 31.8f', in W. Hallo (ed.), *Essays in Memory of E.A. Speiser* (New Haven: American Oriental Society, 1968), pp. 30-36.

Fishbane, M., 'Composition and Structure in the Jacob Cycle (Genesis 25:19–35:22)', *JJS* 26 (1975), pp. 15-38.

—'The Qumran Pesher and Trails of Ancient Exegesis' (*Proceedings of the VIth World Congress of Jewish Studies*; Jerusalem: World Union of Jewish Studies, 1981 [1977]), p. 97-114.

—*Biblical Interpretation in Ancient Israel* (Oxford: Clarendon Press, 1991 [1985]).

—'The Well of Living Water: A Biblical Motif and its Ancient Transformations', in M. Fishbane and E. Tov (eds.), *Sha'arei Talmon, Studies in the Bible, Qumran, and the Ancient Near East Presented to Shemaryahu Talmon* (Winona Lake, IN: Eisenbrauns, 1992), pp. 3-16.

Fokkelman, J.P., *Narrative Art in Genesis: Specimens of Stylistic and Structural Analysis* (Biblical Seminar, 12; Sheffield: JSOT Press, 1991 [1975]).

Frankfort, H., *Kingship and the Gods: A Study of Ancient Near Eastern Religion as the Integration of Society and Nature* (Chicago: University of Chicago Press, 1978 [1948]).

Frankfurt, H., *The Importance of What We Care About* (Cambridge: Cambridge University Press, 1988).

Geller, S., 'The Sack of Shechem: The Use of Typology in Biblical Covenant Religion', *Prooftexts* 10 (1990), pp. 3-15.

Gibson, J.C.L. (ed.), *Canaanite Myths and Legends* (Edinburgh: T. & T. Clark, 1978).

Glenn, M.G., 'The Word לוז in Gen. 28:19 in the LXX and in the Midrash', *JQR* 59 (1968–69), pp. 73-76.

Gnuse, R.K., 'A Reconsideration of the Form-critical Structure in I Samuel 3: An ANE Dream Theophany', *ZAW* 94 (1982), pp. 379-89.

—*The Dream Theophany of Samuel: Its Structure in Relation to Ancient Near Eastern Dreams and its Theological Significance* (Lanham: University Press of America, 1984).

Gordon, R.P., 'Aleph Apologeticum', *JQR* NS 59 (1979), pp. 112-16.

Gossai, H., *Power and Marginality in the Abraham Narrative* (Lanham: University Press of America, 1995).

Greenberg, M., 'Another Look at Rachel's Theft of the Teraphim', *JBL* 81 (1962), pp. 239-49.

Greenspahn, F., *When Brothers Dwell Together: The Pre-eminence of Younger Siblings in the Hebrew Bible* (New York: Oxford University Press, 1994).

—'A Mesopotamian Proverb and its Biblical Reverberations', *JAOS* 114 (1994), pp. 33-38.

Greenstein, E.L., 'An Equivocal Reading of the Sale of Joseph', in K. Gros Louis (ed.), *Literary Interpretations of Biblical Narratives*, II (Nashville, TN: Abingdon Press, 1982), pp. 114-25.

Griffiths, G.J., 'The Celestial Ladder and the Gate of Heaven in Egyptian Ritual', *ExpTim* 78 (1966), pp. 54-55.

Guillaume, A., *Prophecy and Divination among the Hebrews and Other Semites* (London: Hodder and Stoughton, 1938).

Gunkel, H., *Genesis* (Göttingen: Vandenhoeck & Ruprecht, 1966 [1901]).

—*Legends of Genesis* (trans. W.H. Carruth; New York: Schocken Books, 1964).

Ha, J., *Genesis 15: A Theological Compendium of Pentateuchal History* (BZAW, 181; Berlin: W. de Gruyter, 1989).

Habel, N.C., *The Land is Mine: Six Biblical Land Ideologies* (Minneapolis: Fortress Press, 1995).

Hagelia, H., *Numbering the Stars: A Phraseological Analysis of Genesis 15* (ConBOT, 39; Stockholm: Almqvist & Wiksell, 1994).

Hamilton, V., *The Book of Genesis: Chapters 1–17* (NICOT; Grand Rapids, MI: Eerdmans, 1990).

Halpern-Amaru, B., *Rewriting the Bible: Land and Covenant in Postbiblical Jewish Literature* (Valley Forge, PA: Trinity Press International, 1994).

Haran, M., *Temples and Temple Service in Ancient Israel: An Inquiry into the Cult Phenomenon and the Historical Setting of the Priestly School* (Oxford: Clarendon Press, 1978).

Hardy, T., *The Complete Poems of Thomas Hardy* (ed. J. Gibson; London: Macmillan, 1983 [1976]).

Hendel, R.S., *The Epic of the Patriarch: The Jacob Cycle and the Narrative Traditions of Canaan and Israel* (HSM, 42; Atlanta: Scholars Press, 1987).

Hillers, D., *Covenant: The History of a Biblical Idea* (Baltimore: The Johns Hopkins University Press, 1989 [1969]).

Hilton, M., 'Babel Reversed—Daniel Chapter 5', *JSOT* 66 (1995), pp. 99-122.

Holmgren, F., 'Faithful Abraham and the *'amâna* Covenant in Nehemiah 9:6–10:1', *ZAW* 104 (1992), pp. 249-54.

Houtman, C., 'What Did Jacob See in his Dream at Bethel?: Some Remarks on Genesis 28:10-22', *VT* 27 (1977), pp. 337-51.

Hurowitz, V.A., *I Have Built You an Exalted House: Temple Building in the Light of Mesopotamian and Northwest Semitic Writings* (JSOTSup, 115; Sheffield: JSOT Press, 1992).

—'Eli's Adjuration of Samuel (1 Sam. 3:17-18) in the Light of a "Diviner's Protocol" from Mari (AEM 1/1, 1), *VT* 44 (1994), pp. 493-97.

Husser, J.M., *Le songe et la parole: Etude sur le rêve et sa fonction dans l'ancien Israël* (Berlin: W. de Gruyter, 1994).

Japhet, S., 'People and Land in the Restoration Period', in G. Strecker (ed.), *Das Land Israel in biblischer Zeit* (Göttingen: Vandenhoeck & Ruprecht, 1983), pp. 103-25.

Jeffers, A., 'Divination by Dreams in Ugaritic Literature and in the Old Testament', *IBS* 12 (1990), pp. 167-83.

Jenks, A.W., *The Elohist and North Israelite Traditions* (SBLMS, 22; Montana: Scholars Press, 1977).

Jirku, A., 'Ein Fall von Inkubation im Alten Testament (Ex. 38:8)', *ZAW* 33 (1913), pp. 151-53.

Jones, G.H., 'Abraham and Cyrus: Type and Anti-type?', *VT* 22 (1972), pp. 304-19.

Kapelrud, A., 'Temple Building: A Task for Gods and Kings', *Or* 32 (1963), pp. 56-62.

Kaufmann, Y., *The Religion of Israel: From its Beginning to the Time of the Babylonian Exile* (trans. and abridged M. Greenberg; Chicago: Schocken Books, 1972 [1960]).

Kautzsch, E., *Gesenius' Hebrew Grammar* (New York: Oxford University Press, 1990 [1909]).

Koch, K., *Was ist Formgeschichte? Methoden der Bibelexegese* (Neukirchen–Vluyn: Neukirchener Verlag, 1974 [1964]).

—*The Growth of Biblical Tradition: The Form Critical Method* (trans. S.M. Cupitt; London: A. & C. Black, 1969).

—'The Ancestress of Israel in Danger', in Koch, *The Growth of Biblical Tradition*, pp. 111-28.

Kogut, S., 'הנה in Biblical Literature', in S. Japhet (ed.), *Studies in Bible* (Scripta Hierosolymitana, 31; Jerusalem: Magnes Press, 1986), pp. 133-54.

Kraus, H., *Worship in Israel* (trans. G. Buswell; Oxford: Basil Blackwell, 1966).

Kreutzer, S., '430 Jahre, 400 Jahre oder 4 Generationen—Zu den Zeitangaben über den Ägyptenaufenthalt der "Israeliten" ', *ZAW* 98 (1986), pp. 199-210.

Kruger, S.F., *Dreaming in the Middle Ages* (Cambridge: Cambridge University Press, 1992).

Laato, A., 'Assyrian Propaganda and the Falsification of History in the Royal Inscriptions of Sennacherib', *VT* 45 (1995), pp. 198-226.

Labuschagne, C.J., 'Teraphim: A New Proposal for its Etymology', *VT* 16 (1966), pp. 115-17.

Leibowitz, N., *Studies in Bereishit* (trans. A. Newman; Jerusalem: World Zionist Organization, 1972).

Lemche, N., *Early Israel: Anthropological and Historical Studies on Israelite Society Before the Monarchy* (VTSup, 37; Leiden: E.J. Brill, 1985).

Lewis, N., *The Interpretation of Dreams and Portents* (Toronto: Hakkert and Co., 1976).

Lichtenstein, M., 'Dream Theophany and the "E" Document', *JANESCU* 1-2 (1969), pp. 45-54.

Lindblom, J., 'Theophanies in Holy Places in Hebrew Religion', *HUCA* 32 (1961), pp. 91-106.

Loewenstamm, S.E., 'Zur Traditionsgeschichte des Bundes zwischen den Stucken', *VT* 18 (1969), pp. 500-506.

McAlpine, T.H., *Sleep, Divine and Human, in the Old Testament* (JSOTSup, 38; Sheffield: JSOT Press, 1987).

Mendenhall, G., *Law and Covenant in Israel and the Ancient Near East* (Pittsburgh: The Biblical Colloquium, 1955).

Meyers, C., 'Jachin and Boaz in Religious and Political Perspective', *CBQ* 45 (1983), pp. 167-78.

Meyers, C.L., and E.M. Meyers, 'Jerusalem and Zion after the Exile: The Evidence of First Zechariah', in M. Fishbane and E. Tov (eds.), *Sha'arei Talmon: Studies in the Bible, Qumran and the Ancient Near East Presented to Shemaryahu Talmon* (Winona Lake: Eisenbrauns, 1992), pp. 121-35.

Millard, A.R., 'The Celestial Ladder and the Gate of Heaven (Gen. 28:12,17)', *ExpTim* 78 (1966), pp. 85-87.

Miller, J.E., 'Dreams and Prophetic Visions', *Biblica 71* (1990), pp. 410-404.

Moberly, W., *The Old Testament of the Old Testament: Patriarchal Narratives and Mosaic Yahwism* (Minneapolis: Fortress Press, 1992).

Oliva, M., *Jacob en Betel: Visión y voto* (Madrid: Universidad Pontificia Comillas, 1975).

Oppenheim, A.L., 'The Interpretation of Dreams in the Ancient Near East: With a Translation of an Assyrian Dream Book', *Transactions of the American Philosophical Society* NS 46 (1956), pp. 179-373.

Parrot, A., *The Tower of Babel* (trans. E. Hudson; London: SCM Press, 1955).

—*Babylon and the Old Testament* (trans. B. Hooke; London: SCM Press, 1958).

Pedersen, J., *Israel I–II: Its Life and Culture* (London: Oxford University Press, 1959).

Plato, *Collected Dialogues* (ed. E. Hamilton and H. Cairns; Princeton: Princeton University Press, 1971 [1961]).

Polzin, R., '"The Ancestress of Israel in Danger" in Danger', *Semeia* 3-4 (1975), pp. 81-97.

Postgate, J.N., 'Some Old Babylonian Shepherds and their Flocks', *JSS* 20 (1975), pp. 1-21.

Pritchard, J. (ed.), *Ancient Near Eastern Texts Relating to the Old Testament* (Princeton: Princeton University Press, 1969 [1950]).

Pury, A. de, *Promesse divine et légende cultuelle dans le cycle de Jacob* (Paris: J. Gabalda, 1975).

Rad, G. von, *Das Erste Buch Mose, Genesis* (Göttingen: Vandenhoeck & Ruprecht, 1953).

—*Genesis* (trans. J.H. Marks; London: SCM Press, 1987 [1961]).

—*Theologie des Alten Testaments 1* (Munich: Chr. Kaiser Verlag, 1958).

—*Old Testament Theology*, I (2 vols.; trans. D.M.G. Stalker; London: SCM Press, 1989).

Reif, S.C., 'A Root to Look Up: A Study of the Hebrew *ns' 'yn'* (VTSup, 36; Leiden: E.J. Brill, 1985), pp. 230-44.

Resch, A., *Der Traum im Heilsplan Gottes: Deutung und Bedeutung im Alten Testament* (Freiburg: Herder, 1964).

Richter, W., 'Traum und Traumdeutung im Alten Testament: Ihre Form und Verwendung', *BZ* 1 (1963), pp. 202-20.

Robinson, M.G., 'Dreams in the Old Testament' (unpublished PhD thesis; University of Manchester, 1987).

Safren, J.D., 'Balaam and Abraham', *VT* 38 (1988), pp. 105-28.

Sarna, N., *Understanding Genesis: The Heritage of Biblical Israel* (New York: Schocken Books, 1966 [1972]).

Sasson, J., 'Mari Dreams', *JAOS* 103 (1983), pp. 283-93.

Schwartz, J., 'Jubilees, Bethel and the Temple of Jacob', *HUCA* 56 (1985), pp. 63-85.

Selman, M., 'The Social Environment of the Patriarchs', *TynBul* 27 (1976), pp. 114-36.

Shanks, H. (ed.), *Ancient Israel: A Short History from Abraham to the Roman Destruction of the Temple* (London: SPCK, 1989).

Shelley, P.B., *Poetical Works* (London: F. Warne, n.d.).

Sherwood, S., *'Had God Not Been On My Side': An Examination of the Narrative Technique of the Story of Jacob and Laban: Genesis 29:1–32:2* (Frankfurt: Peter Lang, 1990).

Shinan, A., and Y. Zakovitch, 'Midrash on Scripture and Midrash within Scripture', in S. Japhet (ed.), *Studies in Bible* (Scripta Hierosolymitana, 31; Jerusalem: Magnes Press, 1986), pp. 257-77.

Skinner, J., *Genesis* (ICC; Edinburgh: T. & T. Clark, 1980 [1910]).

Smelik, K., *Writings From Ancient Israel* (trans. G.I. Davies; Edinburgh: T. & T. Clark, 1991).

Soggin, J.A., 'Jacob in Shechem and Bethel (Genesis 35:1-7)', in M. Fishbane and E. Tov (eds.), *Sha'arei Talmon: Studies in the Bible, Qumran and the Ancient Near East Presented to Shemaryahu Talmon*, (Winona Lake, IN: Eisenbrauns, 1992), pp. 195-98.

Speiser, E.A., *Genesis* (New York: Doubleday, 1986 [1962]).

—'The Wife-Sister Motif in the Patriarchal Narratives', in A. Altmann (ed.), *Biblical and Other Studies* (Cambridge, MA: Harvard University Press, 1963), pp. 15-28.

Sperber, A., 'Zu Gen. 30:27b', *OL* 16 (1913), pp. 389-90.

Sternberg, M., *The Poetics of Biblical Narrative: Ideological Literature and the Drama of Reading* (Bloomington: Indiana University Press, 1987).

Taylor, J., 'The Asherah, the Menorah and the Sacred Tree', *JSOT* 66 (1995), pp. 29-54.

Tollington, J., *Tradition and Innovation in Haggai and Zechariah 1–8* (JSOTSup, 150; Sheffield: Sheffield Academic Press, 1993).

Toorn, K., van der, 'The Nature of the Biblical Teraphim in the Light of Cuneiform Evidence', *CBQ* 52 (1990), pp. 203-22.

Torczyner, H., 'Zu נחשתי Gen. 30:27', *OL* 20 (1917), pp. 10-12.

Van Seters, J., 'Confessional Reformulation in the Exilic Period', *VT* 22 (1972), pp. 448-59.

—*Abraham in History and Tradition* (New Haven: Yale University Press, 1975).

—'The Religion of the Patriarchs in Genesis', *Biblica* 61 (1980), pp. 220-33.

—*Prologue to History* (Louisville, KY: Westminster/John Knox Press, 1992).

Waldman, N., 'A Note on Gen. 30:27b', *JQR* 55 (1964), pp. 164-65.

Walton, J.H., *Ancient Israelite Literature in its Cultural Context: A Survey of Parallels Between Biblical and Ancient Near Eastern Texts* (Regency Reference Library; Grand Rapids, MI: Zondervan, 1989).

Weinfeld, M., 'The Covenant of Grant in the Old Testament and in the Ancient Near East', *JAOS* 90 (1970), pp. 184-203.

—*Deuteronomy and the Deuteronomic School* (Oxford: Clarendon Press, 1983 [1972]).

—'Sarah and Abimelech (Genesis 20) Against the Background of an Assyrian Law and the Genesis Apocryphon', *AOAT* (1985), pp 421-36.

—*The Promise of the Land: The Inheritance of the Land of Canaan by the Israelites* (Berkeley: University of California Press, 1993).

Weingreen, J., 'הוצאתיך in Genesis 15:7', in P. Ackroyd (ed.), *Words and Meanings: Essays Presented to David Winton Thomas* (Cambridge: Cambridge University Press, 1968), pp. 209-215.

Weiss, M., 'The Contribution of Literary Theory to Biblical Research Illustrated by the Problem of She'ar-Yashub', S. Japhet (ed.), *Studies in Bible* (Scripta Hierosolymitana, 31; Jerusalem: Magnes Press, 1986), pp. 373-86.

Wellhausen, J., *Der Text der Bücher Samuelis* (Göttingen: Vandenhoeck & Ruprecht, 1871).

Wenham, G., 'The Religion of the Patriarchs', in A.R. Millard and D. Wiseman (eds.), *Essays on the Patriarchal Narratives* (Leicester: Inter-Varsity Press, 1980), pp. 157-88.

Westermann, C., *Die Verheißung an die Väter* (Göttingen: Vandenhoeck & Ruprecht, 1976).

—*The Promises to the Fathers* (trans. D. Green; Philadelphia: Fortress Press, 1980).

—*Genesis 12–36* (Neukirchen–Vluyn: Neukirchener Verlag, 1981).

—*Genesis 12–36: A Commentary* (trans. J.J. Scullion; London: SPCK, 1985).

White, M., 'The Elohistic Depiction of Aaron: A Study in the Levite-Zadokite Controversy', in J.A. Emerton (ed.), *Studies in the Pentateuch* (VTSup, 30; Leiden: E.J. Brill, 1990), pp. 149-59.

Whybray, R.N., *The Making of the Pentateuch* (JSOTS, 53; Sheffield: JSOT Press, 1987).

Wilson, R.R., *Prophecy and Society in Ancient Israel* (Philadelphia: Fortress Press, 1970).

Woolf, V., *To the Lighthouse* (London: Hogarth Press, 1977 [1927]).

Wyatt, N., 'Where Did Jacob Dream his Dream?', *SJOT* 2 (1990), pp. 44-57.

Yadin, Y., *The Temple Scroll*, I (3 vols.; Jerusalem: Israel Exploration Society, 1983).

Yarden, L., 'Aaron, Bethel and the Priestly Menorah', *JJS* 26 (1975), pp. 39-47.

Zakowitz, Y., 'Reflection Story: Another Dimension of the Evaluation of Characters in Biblical Narrative', *Tarbiz* 54 (1985), pp. 165-76 (Hebrew).

—'Through the Looking Glass: Reflections/Inversions of Genesis Stories in the Bible', *BibInt* 2 (1993), pp. 139-52.

Zeitlin, S. 'Dreams and their Interpretation from the Biblical Period to the Tannaitic Time: An Historical Study', *JQR* 66 (1975–76), pp. 1-17.

Zornberg, A. Gottlieb, *Genesis: The Beginning of Desire* (Philadelphia: Jewish Publication Society, 1995).

Bibles and Rabbinic Bible Commentaries

Babylonian Talmud (Artscroll; New York: Mesorah, 1990).

Bereishis 1 & 2 (Artscroll Tanach Series; Brooklyn: Mesorah, 1989 [1977]).

Biblia Hebraica Stuttgartensia (Stuttgart: Deutsche Bibelgesellschaft, 1990 [1967]).

Genesis Rabbah, in C. Albeck (ed.), *Midrash Rabbah* (Berlin: Akademie Verlag, 1965 [1929]).

Holy Bible, New Revised Standard Version (Oxford: Oxford University Press, 1989).

Jewish Publication Society Torah Commentary, Genesis (ed. N. Sarna; Philadelphia: Jewish Publication Society, 1989).

Midrash HaGadol (ed. S. Schechter; Cambridge: Cambridge University Press, 1902).

Pirke de Rabbi Eliezer (ed. D. Luria; Warsaw: 1852).

Tanakh, The Holy Scriptures (Philadelphia: Jewish Publication Society, 1985).

INDEXES

INDEX OF REFERENCES

HEBREW BIBLE

OTHER ANCIENT REFERENCES

INDEX OF AUTHORS

White, M. 107
Whybray, R.N. 179, 214
Woolf, V. 50
Wyatt, N. 107, 110-12

Yadin, Y. 93
Yarden, L. 106

Zakovitch, Y. 212, 213
Zakowitz, Y. 55, 99
Zeitlin, S. 52
Zornberg, A.G. 73

JOURNAL FOR THE STUDY OF THE OLD TESTAMENT
SUPPLEMENT SERIES